HOTEL MANAGEMENT AND SECURITY

HOTEL MANAGEMENT AND SECURITY

Vinod Nair

CYBER TECH PUBLICATIONS
4264/3, Ansari Road, Daryaganj, New Delhi-110002 (India)
Ph.: 011-23244078, 011-43559448 Fax: 011-23280028
E-Mail: cyberpublicationsdelhi@yahoo.com
Website: www.cybertechpublications.com

HOTEL MANAGEMENT AND SECURITY

Vinod Nair

First Edition 2011

Published by :

G.S. Rawat for **Cyber Tech Publications**
4264/3, Ansari Road, Daryaganj, New Delhi-110002 (India)
Ph.: 011-23244078, 011-43559448 Fax: 011-23280028
E-Mail: cyberpublicationsdelhi@yahoo.com
Website: www.cybertechpublications.com

CONTENTS

Preface

A history of the founders of the hotel industry provides an opportunity to reflect on our heritage. Learning about the founding giants such as Statler, Hilton, Marriott, Wilson, and Schultz, to name a few, allows a student of the industry to discover the interesting lin-eage of hoteliers. Studying the efforts of the innovators who carved out the modern hotel industry may help future professionals with their own career planning.

To begin to understand the history of the modern hotel industry, let's look at its early entrepreneurs, who were motivated by wealth and fame on a grand scale. Ellsworth M. Statler (1863-1928) developed the chain of hotels that were known as Statlers, beginning with a hotel in Buffalo, New York, built for the 1901 Pan-American Exposition. Eventually there were Statler hotels in Boston, Cleveland, Detroit, New York City, St. Louis, and other locations. In 1954, he sold the Statler chain to Conrad Hilton.

Statler devised a scheme to open an incredible two-story, rectangular wood structure that would contain 2,084 rooms and accommodate 5,000 guests. It was to be a temporary structure, covered with a thin layer of plaster to make it appear substantial, although simple to tear down after the fair closed.

The front office is the nerve center of a hotel property. Communications and accounting are two of the most important functions of a front desk operation. Effective communications-with guests, employees, and other departments of the hotel-are paramount in projecting a hospitable image. Answering guest inquiries about hotel services and other guests, marketing and sales department requests for information on guest room availability, and housekeeping department inquiries concerning guest reservations are but a few of the routine tasks performed almost constantly by a hotel front desk in its role as communications hub. Accounting procedures involving charges to registered and nonregistered hotel guest accounts are also important in the hospitality field. Itemized charges are necessary to show a breakdown of charges if a guest questions a bill.

Services for which fees are charged are available 24 hours a day in a hotel property. Moreover, because guests may want to settle their accounts at any time of the day, accounts must be current and accurate at all times. Keeping this data organized is a top priority of good front office management.

—Author

1

Introduction

The mere mention of the word hotel conjures up exciting images: a busy lobby filled with international dignitaries, celebrities, community leaders, attendees of conventions and large receptions, businesspersons, and family vacationers. The excitement you feel in a hotel lobby is something you will have forever in your career. Savor it and enjoy it. It is the beginning of understanding the concept of providing hospitality to guests. As you begin to grasp the principles of a well-operated hotel, you will discover the important role the front office plays in keeping this excitement intact.

The front office is the nerve center of a hotel property. Communications and accounting are two of the most important functions of a front desk operation. Effective communications-with guests, employees, and other departments of the hotel-are paramount in projecting a hospitable image. Answering guest inquiries about hotel services and other guests, marketing and sales department requests for information on guest room availability, and housekeeping department inquiries concerning guest reservations are but a few of the routine tasks performed almost constantly by a hotel front desk in its role as communications hub. Accounting procedures involving charges to registered and nonregistered hotel guest accounts are also important in the hospitality field. Itemized charges are necessary to show a breakdown of charges if a guest questions a bill.

Services for which fees are charged are available 24 hours a day in a hotel property. Moreover, because guests may want to settle their accounts at any time of the day, accounts must be current and accurate at all times. Keeping this data organized is a top priority of good front office management.

FOUNDERS OF HOTEL INDUSTRY

A history of the founders of the hotel industry provides an opportunity to reflect on our heritage. Learning about the founding giants such as Statler, Hilton, Marriott, Wilson, and Schultz, to name a few, allows a student of the industry to discover the interesting lin-eage of hoteliers. Studying the efforts of the innovators who carved out the modern hotel industry may help future professionals with their own career planning.

To begin to understand the history of the modern hotel industry, let's look at its early entrepreneurs, who were motivated by wealth and fame on a grand scale. Ellsworth M. Statler (1863-1928) developed the chain of hotels that were known as Statlers, beginning with a hotel in Buffalo, New York, built for the 1901 Pan-American Exposition. Eventually there were Statler hotels in Boston, Cleveland, Detroit, New York City, St. Louis, and other locations. In 1954, he sold the Statler chain to Conrad Hilton.

Statler devised a scheme to open an incredible two-story, rectangular wood structure that would contain 2,084 rooms and accommodate 5,000 guests. It was to be a temporary structure, covered with a thin layer of plaster to make it appear substantial, although simple to tear down after the fair closed.

Conrad Hilton

Conrad Hilton (1887-1979) became a successful hotelier after World War I, when he purchased several properties in Texas during its oil boom. In 1919, he bought the Mobley Hotel in Cisco, Texas. In 1925, he built the Hilton Hotel in Dallas, Texas. His acquisitions during and after World War II included the 3,000-room Stevens Hotel (now the Chicago Hilton) and the Palmer House in Chicago and the Plaza and Waldorf=Astoria in New York City. In 1946, he formed the Hilton Hotels Corporation, and in 1948, he formed the Hilton International Company, which came to number more than 125 hotels. With the purchase of the Statler chain in 1954, Hilton created the first major chain of modern American hotels-that is, a group of hotels that follow standard operating procedures in marketing, reservations, quality of service, food and beverage operations, housekeeping, and accounting. Hilton Hotels now includes Hilton Garden Inns, Doubletree, Embassy Suites, Hampton Inns, Harrison Conference Centers, Homewood Suites by Hilton, Red Lion Hotels and Inns, and Conrad International.

Cesar Ritz

Cesar Ritz was a hotelier at the Grand National Hotel in Lucerne, Switzerland. Because of his management abilities, "the hotel became one of the most popular in Europe and Cesar Ritz became one of the most respected hoteliers in Europe."

William Waldorf Astor and John Jacob Astor IV

In 1893, William Waldorf Astor launched the 13-story Waldorf Hotel at Fifth Avenue near Thirty-fourth Street in New York City. The Waldorf was the embodiment of Astor's vision of a New York hostelry that would appeal to his wealthy friends by combining the opulence of a European mansion with the warmth and homey qualities of a private residence.

Four years later, the Waldorf was joined by the 17-story Astoria Hotel, erected on an adjacent site by William Waldorf Astor's cousin, John Jacob Astor IV. The cousins built a corridor that connected the two hotels, which became known by a single hyphenated name, the Waldorf-Astoria.

In 1929, after decades of hosting distinguished visitors from around the world, the Waldorf-Astoria closed its doors to make room for the Empire State Building.

The 2,200-room, 42-floor Waldorf=Astoria Hotel was rebuilt on its current site at Park and Lexington avenues between Forty-ninth and Fiftieth streets. Upon the hotel's opening, President Herbert Hoover delivered a message of congratulations.

President Hoover later became a permanent resident of the Waldorf Towers, the luxurious "hotel within a hotel" that occupies the twenty-eighth through the forty-second floors. Conrad N. Hilton purchased the hotel in 1949 and then the land it stands on in 1977. In 1988, the hotel underwent a $150 million restoration. It was designated a New York City landmark in January 1993.

Kemmons Wilson

Kemmons Wilson started the Holiday Inn chain in the early 1950s, opening the first in Memphis, Tennessee. He wanted to build a chain of hotels for the traveling family and later expanded his marketing plan to include business travelers. His accomplishments in real estate development coupled with his hotel management skills proved a highly successful combination.

Wilson blazed a formidable path, innovating with amenities and high-rise architecture, including a successful round building concept featuring surprisingly functional pie-shaped rooms. Wilson also introduced the in-house Holidex central reservation system, which set the industry standard for both the volume of business it produced and the important byproduct data it generated (allowing it, for example, to determine feasibility for new locations with cunning accuracy).

Wilson died in February 2003 at the age of 90. His legacy to the lodging industry will be serving the traveling public with comfortable, safe accommoations while making a profit for investors.

J. W. Marriott and J. W. Marriott Jr.

J. W. Marriott (1900-1985) founded his hotel empire in 1957 with the Twin Bridges Marriott Motor Hotel in Virginia, near Washington, D.C. Marriott Hotels and Resorts had grown to include Courtyard by Marriott and American Resorts Group at the time of J. W. Marriott's death in 1985, at which time J. W. Marriott Jr. acquired the Howard Johnson Company; he sold the hotels to Prime Motor Inns but retained 350 restaurants and 68 turnpike units.

In 1987, Marriott completed expansion of its Worldwide Reservation Center in Omaha, Nebraska, making it the largest single-site reservations operation in U.S. hotel history. Also in 1987, Marriott acquired the Residence Inn Company, an all-suite hotel chain targeted at extended-stay travelers. With the introduction of limited-service hotels-hotels built with guest room accommodations and limited food service and meeting space-Marriott entered the economy lodging segment, opening the first Fairfield Inn in Atlanta, Georgia, in 1987.

Ernest Henderson and Robert Moore

Ernest Henderson and Robert Moore started the Sheraton chain in 1937, when they acquired their first hotel, the Stonehaven, in Springfield, Massachusetts. Within two years, they purchased three hotels in Boston and soon expanded their holdings to include properties from Maine to Florida. At the end of its first decade, Sheraton was the first hotel chain to be listed on the New York Stock Exchange. In 1968, Sheraton was acquired by ITT Corporation as a wholly owned subsidiary, and ambitious development plans were put into place to create a truly global network of properties. In the 1980s, under the leadership of John Kapioltas, Sheraton's chairman, president, and chief executive officer, the company received international recognition as an industry innovator in offering modern hotel accommodations. The Sheraton chain is currently owned by Starwood Hotels &C Resorts Worldwide.

Ray Schultz

In the early 1980s, Ray Schultz founded the Hampton Inn hotels, a company in the Holiday Inn Corporation. These hotels were tagged as limited-service, meeting the needs of cost-conscious business travelers and pleasure travelers alike. Schultz's pioneering efforts in developing a product and service for these market segments have proved a substantial contribution to the history of the hotel industry.

At a 1998 celebration of the expansion of the Hampton Inn hotel corporation to more than 800 properties, Schultz said:

We started the Hampton Inn chain in 1884 to provide guests with a quality room and special amenities like a free continental breakfast and free local phone calls, all at an exceptional value. The opening of this hotel today tells us that we understood our guests' needs and that price/value is still a viable concept nearly 15 years later. Hampton Inn has been, and is committed to remaining, the standard against which all mid-priced, limited-service hotel brands are measured.

Historical Developments

The history of the hotel industry is filled with concepts that shaped the products and services offered.

The atrium concept design, limited-service hotels, and technology were notable innovations. Management concepts such as marketing and total quality management (TQM) offered managers a new way to do business in hotels. The major U.S. economic reorganization in the late 1980s shaped the way hotels could be profitable. Also, in the 1990s, a new financial approach-real estate investment trusts (REITs)-changed the financial structuring and operation of hotels.

The terrorist events of September 11, 2001, continue to affect how hotels market their products and services and deliver hospitality.

Atrium Concept

The hotel industry has seen many notable developments over the past years. The atrium concept, an architectural design in which guest rooms overlook the lobby from the first floor to the roof, was first used in the 1960s by Hyatt Hotels.

The dramatic approach to hotel style [was] exemplified by the Hyatt Regency in Atlanta. Designed by architect John Portman, with a striking and impressive atrium soaring up its 21 stories, the hotel literally changed the course of upscale hotel design. As a result hotels became more than a place to rest one's head. They became hubs for excitement, fun, relaxation and entertainment.

This 1,260-room hotel "is now one of the nation's premier convention and trade show facilities with 180,000 square feet of ballroom, exhibit, meeting and hospitality space."

Limited-Service Hotels

The movement of hotel construction from the downtown, center-city area to the suburbs in the 1950s coincided with the development of the U.S. highway system. The limited-service concept-hotels built with guest room accommodations and limited food service and meeting space-became prominent in the early 1980s, when many of the major chains adopted this way to serve business travelers and travelers on a limited budget. Hampton Inn revolutionized the hotel industry with the creation of the first national brand targeted to the new limited-service hotel segment. The hotels featured spacious, comfortable rooms but eliminated or reduced other elements common to hotels at that time, such as restaurants, lounges, and meeting and lobby space, passing the resulting cost savings on to guests in the form of lower rates.

The company pioneered a number of ideas, including the mounting of the first site by a hotel brand on the Internet. In 1989, Hampton Inn became the first national brand to offer guests an unconditional 100 percent satisfaction guarantee, which today is the cornerstone of all Promus brands and a testament to the company's commitment to quality.

Technological Advances

Technology has played a major role in developing the products and services offered to guests. Reservations systems, property management systems, and in-room guest checkout are only the most obvious advances in technology.

Recent additions to the list include applications of wireless technology that allow front office staff to alert others on VIP check-ins, housekeeping staff to report guest room cleaning and release, marketing staff to maintain guest profiles, and bell staff to process baggage handling. Guests have also found technology in the 2000s to increase their ability to work and play at the same time; they can check email and print documents as needed from so-called hot spots, or designated wireless transmission and reception areas in the hotel.

Marketing Emphasis

An emphasis on niche marketing to guests was the theme in the 1970s. This technique surveyed potential guest markets and built systems around the needs of identified segments.

The larger hotel-management and franchise companies also were discovering the advantages of forging strong reservations and marketing systems. For a guest, this meant that by calling a single phone number, he or she could be assured of a reservation and feel confident of the quality of accommodations expected.15

The marketing emphasis continues in the 2000s through the routine use of the Internet to place guest reservations. A research study of PhoCusWright data indicated "Internet reservations consisted of about 13 percent of all U.S. hotel reservations in 2003."

LodgeNet Entertainment (interactive video games)

Interactive guest room shopping, interactive visitor's guide, fax delivery on TV, interactive guide to hotel's facilities and activities, reservations from the guest room for other hotels within the same organization, and interactive weather reports

Total Quality Management

Total quality management (TQM), a technique that helps managers look at processes used to create products and services with a critical eye on improving those processes, is practiced in hotels today. This emphasis on analyzing the delivery of services and prod-ucts, with decision making at the front lines, in the 1990s and continues today under terms such as quality assurance and service quality. These concepts are discussed in more detail in chapter 11.

Major Reorganization, 1987-1988

The economic period of 1987-1988 saw a major reorganization of the hotel industry. 1986 Congress unraveled what it had stitched together in 1981. The revised Tax Act made it clear that passive losses on real estate were no longer deductible. Hotels that were previously economically viable suddenly were not. At this time, there were plenty of Japanese who seemed intent on buying up, at astronomical prices, any piece of U.S. property with a hotel or golf course on it. As a result, the value of American hotel properties continued to increase. Between 1990 and 1995, the recession began and ended, and the full impact of the 1986 law and overbuilding were experienced. Some investors who had built properties in the early 1980s found their properties sales or replacement value had fallen to 50 percent or less of original cost. Some owners simply abandoned their properties to their mortgage holders-which in many cases turned out to be Uncle Sam, because of the simultaneous S&L debacle.

Hotel Investment

Real estate investment trusts (REITs) provide an investment opportunity for hoteliers. In the Spring 2000 Virginia Hospitality and Leisure Executive Report, P. Anthony Brown of Arthur

Andersen wrote the following about the U.S. Tax Relief Extension Act of 1999. This information will be useful as you plan your career.

The most significant provision, however, is creation of a new type of corporation-a "Taxable REIT Subsidiary" (effective January 1, 2001)-which will allow REITs to create new incremental income streams. With new growth opportunities, shareholders should be rewarded with higher stock prices since companies with increased growth rates typically trade in the market at higher earnings multiples.

Under the terms of the 1999 legislation, Taxable REIT Subsidiaries can provide non-customary services to tenants through their subsidiaries. This legislation should enable REITs to provide better customer service, create stronger customer loyalty and sell new, non-customary services to tenants. In addition these new subsidiaries can lease lodging facilities from REITs. However, the lodging facilities must be managed by an independent contractor that is actively engaged in the trade or business of operating lodging facilities for any person other than the REIT.

With these changes, hotel REITs will be able to reorganize their structure in order to retain more of the income generated by their hotels. For example, FelCor Lodging Trust Inc., a hotel REIT based in Irving, Texas, currently leases its hotels to two tenants: 1) a company owned by its executives and directors; and 2) Bristol Hotels and Resorts, a publicly traded company. With the new legislation, FelCor will be able to form a new Taxable REIT Subsidiary and transfer the leases of its hotels to this new subsidiary. Accordingly, the net income of the existing lessee would be transferred to the new Taxable REIT Subsidiary. However, a management company (not owned by FelCor) must manage the hotels and must be actively engaged in the trade or business of operating lodging facilities for any person other than the REIT.

September 11, 2001

The terrorist events of September 11, 2001, will have a lasting effect on how a hotel markets its products and services and delivers hospitality. The immediate impact of the terrorist attacks was a decrease in the number of people willing to fly and, thus, a decrease in demand for hotel rooms. Hotels (as well as restaurateurs, tourist attractions, government agencies, and the like) and the federal, regional, and state tourism associations continue to cooperate to address the issue of fear as it relates to travel and tourism.

Hoteliers reviewed their marketing plans and determined how to attract the post-9/11 corporate traveler. The huge corporate guest market can no longer be taken for granted. Corporate executives, travel planners, and traffic managers now must be greeted person-ally by hotel staff and asked when business might be expected. New methods of attracting markets such as local and regional residents are being developed. These efforts include special packages emphasizing local history and culture, businesses, sporting events, and natural attractions and are combined with the products and services of an individual hotel. Is this an easy challenge? Indeed no, yet it is one that hoteliers had to grasp with eagerness and enthusiasm in order to succeed.

R. Mark Woodworth reports that this effort is indeed a formidable task in light of the data revealed in Trends in the Hotel Industry-USA, published by PKF Consulting and the Hospitality Research Group (HRG). The 2003 edition reported that "the operating profit for the average U.S. hotel dropped 9.6 percent in 2002, this after a 19.4 percent decline in profits in 2001."

Rick Swig of RSBA &C Associates notes that although hotel revenues increased by 2 percent from 2003 to 2004, "other issues such as supply of hotel rooms of 4.4% since June 2001 versus average number of rooms sold increasing only by 3.3%." He urges, "Hotel operators should focus on pricing power for the next 24 months until occupancy returns to pre-2001 levels and compression begins to build. . . . National consortium and high volume travel contracts are being finalized for 2005. Hotels will have to be successful in achieving significant rate hikes through these conduits, since the past two years of negotiations have yielded little or no rate increase as operating expense inflated."

Further insight into the challenge facing hoteliers is expressed by Tom Belden of The Philadelphia Inquirer, who relates that 94 percent of the 112 corporations surveyed by the Business Travel Coalition of Radnor, Pennsylvania, cut their travel spending over a three-year period. He reports that one participant increased its use of web-based meeting software by 50 percent in one particular year.

The delivery of hospitality in hotels has also come under review. For example, hoteliers are reviewing security plans to include the front-line employee who must take immediate action based on observations at the front desk, in the dining room and recreational areas, and on guest and public floors. The front-line employee who sees uncommon activities has to know the importance of reporting concerns to supervisors. Special training in what to look for in guest interactions in public areas and on guest floors assists the front-line person in becoming proactive.

Hoteliers must also be concerned with how to support hospitality as part of responsible community citizenship. Hotel general managers should develop emergency plans that allow immediately offering public space to medical personnel and disaster victims. Short-term concerns such as feeding disaster victims and emergency personnel and long-term commitments such as housing displaced members of the community are among the many issues faced by the hotel industry.

Liability implications for the owner, management contractor, or lessee with respect to repair of facilities have arisen in addition to concerns for the safety of guests resulting from terrorism. Andrew MacGeoch, reporting in Hotel, notes:

The obligation of an owner to repair the hotel under a management agreement usually depends on the extent of the damage. In general, if the costs of repair do not exceed a certain threshold specified in the management agreement [which is usually a certain percentage of the replacement costs of the hotel], the owner will be obliged to repair the hotel to its condition prior to the destruction. However, if the costs of repair exceed the specified threshold, the owner will have the right to choose not to undertake the repair and to terminate the management agreement.

MacGeoch continues with a note on liability toward guests by acts of terrorism.

Generally, neither the operator nor the owner would be held liable for any injury or death caused by terrorist activities, unless the owner or operator has failed to exercise reasonable care for the safety and security of their guests. Therefore, to make sure that the reasonable-care standard is met, it is necessary and advisable for owners and operators to take reasonable and necessary steps to protect the safety of guests, including implementing appropriate security policies and measures and providing crisis-management training to all employees.

These issues of marketing, delivering hospitality and the ramifications of possible terrorism are ongoing concerns that hoteliers must continue to discuss. They must focus on goals and subsequent planning for implementation of a safe environment for guests and employees.

OVERVIEW OF THE HOTEL INDUSTRY

A working knowledge of the classifications used in the hotel industry is important to understanding its organization. The various types of properties, their market orientation and location, sales indicators, occupancy, and revenues as they relate to levels of service and various types of business affiliations are all means of classifying hotel properties.

Types of Lodging Facilities

Classification of hotel facilities is not based on rigid criteria. The definitions can change depending on market forces, legal criteria, location, function, and, in some cases, personal preference, but the definitions that follow are generally accepted and are the ones intended for these classifications throughout this text.

Hotels

A hotel usually offers guests a full range of accommodations and services, which may include reservations, suites, public dining and banquet facilities, lounge and entertainment areas, room service, cable television, personal computers, business services, meeting rooms, specialty shops, personal services, valet, laundry, hair care, swimming pool and other recreational activities, gaming/casino operations, ground transportation to and from an airport, and concierge services. The size of the property can range from 20 to more than 2,000 rooms. Hotels are found in center-city, suburban, and airport locations. Guest stays can be overnight or long-term, as much as several weeks in length. Properties sometimes specialize in catering to particular markets, such as conventions or gambling. Casino hotels usually take a secondary role to the casino operation, where the emphasis is on profitable gaming operations. Marriott's hotels operated as JW Marriott Hotels & Resorts and Renaissance Hotels, as well as Hyatt Hotels &C Resorts brands operated as Hyatt Regency, Grand Hyatt, and Park Hyatt Hotels, are examples in this category.

Motels

Motels offer guests a limited range of services, which may include reservations, vending machines, swimming pools, and cable television. The size of these properties averages from 10 to 50 units. Motels are usually in suburban highway and airport locations. Guests typically stay overnight or for a few days. Motels may be located near a freestanding restaurant.

All-Suites

The all-suites concept was developed in the 1980s as a separate marketing concept. These hotels offer guests a wide range of services that may include reservations, living room and separate bedroom, kitchenette, optional public dining room and room service, cable television, videocassette players and recorders, specialty shops, personal services, valet and laundry, swimming pool, and ground transportation to and from an airport. The size of the operation can range from 50 to more than 100 units. This type of property is usually found in center-city, suburban, and airport locations. The length of guest stay can be overnight, several days, or long term. Although this type of hotel may seem new, many downtown, center-city hotels have offered accommodations with in-room kitchenette and sitting room since the early 1900s. Now with mass marketing-advertising products and services through mass communications such as television, radio, and the Internet- this type of hotel is considered "new." Examples of the all-suite concept include Hilton's Embassy Suites and InterContinental's Candlewood Suites.

Limited-Service Hotels

Limited-service hotels appeared in the mid-1980s. Hampton

Inn and Marriott were among the first organizations to offer limited-service properties.

The concept of limited service was developed for a specific segment of the market: business and cost-conscious travelers. The range of accommodations and services may include reservations, minimal public dining and meeting facilities, cable television, personal computers, personal services (valet and laundry), and ground transportation to and from an airport. The size of the property can range from 100 to more than 200 rooms. Limited-service hotels are found in center-city, suburban, and airport locations. They are usually located near restaurants for guest convenience. Guest stays can be overnight or long term. These properties sometimes specialize in catering to the business traveler and offer special business technology centers. Limited-service hotel properties include Holiday InnExpress, operated by InterContinetal Hotels Group; Comfort Inn, by Choice Hotels International; and Marriott's Fairfield Inn.

Extended-Stay Hotels

Extended-stay properties were designed to offer guests a home-away-from-home atmosphere over long stays precipitated by business, leisure, or personal necessity. For example, a person may have to attend to a business project for several days or weeks; another may want to visit with relatives whose home does not have adequate accommodations for visitors; a third may be accompanying a relative or friend receiving an extended health treatment at a medical center and require overnight accommodations. The patient himself may appreciate the homelike atmosphere of the extended-stay hotel in which to recover between treatments.

Leon Stafford of The Atlanta Journal-Constitution writes, "The big, fancy hotels . . . have struggled to get 60 percent of their rooms filled since 2001. Meanwhile, extended-stays . . . have remained at least 70 percent filled." He adds an interesting concept for your career development consideration: "About three extended-stay lodges were built for every traditional hotel constructed between 2001 and 2004." At Hilton's Homewood Suites, the following room amenities are included: king-size bed or two double beds in the bedroom and foldout sofa in the living room; two remote-controlled color televisions; fully equipped kitchen with a microwave, refrigerator with ice maker, coffeemaker, twin-burner stove, and kitchen utensils; a spacious, well-lit dining area; and ceiling fans and iron and ironing board. Additional hotel services include a business center, an exercise room, and a pool. This hotel concept also structures its room rates to attract the long-term guest.

Market Orientation

Market orientation in the hotel industry is categorized into two segments: (1) residential hotels, which provide guest accommodations for the long term; and (2) commercial hotels, which provide short-term accommodations for traveling guests.

Residential properties include hotels, all-suites, limited-service, and extended-stay properties. Services may include (but are not limited to) public dining, recreational facilities, social activities, and personal services. These hotels are usually located in center-city and suburban areas where other activities (shopping, arts and entertainment, business services, public transportation) are available to round out the living experience.

Commercial properties service the short-term transient guest. Services include (but are not limited to) computerized reservation systems, public dining, banquet service, lounge and entertainment areas, personal services, and shuttle transportation to airports. These hotels may be located almost anywhere.

It is essential to note the gray areas where these two categories overlap. A commercial lodging establishment may have a certain percentage of permanent residents. Likewise, a residential hotel may have nightly rentals available. Owners and general managers must exhibit a great deal of flexibility in meeting the needs of the available markets.

Sales Indicators

Sales indicators, including hotel occupancy and average daily rate, are another way of describing hotels. This information is necessary for business investors to estimate the profitability of a hotel. Four factors measure a hotel's degree of financial success: occupancy percentage, average daily rate, yield percentage, and revenue per available room (RevPAR). Occupancy percentage is the number of rooms sold divided by the number of rooms available. Average daily rate (ADR) is the total room revenue divided by the number of rooms sold. Yield percentage, the effectiveness of a hotel at selling its rooms at the highest rate available to the most profitable guest, reveals a facility's success in selling its room inventory on a daily basis. RevPAR is used to indicate the ability of each guest room to produce a profit. Once the daily sales opportunity has presented itself, it cannot be repeated (excluding the opportunity to sell a room at a half-day rate).

Occupancy

Occupancy percentages measure the effectiveness of the marketing and sales department as well as the external and internal marketing efforts of the front office. Occupancy percentage is also used by investors to determine the potential gross income, or the amount of sales a hotel might obtain at a given level of occupancy, average daily rate, and anticipated yield. However, it is important not to assume that occupancy is standard each night. Variations occur daily and seasonally.

Average Daily Rate

The average daily rate (sometimes referred to as average room rate) is also used in projecting room revenues-the amount of room sales received-for a hotel. However, this figure also affects guests' expectations of their hotel experience. Guests expect higher room rates to correlate with higher levels of service; the hotel with a rate of $175 per night is expected to offer more services than a hotel in the same geographic area with a rate of $85 per night. These expectations have been extensively capitalized on by major hotel chains, which develop different properties to meet the expectations of various segments of the hotel market.

Yield Percentage

Yield percentage measures a hotel manager's efforts in achieving maximum occupancy at the highest room rate possible. This term is discussed more fully in chapter 6. It is sufficient to note here that this concept is relatively new in the hotel industry. Prior to the 1990s, hotel managers relied on occupancy and average daily rate as indicators of meeting financial goals. Yield percentage forces managers to think in more active terms.

RevPAR (Revenue per Available Room)

RevPAR is determined by dividing room revenue received for a specific day by the number of rooms available in the hotel for that day. The formulas for determining RevPAR are as follows:

Room Revenue

Number of Available Rooms

or

Hotel Occupancy x Average Daily Rate

For example, RevPAR for a hotel that has $10,000 in room revenue for the night of September 15 with 200 rooms available equals $50 ($10,000 ÷ 200 = $50).

This same hotel on September 15 with 200 rooms, room revenue of $10,000, 125 rooms sold at an average daily rate of $80 ($10,000 ÷ 125 = $80), and with hotel occupancy of 62.5 percent (125 rooms sold ÷ 200 rooms available x 100 = 62.5 percent), produces the same RevPAR (0.625 x $80 = $50).

RevPAR is used in hotels to determine the amount of dollars each hotel room produces for the overall financial success of the hotel. The profit from the sale of a hotel room is much greater than that from a similar food and beverage sale. However, the food and beverage aspect of the hotel industry is essential in attracting some categories of guests who want conference services.

Consider the following article, "January RevPAR Grows Nearly Ten Percent at Suburban Lodge Company-Owned Hotels," which was published online. It shows how RevPAR is dependent on hotel occupancy. This article also addresses the importance of using RevPAR to present a fuller financial picture based on factors that affect room sales, such as economic conditions, weather patterns, and business travel, and ownership.

NEW YORK, September 16, 2004: PricewaterhouseCoopers forecasts revenue per available room (RevPAR) to increase by 6.3 percent in 2004, the largest increase in 20 years. The 3.7 forecast increase in average daily rate in 2004 will contribute almost 60 percent of the total forecast RevPAR gain for the year. Many factors support the favorable outlook for ADR:

1. upward revisions to inflation forecasts;
2. acceleration of business travel and the consequent increase in higher-rate lodging demand;
3. consolidation of ownership, and therefore, more properties under pricing discipline;
4. dramatic increase in control being exercised by hotel companies and owners over rate integrity and inventory, leading to less discounting on third-party distribution channels; and
5. aftermath of hurricanes in Florida, generating room demand from people involved in damage assessment, insurance, and reconstruction in otherwise low-occupancy months, with especially positive effects on room rates.

The lodging expansion that is underway will bring lodging demand to 2.71 million daily occupied rooms in 2004, or 2.1 percent above the previous peak level recorded in the 2000. With supply expanding by only 1.3 percent in 2004 amid 3.7 percent demand growth, occupancy will advance to 60.6 percent, an increase of 1.5 occupancy points from 2003.

"We were criticized for being too negative in 2002 and 2003, but our forecasts were almost exactly the actual results, and for 2004 and 2005 we have been criticized for being too positive. But this regularly scheduled quarterly update is for even more positive growth in rate; our demand forecast for 2004 is unchanged," said Dr. Bjorn Hanson, Global Practice Leader of PricewaterhouseCoopers Hospitality &C Leisure Practice.

Real GDP is forecast by Macroeconomic Advisers to grow by 4.4 percent in 2004, followed by 3.9 percent growth in 2005 and 3.6 percent growth in 2006. Consumer prices are expected to advance by 2.7 percent in 2004, followed by 2.2 percent annual increases in both 2005 and 2006. These new forecasts represent slightly slower real GDP growth and an acceleration in inflationary pressures, compared to the macro-economic forecasts underlying our June 2004 forecasts. Demand growth is expected to moderate in the next two years to the long-term annual growth rate of approximately 2.8 percent. Occupancies will improve to 62.1 percent by 2006, as supply growth remains moderate at 1.5 percent in 2005 and 1.7 percent in 2006.

After achieving 3.7 percent growth in 2004, ADR will increase by 3.5 percent in 2005 and 3.4 percent in 2006, making ADR increases the primary driver of the robust forecast RevPAR growth of 5.0 percent in 2005 and 4.5 percent in 2006.

Levels of Service

The four commonly used market segments-identifiable groups of customers with similar needs for products and services-are full service, all-suites, limited service, and extended stay. There is a great deal of overlap among these divisions, and much confusion, some of which occurs because leaders in the hotel industry do not agree on terminology. Some industry leaders avoid the "budget" tag because of its connotations of cheapness and poor quality. Others welcome the label because it appeals to travelers looking for basic accommodations at inexpensive rates. Nevertheless, the following definitions provide some idea of what is offered at each level of service.

Full service is a level that provides a wide range of conveniences for the guest. These services include, but are not limited to, reservations, on-premises dining, banquet and meeting facilities, and recreational facilities. Examples of full-service hotels include Marriott Hotels and Resorts, Renaissance Hotels, and Holiday Inns. As discussed earlier, the all-suites category indicates a level of service appropriate for a guest who desires an at-home atmosphere. Services include separate sleeping and living areas or working areas, kitchenette facilities, wet bars, and other amenities at the mid-price level. This concept appeals to the business traveler as well as to families. Marriott's SpringHill Suites and Embassy Suites Hotels are examples of all-suite hotels. It is interesting to note that this concept is also employed in older center-city commercial hotels, in which rooms adjoining the bedroom and bath have been remodeled as living rooms and kitchenettes to create suites.

Limited service emphasizes basic room accommodations, guest amenities, and minimal public areas. A continental breakfast and/

or an evening cocktail is often included in the price of the room. The guest has the opportunity to trade the public meeting room for free in-room movies, the dining room for free local phone calls. Hampton Inns and Holiday Inn Express Limited are examples of limited-service hotels.

Extended stay is a level of service that offers a home-away-from-home atmosphere for business executives, visitors, and families who are planning to visit an area for an extended period. A fully equipped kitchenette allows international guests to prepare com-forting foods in a new environment. The spacious bedrooms and living areas provide work and recreational areas. Light breakfast and evening meals included. Examples of this level of service include Hilton's Homewood Suites hotels, InterContinental's Stay-bridge Suites, and Choice Hotels International's MainStay Suites.

Business Affiliations

Business affiliations, which indicate either chain or independent ownership of hotels, also categorize the hotel industry. These classifications are the most easily recognizable by consumers with regard to such features as brand name, structural appearance, and ambience. Long-lasting marketing effects develop a brand loyalty and acceptance that are most important to the long-term profitability for a hotel.

Chain Affiliation

When asked to name several chain operations (a group of hotels that follow standard operating procedures such as marketing, reservations, quality of service, food and beverage operations, housekeeping, and accounting), most people would probably mention Holiday Inn, Marriott, Sheraton, Days Inn, Hyatt, Hilton, or Econo Lodge. Students should stay up to date regarding developments in the industry, such as acquisitions, restructuring, and other changes in these organizations. This information, important to know when making career decisions, can be obtained from trade journals such as Hotels (published by Cahners, Des Plaines, Illinois), whose annual July issue includes a listing of hotel chains, addresses, and number of rooms; the Wall Street

Journal; and other newspapers, magazines, and websites. Chain affiliations, which include hotels that purchase operational .and marketing services from a corporation, are further divided into franchisee, referral, company-owned properties, and management contract companies. Franchise corporations offer support to the franchisee, who is the owner of the land and building, in the form of reservation systems, advertising, operations management, and management development. In return for these services, the franchisee pays fees for items such as initial startup, rental of signs and other equipment, use of the corporation's reservation referral system, and national advertising.

Anyone wishing to enter the hotel business by investing personal funds wants to be sure of realizing a profit. Perhaps due to lack of experience in operating a hotel or motel, a lack of business acumen, a poor credit rating, or limited knowledge of real estate devel-opment, this type of entrepreneur may need to seek the guidance of others. He or she can receive direction from a corporation, such as Days Inn, Sheraton, or Hilton, concerning land, building, and management development.

Referral Property

Sometimes a hotel organization chooses to become a referral property-that is, to operate as an independent in association with a certain chain. Because the property is already physically developed, the entrepreneur may want assistance only with management, marketing and advertising, or reservation referral. Likewise, the fees are based on services required. The chain's quality assurance standards must, however, be met by the referral property.

Company-Owned Property

A company-owned property, a hotel that is owned and operated by a chain organization, allows the hotel company developer to act as an independent entrepreneur. The hotel company developer operates the hotel property in competition with all other properties in the area. It uses its own expertise in site selection, property development, marketing and advertising, and operations management. The hotel company developer recruits talented professions into the organization to manage such properties. It uses the chain's reservation system. The hotel company developer may set a limit on the number of franchises so that a majority of the properties remain company-owned.

Management Contract Property

A management contract property, a hotel operated by a consulting company that provides operational and marketing expertise and a professional staff, is similar to a referral property. Several management contract organizations develop business relationships with existing hotels and operate the hotels as their own. Their business relationship requires financial accountability and profitability. Management contract companies may choose to operate each hotel as a member of a franchise or as an independent.

Brands

Hotel brands are an important part of the lodging industry, especially in consumer marketing. Branding allows a hotel company to create a concept in the mind of a consumer. This mind-concept helps the consumer classify a hotel's offerings. For example, a ficti-tious brand such as the Hotel Flower Chain may have three distinct offerings in its portfolio of lodgings: the Tulip Extended Stay, the Rose Limited Inn, and the Violet All-Suites. Another fictitious brand such as the Timber Chain may have seven more brands in their chain with similar facilities, such as the Pine All-Suites, the Maple All-Suites, the Sunset Extended-Stay Suites, the Timber Express, the Timber Grand Hotels, the Timber Falls, and the Pine Limited Service.

Each of these brands has distinct product and service offerings such as communication via website, reservation service, reservation reward point program, room accommodations, food service, personal fitness and business equipment, and meeting and convention facilities. Therefore, when guests have certain needs for business or pleasure traveling, they can match them up to a certain brand.

The following is a list of major hotel brands. Further information can be accessed on each of the hotel companies on the Internet.

Independent Properties

An independent hotel is one that is not associated with a franchise. It provides a greater sense of warmth and individuality than does a property associated with a chain. Independent hotel characteristics include an owner who functions as a manager, room rates similar to chain properties, rooms decorated in different styles, and inviting dining rooms. These hotels may be residential or commercial, with locations in the center city, suburbia, along the highway, or near an airport. The number of rooms can range from 50 to 1,000. They may offer full services to the guest, including suites, dining room, room service, banquets, gift shop, beauty shop, athletic facilities, swimming pool, theaters, valet services, concierge, and airport shuttle service. Some older independent hotels have refurbished their suites to capture a share of the all-suites market.

With all of these advantages, why aren't all lodging properties independent? The answer lies with the U.S. economy. The development of large chains and of smaller properties often brings tax advantages and improved profits to investors. Millions of dollars in capital are required to develop a 2,000-room full-service property. Business, financial, and managerial expertise is more readily available in a company in which there is a pool of skilled experts. Large corporations can also offset financial losses in certain fiscal years or from certain properties against financial gains of other companies or properties in their diversified portfolios.

The independent entrepreneur operates his or her business without the advantages of consultation and assistance. This person may have worked for a large chain or gained a great deal of operations and development experience in the industry. He or she may also purchase a hotel property to balance an investment portfolio. As for any financial investment, the entrepreneur seeks a professional to manage and operate the establishment. The person chosen for this job must manage all aspects of the business: room, food and beverage, housekeeping, security, maintenance, parking, controller's office, and marketing and sales. All business decisions on expenditures must be coordinated with a profit-and-loss statement and a balance sheet. Every sale of a guest room, every guest purchase of food and beverage, occurs because the management of that property has been able to market and manage the property effectively. The challenge of managing an independent property can be overwhelming. It can, however, also offer enormous satisfaction and financial independence.

Trends That Foster Growth

Future professionals in the hotel industry must be able to analyze who their customers will be and why they will have customers. Marketing classes teach how to determine the buyers of a particular product-who the potential guests of a particular hotel property are. Such courses show how to evaluate demographic data (the size, density, distribution, and vital statistics of a population broken down into, for example, age, sex, martial status, and occupation categories) and psychographic data (emotional and motivational forces that affect a service or product) for potential markets.

The second question-why there will be customers-is an important one. Students will explore this question many times during their career in the lodging industry. A manager must plan for profitable results. This plan must take into account the reasons customers purchase a product-what trends will increase or decrease the need for hotel facilities? Factors include the growth of leisure time, the development of the me/pleasure concept, increases in discretionary income, the trend toward smaller families, changes in business travel, and expansion of the travel experience. Other economics and political trends- such as public liability, insurance costs, overbuilding, the value of the U.S. dollar overseas, gasoline prices, safety from random danger while traveling, and legislation-affect commerce; labor and the airline industry also have an impact on current sales as well as growth in the lodging industry.

Leisure Time

The trend toward increased leisure time-in the form of three-day weekends, paid vacations and personal days, a workweek of 40 hours or less, and early retirement-sets the stage for the growth of the lodging industry. As more people have available leisure time to explore new geographical areas, try new hobbies, sample culinary trends, participate in sporting events, and just relax, the customer base of the hotel industry expands.

Workers are spending fewer years in the labor force as the concept of early retirement becomes more popular. As the population segment known as the baby boom ages, the number of retirees is projected to soar. Many of them will take on a second career, but part-time jobs will likely be more common. With the two prime ingredients for using hotel facilities-time and money-readily at hand, these people will be a primary market for the hotel industry.

Me/Pleasure Concept

The idea of deserving recreation away from the job to restore mental acuity and improve attitude has evolved over the years. The work ethic of the eighteenth and nineteenth centuries strongly influenced the way Americans played, as recreation and leisure were considered privileges reserved for the wealthy. Today, most workers enjoy vacations and the feeling of getting away from it all. This trend toward fulfilling personal needs continues in the twenty-first century.

The isolated nature of many jobs increases the need for respite. As more and more people find themselves spending more time communicating via computer and other machinery rather than face to face, social needs continue to grow. Workers need the away-from-job experience to balance their social and mental needs with their daily-life demands. Travel helps satisfy these needs, and the hotel industry benefits as a result.

Discretionary Income

Discretionary income, the money remaining from wages after paying for necessities such as food, clothing, and shelter, is the most important of all the trends that support the growth of the hospitality industry. One of the main reasons for the increase in discre-tionary income of American families is the emergence of the two-income family. An almost double-income family unit has emerged over the years as more married women join or stay in the labor force. The strong growth in this labor segment will undoubtedly continue. As more income becomes available to pay for the necessities of life, discretionary income for leisure time and corresponding goods and services also becomes available.

Discretionary income is not a constant. It is strongly affected by economic factors; an economic downturn with increased unemployment reduces discretionary income, for example. Different economic conditions tend to favor different ways of spending discretionary income; for example, low interest rates, which make the purchase of high-ticket items (such as homes, cars, boats, and aircraft) more desirable, make less discretionary income available for short vacations or quick day trips. Students of the U.S. economy need only review the effects of recessions, the energy crisis of the 1970s, and September 11, 2001, to see how quickly discretionary income formerly directed to the hospitality industry can evaporate.

Family Size/Household Size

The current trend toward smaller families also indicates growth for the hospitality industry. The discretionary income available for a family with two children is greater than that for a family with five children when total incomes are equal. Household size-the num-ber of persons in a home-has decreased over the years. Like the trend toward smaller families, the increased number of small households indicates that more discretionary income is available. The costs associated with a one- or two-person household are less than those for a household of four or more people. Moreover, people who live in smaller households are more likely to dine out, travel, and participate in leisure-time activities.

Business Travel

Corporate business travel should not be taken for granted by hotel managers in today's world of high energy prices and speedy communication. Oil prices significantly affect business travel; as the cost of fuel oil rises, higher prices for air travel and other means of transportation result. A business is not always willing or able to increase its travel budget. When travel costs increase, less travel is undertaken and the necessity for any business travel is reviewed. Executives no longer hop the next plane to clinch a deal if the same task can be accomplished via a phone call, (conference call) in which three or more persons are linked by telephone (or PictureTel, which is the use of telephone lines to send and receive video and audio impressions). Shorter trips (day trips or one-night stays) are another response to the increased cost of travel.

Business travel often represents the largest portion of the regular income of a hotel property. This prime market must be constantly reviewed for economic details that affect its viability.

Female Business Travel

Female business travelers represent an increasing segment of the corporate travel market. As previously discussed, their travel is affected by energy prices and speedy communication. This particular market segment requires close attention to fulfilling special needs. Female travelers request particular amenities and demand close attention to safety. Marketing and sales managers must develop products and services to capture this growing market segment.

Travel as Experience

At one time, people traveled primarily out of necessity; business and family visits were the usual reasons for traveling. Today, people travel for many reasons, including education, culture, and personal development. Many people want to learn more about the society in which they live. They have studied American or world history and want to see the places they have read about. Cultural pursuits-art, theater, music, opera, ballet, and museums-can attract a constant flow of people. Sports and nature attract travelers who want to enjoy the great outdoors as well as those who prefer to watch their favorite teams. The push for lifelong learning has provided an incentive for many to take personal development/enrichment courses, whether to update professional skills or to increase knowledge of a particular hobby. Ecotourists, people who plan vacations to study the culture and environment of a particular area, want to enjoy nature in its unblemished and unsullied form.

Career Development

An introductory chapter on hotel management would not be complete without attention to career development. People planning a career in the hotel industry need to review the fundamentals of career development, which revolve around five important concepts:

educational preparation, practical experience, membership in professional organizations, ports of entry, and growth areas for the industry.

Educational Preparation

The educational base you build now will serve you well over time. The classes you are taking in your major course of study-including management and supervision, cost control, human resources management, quantity food production, hotel management, purchasing, sanitation, layout and design, accounting, and marketing-constitute a strong foundation for your continued development of technical skills. Courses outside your major-such as English, speech communication, computer training, arts, economics, psychology, sociology, nutrition, science, and math-will help develop the skills you need to cope in the professional world. The formal education you receive in your classroom study will be enhanced by extracurricular activities such as clubs, student government, sports, and other areas of special interest. These activities are a microcosm of the environment in which you will apply your technical, liberal arts, and science courses. Clubs associated with your major, in particular, allow you to apply theoretical concepts learned in class to a real-life business environment.

Your educational experience will open the door to your career. You must apply your skills and knowledge after graduation to be an effective, successful employee in the hotel industry. Use your degree as a starting point for an exciting career in hospitality.

The educational experience you are now obtaining must be nurtured beyond graduation day. There are many opportunities for in-service education, which are courses that update a professional's educational background for use in current practice; these are offered by professional organizations, sponsors of trade shows, community colleges and universities, technical schools, correspondence schools, trade journals, and other industry groups, providing the professional an opportunity to stay current in industry practices.

Just as professionals in other industries take classes to refresh their skills and learn new concepts and procedures, so must professionals in the hotel industry maintain awareness of industry advances. One particularly relevant area is computer training. Professionals who attended school before the early 1980s had little exposure to computers and their ever-changing technology; even recent graduates are not always aware of the most current trends and advances. The professional has the choice of overlooking this need or enrolling in computer applications courses. The next choice is to determine whether these new procedures and equipment are applicable to a particular establishment.

Professional organizations-such as the American Hotel & Lodging Association, the Hotel Sales and Marketing Association International, and the National Restaurant Association-offer professionals continuing education opportunities through correspondence courses and seminars. The American Hotel &C Lodging Association offers opportunities for hotel employees to become a Certified Hotel Administrator (CHA) and Certified Rooms Division Executive (CRDE), among other certifications. Trade shows sponsored by these organizations promote the latest concepts in technology, products, and supplies as well as providing miniseminars on how to use current technology in human resources management, food production, marketing, and general management. Community colleges and technical schools offer special-interest courses in management and skills application to keep you and your staff abreast of new areas and to review basic concepts. Attending these courses can provide new insight into operational problems. Each of these professional organizations sponsors a website and provides opportunities to access the abovementioned career information.

Correspondence courses are another way to learn new skills and understand new areas. New technology in distance learning-classes offered via satellite broadcasts, cable, PictureTel, or online computer interaction-is offered by colleges, universities, and professional groups.

Trade journals are also extremely helpful in keeping professionals up to date with new management concepts, technical applications, marketing principles, equipment innovations, and the like. The isolation experienced by managers in out-of-the-way hotel estab-lishments can be alleviated by reading trade journals.

Such journals help all managers feel connected to the community of hotel industry professionals, perhaps providing insight into solving technical problems as well as boosting morale. Some trade journals are offered free on the Internet.

Education is a lifelong venture; it does not stop with the attainment of a degree from a university or community college. The degree is only the beginning of a commitment to nurturing your career.

Work Experience

The practical experience you obtain from entry-level hotel jobs-whether you are a desk clerk, waiter/waitress, host/hostess, maid/houseman/room attendant, bellhop, or groundskeeper-will be invaluable as you plan and develop your career in the hotel industry. It will give you an opportunity to learn what hotel employees do and how departments interact, and it will expose you to the momentum of a hotel-the time frame of service available for the guest, management applications, and service concept applica-tions, to name just a few.

Your work experience will enable you to evaluate theoretical concepts offered in the classroom. You will have a basis for comparing your work experiences with those of other students. You will also develop your own beliefs and behaviors, which can be applied to other hotel properties throughout your career. At times, you will have to think on your feet in order to resolve a guest complaint, evaluate equipment proposals, reorganize work areas for efficiency, or achieve cost-effective spending. Your work experience provides you with the proper foundation on which to base a successful career.

Professional Memberships

A professional trade organization is a group of people who voluntarily pool their efforts to achieve a set of goals. These goals may have a political nature, such as lobbying legislators or providing certification of achievement.

Professional trade organizations in the hospitality industry serve members in many ways. First and foremost, they are a political voice in government. Through use of membership fees, trade organizations are able to lobby local, state, and federal legislators to be sure the entrepreneur's views are recognized. Members can opt not to have their membership fee used to support legislators who they don't politically support on personal issues. These organizations also offer significant opportunities for continuing education by sponsoring seminars and trade shows. They offer group plans for insurance and other programs that can be cost-efficient to the entrepreneur. Professional trade associations also allow you to interact with others in the industry on both a professional and a social level. Valuable advice and rewarding friendships often result.

Ports of Entry

A review of the organizational structure of a hotel shows many departmental managers in a large organization. Which area is the best for you to enter to develop your career goals? Four of the ports of entry are marketing and sales, front office, food and beverage, and controller. It is impossible to say which the best port of entry is; all are avenues for career development.

The hotel industry demands a great deal of its professionals. All employees must have extensive knowledge of all areas of the facility, and they must understand the overall function of all departments. This understanding must be reflected in professional business plans. Employees must also have good communication skills and good interpersonal skills. The industry requires great flexibility in scheduling work responsibilities and personal life. It demands that the professional understand the entrepreneurial role of corporate owners while operating within budgeted resources.

Students who enter the lodging industry will find that each area in which they work contributes to a good background for the ultimate position of general manager. When trying to decide where to begin, consider reviewing the job responsibilities of department managers to learn what tasks are required to complete each job and who is involved in doing so.

Try to work in as many areas as you can before taking the leap into a general manager position. The job will be a lot easier, and you will go a long way toward meeting the establishment's goals if you are well prepared. You will make mistakes, no matter how much experience you have had; however, your success rate will be much higher if you have a varied background in many departments.

Researching Growth Areas in the Hospitality Industry

Areas that offer the most potential for growth should be explored. Because such areas change frequently, it is not possible to list them in a textbook. However, factors that support continued growth and strong business activity are regularly reported in such publications as Trends in the Lodging Industry, by Pannell, Kerr, and Forster.

Hospitality industry futures projections publications usually cover such issues as new hotel developments; hotels under consideration; activities of convention and visitors' bureaus; strength of local economies; development of business, recreation, and arts activities; the need for office space; and area hotel occupancy percentages and average room rates. This information is listed for selected cities both within the United States and at international sites.

The Internet is increasingly used as a method for researching career opportunities in hospitality management. Search engines will produce multiple listings of hospitality recruiters with key words such as "hotel manager," "front office manager," and "hotel careers." Also, professional hospitality organizations usually offer a job-posting service on their websites.

The Internet provides many opportunities for a new graduate to examine trends that are driving the industry and new technologies that will shape a career in hotel management. This information can assist job applicants in exploring the employment possibilities and prospects in different geographic areas.

Your survey of career possibilities should include a review of a potential employer's economic performance on a balance sheet and other features of its profit-and-loss statement. This information is available on computerized business databases. Take the time to research the economic potential of the company you are considering. Your interview preparations should include reviewing the regional economic prospects and the company's economic performance. This preparation could set the stage for an investment that lasts many years, perhaps a lifetime.

Solution to Opening Dilemma

The effort you put into preparing for a visit to a career fair is essential for making this a learning and networking opportunity for you. Questions you could ask a representative of a limited-service hotel include, "What are the typical management responsibilities of an assistant general manager in your organization? What types of visitors frequent your hotels during the week and on the weekend? What is the typical size of your hotels?" Questions you may want to consider asking a representative of a full-service hotel include, "What size staff is employed in your hotel? Do you have any convention hotels in your portfolio? What services do you typically offer in a hotel in your organization?" These types of questions open lines of communication and help you present yourself as a future professional.

2

Hotel Organization and the Front Office Manager

At a recent staff meeting, the general manager of The Times Hotel asked if anyone wanted to address the group. The director of housekeeping indicated he was at a loss in trying to work with the front desk clerks. He had repeatedly called the desk clerks last Tuesday to let them know that general housecleaning would be performed on the seventh and eighth floors on Wednesday morning and that they should not assign rooms on those floors to guests on Tuesday night. When the cleaning crew came to work on Wednesday morning, they were faced with 14 occupied rooms on the seventh floor and 12 occupied rooms on the eighth floor. This cost the hotel several hundred dollars because the cleaning crew was from an outsourced contract company, which charged the hotel a basic fee for failure to comply with the contract. The front office manager retorted that a bus group called two weeks ago and asked if any rooms were available because there was a mix-up in room rates at the group's original hotel. The front office manager indicated something must have gone awry in the computer system. After all, this was a good opportunity to bring in 26 additional room-nights.

Organization of Lodging Properties

The objective of most hospitality establishments is to produce a profit. To meet this goal, factors such as current economic conditions, marketing plans, competition, and staff size and ability are constantly reviewed. The general manager, the person in charge of directing and leading the hotel staff in meeting its financial, environmental, and community responsibilities, develops organization charts that fit his or her plan to meet the goals of the company. The organization charts-schematic drawings that list management positions in an organization-included in this chapter are offered only as instructional examples. An organization chart repre-sents the span of control for the general manager. Not all hotels have every position listed in these organization charts. Persons pursuing a career in the hotel industry will be called on many times throughout their career to develop or restructure an organization. The people who are part of these operational plans will have a direct influence on the type of structure developed or reorganized. The goals of the organization must be paramount in the decision-making process. However, there must be flexibility to make the plan work. This section points out the major organizational features of a lodging property and typical managerial duties of the people within the organization.

It is not uncommon for a general manager of a property to move people from department to department of the hotel. This is done for many reasons. The front office manager, the person responsible for leading the front office staff in delivering hospitality, may express interest in the position of controller, the internal accountant for the hotel, or in a position in the marketing and sales department.

The general manager realizes a candidate must possess certain skills before being placed in any new position. To prepare someone for an opening in the controller's office, the general manager may assign him or her some of the controller's busywork. The front office manager might also spend slack periods with the director of marketing and sales, the person who analyzes available markets and sells products and services at a profit, to become familiar with that department.

The general manager may also use the weekly staff meeting to explain the financial condition and marketing plans of the property. This tactic reinforces the management team concept. By exposing interested employees to the responsibilities of other departments and by keeping the staff informed of the current situation of the property, the general manager enables staff members to meet their career goals within the organization.

Flexibility is the key to hospitality organization. At the operations level, familiarity with the staff's strengths and weaknesses is essential to meeting the demands of the situation. When the property experiences an expected slow period, regrouping may be necessary to maintain full-time positions. The front office manager may have to assist the marketing and sales office in advertising or hosting tour directors for a specific weekend. The food and beverage director might have to spend some time in the controller's office completing reports and developing budgets. This interdepartmental cooperation provides the backdrop for a smooth-running organization. Such flexibility prevents departmental jealousies and territoriality from becoming roadblocks to communication. The general manager receives additional operational support from the director of security, the person who takes a proactive role in establishing and maintaining a safe environment for guests and employees. Because of the precautions necessary in delivering hospitality, the director of security is vital to the operation of the lodging property.

To function as a well-run lodging facility, this property requires the following department heads:

- General manager
- Assistant general manager
- Controller
- Plant engineer
- Executive housekeeper
- Human resources manager
- Director of security
- Recreation director
- Athletics director
- Marketing and sales director
- Gift shop manager
- Front office manager
- Food and beverage director

Garage manager

The corporate owners have entrusted the financial success of this organization to the general manager, who must organize departments to provide optimum service to the guest. Each department is well organized and staffed to allow the supervisor time to plan and develop the major revenue-producing areas. The marketing and sales director, gift shop manager, front office manager, food and beverage director, and garage manager develop programs that increase sales and profits and improve cost-control methods. Those supervisors who do not head income-generating departments-controller, plant engineer, executive housekeeper, director of security, human resources manager, recreation director, and athletics director-provide services to the guest, principally behind the scenes.

For example, the controller develops clear and concise performance reports that reflect budget targets. The plant engineer, the person responsible for the operation and maintenance of the physical plant, establishes an effective preventive maintenance program. The executive housekeeper, the person responsible for the upkeep of the guest rooms and public areas of the lodging property as well as control of guest room inventory items, keeps on top of new trends in controlling costs and effective use of personnel. The director of security provides the training for the staff for front-line safety needs of guests. The human resources manager, the person who assists department managers in organizing personnel functions and developing employees, provides leadership in attracting new hires and maintaining a stable yet progressive approach to utilization of personnel. The recreation director, the person in charge of developing and organizing recreational activities for guests, and the athletics director, who is responsible for supervising physical exercise facilities for guests, provide direct hospitality services for the guest, helping ensure their safe and interesting stay.

This managerial staff seems skeletal compared to that of a large hotel or resort. This type of organization chart is possible because the level of service provided to guests is reduced. At this property, the guest's stay is one or two nights, and a dining room and lounge are provided for convenience. Many of the department heads are working supervisors, which means they participate in the actual work performed while supervising. Laundry and other services are contracted out. The controller provides accounting services as well as human resources management. The maintenance/ groundskeeper oversees indoor and outdoor facilities. The front office manager and the clerks take care of reservations as well as registrations, posting, checkout, and the like. The restaurant manager works closely with the cook and hostess in maintaining quality and cost control and guest services. The housekeeper inspects and cleans rooms and maintains linen and cleaning supply inventories as well as providing leadership for the housekeeping staff. Security services are provided by the general manager and outsourced as needed.

The general manager is a working supervisor in that he or she participates in the actual work performed while supervising at the front desk. The general manager at this type of property assists with marketing plans, reservations, maintenance, and groundskeeping, maintains financial records; and implements cost-control measures. The front office manager works regular shifts to provide coverage along with the night auditor and desk clerks. The housekeeper, also a working supervisor, assists the room attendants, employees who clean and maintain guest rooms and public areas.

The organization charts shown here were developed by evaluating the needs of guests. The organization of departments and the subsequent staffing are influenced by the available labor pool, the economic conditions of the region, and the financial goals of the organization. Each organization chart varies depending on the factors influencing a particular lodging establishment. Flexibility is essential in providing service to the guest and leadership to the staff.

Typical Job Responsibilities of Department Managers

As you begin your career in the lodging industry, you will undoubtedly come in contact with the various department managers in a hotel. Some of the positions seem to be shrouded in mystery, while others are clear. The controller, for example, works behind the scenes, and little about his or her role is obvious. The security director seems to be everywhere in the hotel, but what does this person do, and for what is he or she respon-sible?

The food and beverage director holds a visible position that seems to encompass much. The general manager must be aware of both the forest and the trees, overseeing all operations while staying on top of the small details. How can all of these positions be coordinated to provide hospitality to the guest and profit to the investors?

General Manager

Several years ago I invited a guest speaker to my class. This person was the general manager of an inn in our community. He was well prepared for the lecture and described the organization chart and staff he had developed. After he explained the work that goes on in the various departments and the responsibilities of the respective supervisors, a student asked, "What do you do as the general manager if all the work is being done by your staff?" This honest question made me terribly aware that the role of the general manager is not easy to understand. Indeed, detailing this managerial role could fill volumes and encompass decades of experience. However, the legitimacy of the question compels me to be specific in describing this essential job in the organization chart.

The leadership provided by the general manager is undoubtedly the most important quality he or she brings to this position. The general manager orchestrates the department directors in their efforts to meet the financial goals of the organization through their employees. The general manager is required to use the full range of managerial skills- planning, decision making, organizing, staffing, controlling, directing, and communicat-ing-to develop a competent staff. Performance is judged according to how effectively supervisors are directed to meet the goals of the organization. Efficiency depends not on how well tasks are performed but on how well employees are motivated and instructed to meet the goals and objectives of the plans the general manager and staff have formulated. Figure 2-4 presents a group of managers, supervisors, and frontline employees who carry out the goals of the general manager.

The plans developed by the general manager along with the department supervisors provide the vision the business needs to compete for the hospitality markets. The evaluation of candidates for positions based on a well-structured division of labor begins the process of meeting the goals and objectives of the planning stage. Who should be chosen to lead operations? What skills and strengths are necessary to get the job done? What degree of business acumen must this person have? What vision should be brought to the job? How will the new hire fit into the existing staff? These are just a few questions that a general manager must consider and act upon.

The operational reports-operational data on critical financial aspects of hotel operations-that a general manager must review can be overwhelming in both quantity and complexity. However, the efficient general manager knows which key operating statistics reflect the profitability and efficiency of operations. Do the food cost percentage, labor cost percentage, alcohol beverage cost percentage, and sales item analysis provide enough information to indicate the success of the food and beverage department? Are the daily occupancy percentage, average daily room rate, and total sales for the day adequate to indicate the hotel's profitability? Each general manager develops key indicators that measure the financial success and operational success of the department directors. These concepts are flexible, depending on the goals the corporate ownership established.

Communicating ideas and goals and providing feedback on performance are skills the general manager must develop. The general manager is a pivotal link in the communication process. Each department director works from communications received (or not received) from the general manager. Weekly staff meetings serve as a major vehicle for sharing information. Individual meetings with department directors additionally support the communication process. At one-on-one meetings, the general manager helps the department director transform organizational goals into operational functions.

The general manager offers practical supervisory training to his or her staff. For example, the director of marketing and sales may have set a goal of increasing guest room sales by 10 percent in the next quarter. At an individual meeting with the general manager, the director of marketing and sales agrees to meet that goal over the next three months. What does a general manager do? He or she provides leadership to meet organizational goals of profitability and service. Leadership skills are acquired by studying theories of management and the behavior of other managers as well as practicing leadership and receiving constructive criticism from superiors on efforts expended. The job of general manager is a professional position. It is a career goal the achievement of which is based on operations experience and education.

The role of the general manager, whether in a full-service or limited-service property, must encompass the concepts previously discussed. The general manager in a limited-service property may perform additional hands-on responsibilities, but he or she is required to provide leadership to the other members of the management team. The use of total quality management (TQM), or the application of managerial concepts to understanding operational processes and developing methods to improve those processes (described in chapter 11), allows managers in full-service and limited-service properties to extend leadership to front-line supervisors and employees. In full-service and limited-service properties, where profit margins are based on lean departmental budgets, total quality management is encouraged.

Assistant General Manager

The assistant general manager of a lodging property holds a major responsibility in developing and executing plans developed by the corporate owners, the general manager, and other members of the management staff. The relationship between the general manager and the assistant general manager must be founded on trust, skill, and excellent communication. The assistant general manager works with department directors to meet their respective goals and objectives through efficient operations. Often, he or she is the liai-son between management and operations. The more thoroughly the assistant general manager understands the reasons for management decisions, the better able he or she is to communicate plans to the operations supervisors. The assistant general manager is sometimes referred to as the rooms division manager. He or she is responsible for the entire front office operations, which includes front desk, housekeeping, bell staff, concierge, and parking garage. The assistant general manager may also be called the operations manager.

The assistant general manager often must oversee the beginning of a task and ensure that others complete it. He or she must also complete, review and summarize statistical reports, and share them with the general manager. The assistant general manager is everywhere on the property, checking on operations, providing feedback, and offering assistance as needed. This job requires a wide variety of established operational skills, such as front office, food and beverage, marketing and sales, and accounting. A large property may divide the responsibilities of the assistant general manager between a rooms division manager and an operations division manager.

Limited-service hotels usually do not have an assistant general manager position in their organization chart. The department managers report directly to the general manager to streamline guest services and operational budgets. Again, the general manager of a limited-service property may perform some hands-on tasks, but he or she is required to provide direct leadership to the other members of the management team.

Food and Beverage Director

The food and beverage director is responsible for the efficient operation of the kitchen, dining rooms, banquet service, room service, and lounge. This includes managing a multitude of details with the supervisors of these outlets. Such details include food quality, sanitation, inventory, cost control, training, room setup, cash control, and guest service, to name a few. The food and beverage director keeps a keen eye on new trends in food and beverage merchandising, cost-control factors in food and beverage preparation, and kitchen utilities.

The food and beverage director works closely with the assistant food and beverage director, a highly skilled executive chef, a dining room supervisor, a banquet manager, and a bar manager. This team's goal is to provide high-quality products and services around the clock, every day of the year. Constant supervision of products, employees, and services is essential to ensure a fair return on investment.

Although food and beverages are served at a continental breakfast or cocktail hour at a limited-service property, there is no food and beverage director position; here, the responsibility for serving food and beverages is an extension of the front office manager's duties. However, the same principles of sanitation, food purchasing and storage, marketing, standards of service, and so forth must be followed to provide good service to the guest.

Physical Plant Engineer

The plant engineer is important in the overall delivery of service to the guest. This person oversees a team of electricians, plumbers, heating, ventilating, and air-conditioning contractors, and general repair personnel to provide behind-the-scenes services to the guests and employees of the lodging property. With today's emphasis on preventive maintenance and energy savings, he or she must develop a plan that will keep the lodging property well maintained within budget targets. Knowledge of current advances in equipment and machinery is essential. This position requires a range of experience in general maintenance and a positive attitude about updating skills and management concepts through continuing education.

The plant engineer interacts with all the departments of the hotel. This person is part of the management team and can be relied on to provide sound advice about structural stability, equipment maintenance, and environmental control. He or she can be one of the most treasured assistants in a lodging business.

A role similar to that of the plant engineer in a limited-service property is that of maintenance manager, a staff member who maintains the heating and air-conditioning plant, produces guest room keys, helps housekeeping attendants as required, and assists with safety and security. The limited-service property emphasizes quality in guest service, which is delivered by an efficient staff.

Executive Housekeeper

The executive housekeeper is responsible for the upkeep of the guest rooms and public areas of the lodging property. This person trly must work through other people to get the job done. Each room attendant must be thoroughly trained in cleaning techniques. Each floor inspector, a person who supervises the housekeeping function on a floor of a hotel, and each housekeeping employee must be trained in standard inspection techniques. (Many hotels are moving away from the use of floor inspectors, and are implementing self-inspection systems.) Speed and efficiency are paramount in performing the vital service of maintaining guest rooms and public areas.

Skill in supervising unskilled labor is essential. Survival fluency in foreign languages is important to the executive housekeeper, who must communicate effectively with employees. Accurate scheduling of employees is also necessary to maintain control over labor costs. The executive housekeeper is further responsible for maintaining and controlling an endless inventory of linens, soap, guest amenities, furniture, in-house marketing materials, live and artificial plants, and more. The executive housekeeper, like the plant engi-neer, must stay abreast of new ideas and techniques through trade journals and continuing education courses.

The executive housekeeper supervises the in-house laundry, if one is present. The equipment, cleaning materials, cost controls, and scheduling are handled in cooperation with the laundry supervisor.

The limited-service property depends on this member of the management team to supervise the staff that provides clean rooms and operates an in-house laundry. This hands-on supervisor works with the staff to provide many behind-the-scenes guest services. The housekeeper travels the elevators of high-rise limited-services properties, stopping at each floor to provide employees with constant supervision and motivation.

Interdepartmental cooperation and communication with the front desk and maintenance department are vital for the executive housekeeper in both full-service and limited-service hotels. The release of cleaned rooms for occupancy and the scheduling of periodic maintenance are only two functions demonstrating why interdepartmental cooperation is critical.

In addition, the marketing and sales efforts in hotels depend on the housekeeper to enforce cleanliness and appearance standards in the public areas so guests are attracted to and impressed by the property. More information about the executive housekeeper and that department is detailed in chapter 15 of this textbook.

Human Resources Manager

In a full-service lodging property, the luxury of employing a human resources manager is beneficial for everyone. This person is responsible for administering federal, state, and local employment laws as well as advertising for and screening job candidates and interviewing, selecting, orienting, training, and evaluating employees. Each department director can rely on the human resources manager to provide leadership in the administration of complex personnel programs such as implementation of wage and salary laws. Staffing a hotel involves many time-consuming tasks:

- Writing and placing classified ads
- Screening, interviewing, testing, and selecting candidates
- Orienting, training, and evaluating new employees

The preparation of job descriptions, while perceived by many in the hotel industry as a luxury, is mandatory if the employees are represented by a collective bargaining unit- that is, a labor union. The human resources manager can assist in preparing the job analysis and subsequent job description. This process helps him or her develop realistic job specifications.

The development of employees by providing a plan for the growth of each takes a great deal of planning and evaluating. Each department director works under pressure to meet budget guidelines, quality control levels, sales quotas, and other goals. The human resources manager can assist each director in making plans to motivate employees, to develop career projections for them, to provide realistic pay increases, and to establish employment policies that reflect positively on the employer.

Limited-service properties do not employ a human resources manager but rather divide the responsibilities among department heads. Although the emphasis remains on well-planned and competently delivered human resources activities, the streamlined limited-service property relies on interdepartmental cooperation to accomplish its objectives.

Marketing and Sales Director

In the title of this position, the marketing function is emphasized. The person in this position plays an essential role in all departments of the hotel. An effective director of marketing and sales not only wants to attract external sales such as conventions, small business conferences, wedding receptions, and dining room and lounge business but also provides direction for promoting in-house sales to the guests.

This is an exciting position that requires endless creativity. The director of marketing and sales is constantly evaluating new markets, reviewing the needs of existing markets, watching new promotions by the competition, organizing sales blitzes, working with community and professional groups to maintain public relations, working with other department directors to establish product and service specifications and in-house promotional efforts, and following up on details, details, and more details. This is a high-energy position that not only provides financial vitality but also fosters the attainment of financial goals by all departments.

Some limited-service properties employ a full-time or half-time marketing and sales director. The duties of this position may also be shared by the general manager and front office manager; these duties (with the exception of soliciting food and beverage business) are the same as those of the marketing and sales director. Competition for room sales to the corporate, group, and pleasure travel markets is enormous, and each hotel must address this planning need.

Front Office Manager

The role of the front office manager is detailed more completely later in this chapter. In short, however, the major responsibilities of the front office manager include reviewing the final draft of the night audit, a daily review of the financial accounting procedures at the front desk and other guest service areas during the previous 24-hour period and an analysis of operating results; operating and monitoring the reservation system; developing and operating an effective communication system with front office staff and other department directors; supervising daily registrations and checkouts; overseeing and developing employees; establishing in-house sales programs at the front desk; preparing budgets and cost-control systems; forecasting room sales; and maintaining business relationships with regular corporate and community leaders. The front office manager works with an assistant front office manager, a night auditor, a reservations manager, and a bell captain to tend to the details of running an efficient department.

These are just a few of the responsibilities of the front office manager. The front office is a pivotal point in communication among in-house sales, delivery of service to the guest, and financial operations. The poition requires an individual who can manage the many details of guest needs, employee supervision, interdepartmental communication, and transmittal of financial information. The person who holds this exciting position can develop an overview of the lodging property with regard to finances and communication.

Controller

The controller is the internal accountant of a hotel. He or she is responsible for the actual and effective administration of financial data produced daily in the hotel. In the lodging property, appropriate daily financial information must be available to corporate owners, management, and guests. This requires a well-organized staff, not only to prepare operating statistics but also to assist the general manager in determining the effectiveness of each department manager. Often the general manager relies on the controller for financial insight into the operations of the property, including cash flow, discounts, evaluation of insurance costs, fringe-benefit cost analysis, investment opportunities, computer technology applications, banking procedures, and more.

The controller's department processes accounts payable (amounts of money the hotel owes to vendors); accounts receivable (amounts of money owed to the hotel by guests); the general ledger (a collection of accounts the controller uses to organize the financial activities of the hotel); statement of cash flows (a projection of income from income-generating areas of the hotel); the profit-and-loss statement (a listing of revenues and expenses for a certain time period); and the balance sheet (a listing of the financial position of the hotel at a particular point in time). This busy department provides financial information to all department directors.

The general manager of a limited-service property acts as the controller with the assistance of the night auditor. (In some properties, the night audit is performed during the day, and the night auditor is replaced with a lower-salaried front desk clerk for late-night coverage.) The ownership of a limited-service hotel may be a part of a larger financial portfolio of a business, which helps the general manager perform the controller's responsibilities by processing accounts payable, accounts receivable, and payroll.

Director of Security

The director of security works with department directors to develop cost-control procedures that help ensure employee honesty and guest safety. This person supervises an ongoing training program in cooperation with department directors to instruct employees in fire, job, and environmental safety procedures. Fictional stories often depict the security director as someone who investigates crimes after the fact. On the contrary, this person's primary responsibility is to implement programs that make employees security-minded, helping prevent crime from occurring.

Unfortunately, the lodging industry has always been involved in lawsuits, which have multiplied in both number and cost in recent years. A substantial body of law provides regulations under which properties must operate. Preventive security precautions are the central theme of the security department today. The director of security's background is usually in police or detective work or in security or intelligence in the armed services. He or she usually has an understanding of the criminal mind and the practices of criminals. This person is constantly on the lookout for suspicious people and circumstances. The responsibilities of this necessary position in a limited-service property are shared by the front office manager and the general manager. Security services for on-site and parking-lot patrol are often outsourced, but this practice does not relieve the general manager of the need to develop and provide ongoing procedures to train employees to become security-minded. More information about the director of security is explained in chapter 14 of this textbook.

Parking Garage Manager

The responsibility of ensuring a safe environment for guests' vehicles falls to the parking garage manager. This person supervises the work of garage attendants and maintains the security of guests and cars in the parking garage. Garage maintenance, in cooperation with the engineering and housekeeping departments, is another responsibility of this position. Often a hotel rents parking spaces to local businesses and professional people, and the associated accounting process involves accurate billing and recording of funds and subsequent deposits. The parking garage manager also has to develop budgets and recruit and train employees. He or she often provides driver assistance to guests when their cars break down and directional information to departing guests. Even though these York C ity, has been em p loy ed by Hilton Corporation for 30 years. He has served in various management positions at the Hilton Short Hills, Chicago Hilton and Towers, Hilton Walt Disney Village, Fontainebleau Hilton Resort, and the Palmer House.

His well-thought-out career with Hilton allowed him to develop a strong network of relationships and vital experience to prepare him for the position he holds today. Mr. Long indicates that there are four major areas of responsibility in his job: finance, marketing, customer service, and human resources management. Although other employees carry out the day-to-day administration of those departments, he feels he is ultimately responsible for their success. For example, he wants to ensure that a marketing and sales plan is current and operating, and he attends an 8:00 A.M. customer feedback meeting each day to review feedback on the previous day's efforts to provide high-quality service. He adds that he wants to ensure that the level of talent in the organization is nurtured through motivation, training, development, and so forth.

Early in Mr. Long's career, his mentor encouraged him to gain expertise in any three areas of the hotel and a solid working knowledge of all the others. He feels that achieving this has been an overriding factor in his career progression. He encourages future hoteliers "to take complete ownership and responsibility for your own career. Don't take promotions just for the sake of the promotion; be selective of the moves that you make. Each move should be weighed against the potential that it will have in growing your career."

Organization of the Front Office Department

Typical Front Office Organization

The staff includes desk clerk, cashier, reservations manager, concierge, night auditor, telephone operator, bell staff, room key clerk, and elevator operator. Not all of these positions are found in every lodging establishment. In some operations, the front desk clerk acts as desk clerk, cashier, telephone operator, and reservations clerk, as required by the volume of business. Many large, full-service hotels, in contrast, employ the complete staff as listed.

Staffing the front desk positions incurs a cost. The front office manager, in consultation with the general manager, usually prepares a personnel budget related to salary levels throughout the lodging establishment.

The responsibilities of the front office staff are quite varied. The position of the desk clerk can encompass many duties, which typically include verifying guest reservations, registering guests, assigning rooms, distributing keys, communicating with the housekeeping staff, answering telephones, providing information about and directions to local attractions, accepting cash and giving change, and acting as liaison between the lodging establishment and the guest as well as the community.

The position of cashier includes processing guest checkouts and guest legal tender and providing change for guests. This position is found in a number of lodging establishments, and it helps make the front desk workload manageable when a full house, a hotel that has its entire guest rooms occupied (sometimes referred to as 100 percent occupancy) is checking out. Given the possibility that every attendee of a 400-guest convention could check out within a few hours, this division of labor is a well-planned concept. Even with the best-planned systems-such as express checkout, whereby the guest uses computer technology in a guest room or a computer in the hotel lobby to check out; prior approved credit, the use of a credit card to establish creditworthiness; or bill-to-account, an internal billing process-the lines at the cashier station can be long and seem longer when a guest is in a hurry.

The reservations manager can be found in many of the larger lodging establishments. This person is responsible for taking incoming requests for rooms and noting special requests for service. The particulars of this position are endless, aimed at providing the guest with requested information and services as well as accurate confirmation of these items. The reservations manager is responsible for keeping an accurate room inventory by using a reservation module of a property management system. This person must communicate effectively with the marketing and sales department. Peak as well as slow periods of sales must be addressed with adequate planning.

The night auditor balances the daily financial transactions. This person may also serve as desk clerk for the night shift (11:00 P.M. to 7:00 A.M.). He or she must have a good grasp of accounting principles and the ability to resolve financial discrepancies. This position requires experience as a desk clerk and good communications with the controller.

The telephone operator has a very important job in the lodging establishment. This person must be able to locate the registered guests and management staff at a moment's notice. He or she also must be able to deal with crises up to and including life-threatening emergencies. With the introduction of call accounting, a computer technology application that tracks guest phone calls and posts billing charges to lodging establishments, the telephone operator's job has been simplified, as the tracking of telephone charges to registered guests can now be done with ease. This person may also assist the desk clerk and cashier when necessary.

The bell captain, with a staff of bellhops and door attendants, is a mainstay in the lodging establishment. The bell staff starts where the computerized property management system stops. They are the people who lift and tote the baggage, familiarize the guest with his or her new surroundings, run errands, deliver supplies, and provide the guest with information on in-house marketing efforts and local attractions. These people also act as the hospitality link between the lodging establishment and the guest. They are an asset to a well-run lodging establishment.

The key clerk can be found in very large, full-service hotels that do not have electronic key systems. This clerk is responsible for issuing keys to registered guests and for related security measures. Often he or she sorts incoming mail for registered guests and the management staff. This position is now obsolete in most hotels.

The elevator operator, a person who manually operates the mechanical controls of the elevator, is almost extinct in the lodging establishment, replaced by self-operated elevators and escalators. Some elevator operators now serve as traffic managers, who direct hotel guests to available elevators in the lobby. In large, full-service hotels, the traffic manager can be a welcome sight; the confusion of check-ins and checkouts can be lessened when he or she is on duty.

The concierge provides guests with extensive information on entertainment, sports, amusements, transportation, tours, church services, and baby sitting in the area. He or she must know the area intimately and be able to meet the individual needs of each guest. This person also obtains theater tickets and makes reservations in restaurants. In most cases, the concierge is stationed at a desk in the lobby of the lodging property.

Limited-Service Hotel Front Office Organization

The organization chart in Figure 2-7 portrays a simpler workforce than that seen with a full-service property. The desk clerks perform multiple duties such as reservations and registrations, and they act as cashiers, telephone operators, and so forth. Whatever guest need is presented, the front desk clerk is called on to meet it with efficiency and professionalism. In limited-service properties, the general manager may also assist, when needed, to process reservation requests, check guests in upon arrival, and check guests out upon departure.

Night Auditor

The night auditor's role in a limited-service property is unlike that of his or her counterpart in a full-service hotel. Because there are usually no departmental transactions from restaurants, banquets, lounges, gift shops, or spas, the night auditor is mainly concerned with posting room and tax charges and preparing statistics for the hotel. With the utilization of computer technology, the completion of the night audit has been reduced to a minimum of time. As previously mentioned, this task may be performed early in the morning prior to guest checkouts.

Function of the Front Office Manager

A successful front office manager conveys the spirit of a particular lodging property to the customer. By applying management principles, he or she works through the front office staff to communicate feelings of warmth, caring, safety, and efficiency to each guest. The front office manager must train personnel in the technical aspects of the property management system (PMS), a hotel computer system that networks the software and hardware used in reservation and registration databases, point-of-sale systems, accounting systems, and other office software. He or she also must maintain the delicate balance between delivery of hospitality and service and promotion of the profit centers, and maintain the details of the communication system.

The front office manager has at his or her disposal the basic elements of effective management practice: employees, equipment, inventory (rooms to be sold), a budget, and sales opportunities. This manager is responsible for coordinating these basic elements to achieve the profit goals of the lodging property.

Front office employees must be trained properly to function within the guidelines and policies of the lodging establishment. The front office manager cannot assume that an employee knows how to do certain tasks. Every employee needs instructions and guidance in how to provide hospitality; front office employees' attitudes are of utmost importance to the industry. To ensure that the proper attitude prevails, employers must provide an atmosphere in which employees are motivated to excel and that nurtures their morale and teamwork.

The property management system gives the front office manager an unlimited opportunity for managerial control. He or she can easily track information such as Zip codes of visitors, frequency of visits by corporate guests, and amount of revenue a particular conference generated, and pass this information on to the marketing and sales department. An unsold guest room is a sales opportunity lost forever. This is one of the major challenges of the front office manager. Cooperation between the marketing and sales department and the front office is necessary to develop profitable advertising and point-of-sale strategies. The subsequent training of front office personnel to seize every opportunity to sell vacant rooms helps ensure that the financial goals of the lodging property are met.

Budgetary guidelines must be developed by the front office manager and the general manager, as the front office manager does have a large dollar volume under his or her control. The budgeting of money for payroll and supplies, the opportunity for improving daily sales, and accurate recording of guest charges require the front office manager to apply managerial skills.

The foremost concept that characterizes a front office manager is team player. The front office manager does not labor alone to meet the profit goals of the lodging property. The general manager sets the goals, objectives, and standards for all departments to follow. The assistant manager offers the department heads additional insight into meeting the operational needs of the establishment. The controller supplies valuable accounting information to the front office manager as feedback on current performance and meeting budgetary goals. The food and beverage manager, housekeeper, and plant engineer provide essential services to the guest. Without cooperation and communication among these departments and the front office, hospitality cannot be delivered. The director of marketing and sales develops programs to attract guests to the lodging property. These programs help the front office manager sell rooms. The human resources manager completes the team by providing the front office with competent personnel to accomplish the goals, objectives, and standards set by the general manager.

Job Analysis and Job Description

A job analysis, a detailed listing of the tasks of a job, provides the basis for a sound job description. A job description is a listing of required duties to be performed by an employee in a particular position. Although almost nothing is typical in the lodging industry, certain daily tasks must be performed. A job analysis is useful in that it allows the person preparing the job description to determine certain daily procedures.

These procedures, along with typical responsibilities and interdepartmental relationships involved in a job, form the basis for the job description. The future professional will find this management tool helpful in preparing orientation and training programs for employees. It also helps the human resources department ensure that each new hire is given every opportunity to succeed.

The following is the job analysis of a typical front office manager:

7:00 A.M. Meets with the night auditor to discuss the activities of the previous night. Notes any discrepancies in balancing the night audit.

7:30 Meets with the reservation clerk to note the incoming reservations for the day.

8:00 Greets the first-shift desk clerks and passes along any information from the night auditor and reservation office. Assists desk clerks in guest checkout.

8:30 Meets with the housekeeper to identify potential problem areas of which the front office staff should be aware. Meets with the plant engineer to identify potential problem areas of which the front office staff should be aware.

9:00 Meets with the director of marketing and sales to discuss ideas for potential programs to increase sales. Discusses with the banquet manager details of groups that will be in-house for banquets and city ledger accounts that have left requests for billing disputes.

9:30 Checks with the chef to learn daily specials for the various restaurants. This information will be typed and distributed to the telephone operators.

9:45 Meets with the front office staff to discuss pertinent operational information for the day. Handles guest billing disputes.

11:00 Meets with the general manager to discuss the development of the next fiscal budget.

12:30 P.M. Works on forecasting sheet for the coming week. Prepares preliminary schedule and anticipated payroll.

1:30 Has a lunch appointment with a corporate business client.

2:15 Works on room blocking-reserving rooms for guests who are holding reservations-for group reservations with the reservations clerk.

2:30 Works with the controller on budgetary targets for the next month. Receives feedback on budget targets from last month. Checks with the housekeeper on progress of room inspection and release.

2:45 Checks with the plant engineer on progress of plumbing repair for the eighteenth floor.

3:00 Greets the second-shift desk clerks and relays operational information on reservations, room assignments, room inventory, and the like.

3:15 Assists the front desk clerks in checking in a tour group.

4:00 Interviews two people for front desk clerk positions.

4:45 Assists the front desk clerks in checking in guests.

5:15 Reviews trade journal article on empowerment of employees.

5:45 Telephones the night auditor and communicates current information pertinent to tonight's audit.

6:00 Checks with the director of security for information concerning security coverage for the art exhibit in the ballroom.

6:30 Completes work order request forms for preventive maintenance on the front office posting machine.

6:45 Prepares "things to do" schedule for tomorrow.

This job analysis reveals that the front office manager has a busy schedule involving hands-on participation with the front office staff and communication with department heads throughout the lodging establishment. The front office manager must be able to project incomes and related expenses, to interview, and to interact with potential business clients.

Based on this job analysis, a job description for a front office manager is easily prepared, as shown in Figure 2-8. The job description is an effective management tool because it details the tasks and responsibilities required of the job-holder. These guidelines allow the individual to apply management principles in the development of an effective front office department. They also challenge the person in the job to use prior experience and theoretical knowledge to accomplish the tasks at hand.

The Art of Supervising

The art of supervising employees encompasses volumes of text and years of experience. Management experts have analyzed the complexities of supervising employees. Some of your other management courses explain in detail the concept of management. This chapter covers a few concepts that will assist you in developing your own supervisory style.

The first step in developing a supervisory style is to examine the manager's position in the context of the management team. As the front office manager, you are assigned certain responsibilities and granted certain authorities. These are areas for participation, growth, and limitation on the management team. Although this is a simplified overview of the management team, it does help clarify managerial intended performance. Early in the new job, a manager should review personal career goals with this organization. The ports of entry to the position of general manager (described in chapter 1) will help an aspiring general manager clarify goals and understand which areas of the hotel will provide good exposure and experience. Once you have clarified your arena of participation and plan for growth, you can decide how best to lead a team to financial success and personal growth.

The first concept a new supervisor should address is employee motivation. What helps each employee perform at his or her best? The emphasis is on each employee; different incentives motivate different people. The better shift scheduling that motivates the second-shift desk clerk may have no effect on the part-time night auditor who is a moonlighter, a person who has a full-time job at another organization and a part-time job at a hotel, two days a week on your property. The young person who prefers the second shift (3:00-11:00 P.M.) because it better fits his or her lifestyle will not be inspired by the possibility of working the first shift.

Tuition reimbursement may motivate the recent graduate of an associate degree program who wants to continue toward a four-year degree; this same benefit will mean little to someone uninterested in higher education. The possibility of promotion to reservations clerk may not have the same motivating effect on a telephone operator who is a recently displaced worker concerned about a schedule that meets the needs of a young family as it does on a front desk clerk who has no dependents. Sometimes a supervisor cannot figure out what motivates a person. It is a manager's ultimate challenge to discover how to motivate each member of his or her staff. By using this knowledge, a manager can promote not just the best interests of the employee but also the best interests of the hotel.

Another supervisory responsibility is to achieve a balance among varying personalities in a group work setting. This is a constant and evolving situation. Very often, a new supervisor does not have time to assess each employee's relationship with others on the team, yet these dynamics are key to establishing a positive and effective team setting. The front office staff may jockey for position with the new boss; this common situation must be addressed as part of the job. Once the new supervisor shows himself or herself capable and competent, the supervisor can move on to the day-to-day tasks. The staff needs this time to learn their new manager's reactions under stress. They also want to make sure their supervisor will be their advocate with top management. All new supervisors are tested in this way. You should not be discouraged by this challenge but embrace it as the first of many to come.

After working out whatever personality clashes exist among the employees, the manager must be objective about the strengths and weaknesses of the staff. Who is the unofficial leader of the group? Who is the agitator? Who is the complainer? Objective views of staff are probably shared by the rest of the team. Often, the staff members are quite aware of the shortcomings of their coworkers. They also know on whom they can rely to check out the full house and check in the convention three hours later. The unofficial leader of the group can assist the supervisor in conveying important ideas.

Some supervisors respond negatively to such accommodation of the staff. Their response is based on the assumption that the supervisor has the first and last word in all that goes on in the front office. Of course, authority is important, but any supervisor who wants to maintain authority and have objectives met by the staff must constantly rework his or her strategy.

Adequate personnel training (discussed in chapter 12) makes the job of a supervisor much easier. When training is planned, executed, and reinforced, the little annoyances of human error are minimized. As previously discussed, each job description lists the major duties of the employees, but the gray areas-handling complaints, delivering a positive image of the lodging property, selling other departments in the hotel, and covering for a new trainee-cannot be communicated in a job description. On-the-job training, employee training that takes place while producing a product or service, and videotape training are excellent methods for clarifying such tasks. These methods serve not only to demonstrate skills but also to communicate the financial goals, the objectives of hospitality and service, and the idiosyncrasies of the lodging property and the people who work in it.

Employees always have special scheduling needs as well as other job-related requests, and supervisors should try to accommodate them. The new hire who made commitments four to six months prior to accepting a position at the front desk will appreciate and return a supervisor's consideration. The individual who wants to change shifts because of difficulties with another person on the job may just need advice on how to handle that person. These individuals may make a good team, but they wear on each other's patience. A longtime employee might ask you how he or she can advance in the organization. You may not have an immediate response, but you can indicate that you will act on the request in the near future. Sometimes employees know that a good thing takes time to develop. Listen to their needs; their requests may answer your problems by fitting into the demands of the job. For example, a desk clerk who needs additional income may request overtime hours. An opportunity may arise for this employee to fill a vacancy caused by another employee's illness or vacation.

The responsibility of communications within the hotel usually rests with the front office. From the guests' perspective, this department is the most visible part of the lodging establishment. The various departments in the hotel realize that the transfer of information to guests is best done through the front office. When such communications fail to reach guests, it is often the front office that bears the brunt of their unhappiness at checkout time.

The more systematic the communication process can become, the better for all concerned. For example, messages that will affect the next shift of desk clerks can be recorded in the message book, a loose-leaf binder in which the front desk staff of any shift can record important messages. This communication tool is vital to keeping all front office personnel informed of additions, changes, and deletions of information and activities that affect the operation of a front office. Additionally, daily function sheets, which list the planned events in the hotel and their updates, must be delivered to the front office on a routine basis. The daily function board or electronic bulletin board in guest rooms available on in-room television or in public areas is usually maintained by the front office. The guest who complains about the maintenance of a room must have the complaint passed along to the right person. The complaint is then reviewed by a member of the staff, front office manager, member of the housekeeping staff, housekeeper, member of the maintenance staff, or maintenance director to ensure it is resolved.

Inquiries about hotel services, reservations, city ledger accounts (a collection of accounts receivable of nonregistered guests who use the services of the hotel), accounts payable, scheduled events, and messages for registered guests constitute only some of the many requests for information. Desk clerks and telephone operators are expected to know the answers to these questions or to whom they should be referred.

Some of this advice is based on my own experience. One of the jobs I was responsible for as a front desk clerk included operating the switchboard. This job was truly stressful, involving accuracy at every contact. Finding the right department head to meet the request of an incoming caller or ensuring that a message is passed along to a guest are only some of the tasks required every minute a person is on the job. If a message is conveyed inaccurately or if an employee fails to complete the communication process, hospitality is not projected to the guest.

Ways of applying employee empowerment concepts are explored in chapter 12. The contemporary front office manager needs extensive training and experience in this vital area to manage a workforce that can deliver hospitality on a daily basis. Ensuring that an employee can conduct business without constant approval from a supervisor is the goal of empowerment. The mastery of empowerment requires a supervisor to train employees and to practice much patience. Employees accustomed to direct supervision on all matters may not readily adapt to a work environment that requires independent thinking to address challenges.

Staffing the Front Office

The schedule for the front office staff is based on both budgetary targets and anticipation of guest check-ins and checkouts. An increase in the frequency of guest requests for information and various front office services may affect the schedule. The front office manager must also determine labor costs by reviewing salaries and hourly wages and respective rates. The resulting figures show if the front office manager has adhered to the projected budget. Table 2-1 (pages 66-67) shows how the costs for staffing are determined. Table 2-2 (page 68) compares these projected costs with the projected revenue generated by room rentals, which allows for a preevaluation of income and labor expenses.

The preparation of the front office schedule is broken into four steps. The first step requires the front office manager to estimate or forecast the needs of his or her department for a certain period. The front office manager must review the sales history of previous events, current functions, current reservations, anticipated walk-ins, stayovers, and check-outs for that period to determine their impact on the labor requirements for the workweek.

He or she has the opportunity to review and thus adjust data for departures, stayovers, arrivals, and walk-ins, which affects the number of rooms sold each night. For example, if the front office manager realizes that on a certain day at 6:30 P.M. there are 25 vacant rooms and no more confirmed or guaranteed reservations are being held, desk clerks can be empowered to negotiate a reasonable room rate with guests to obtain their business (in order to secure a full house). If there were three vacant rooms and eight guaranteed reservations being held, desk clerks would not be so empowered.

Solution to Opening Dilemma

Communication in a hotel is essential to efficiency, delivery of high-quality service, and making a profit. In this case, the front office staff failed to place a room block in the computer system for the additional 26 rooms. Does this happen frequently in the hotel business? Unfortunately, it does. However, the delivery of high-quality service is dependent on the upkeep of a hotel's physical property, and this is an important operational procedure. The front office manager and the director of housekeeping must cooperate in setting up times for taking guest rooms out of available inventory. The front office manager must be made aware of the costs involved in contracted services and work in partnership with the director of housekeeping.

3

Effective Interdepartmental Communications

OPENING DILEMMA

The leader of a workshop in one of the conference rooms is uneasy about his program today. After noticing the connection for the teleconference is not working, he stops by the front desk and asks if the convention representative could come to the conference room. The desk clerk on duty offers to locate the convention representative and send her to the room. After the workshop leader leaves the front desk area, the desk clerk remarks, "You would think we have to be all things to all people all the time!"

Role of the Front Office in Interdepartmental Communications

The front office plays a pivotal role in delivering hospitality to guests. It sets the stage for a pleasant or an unpleasant visit. Guests, often in an unfamiliar setting and wanting to proceed with their business or vacation plans, are eager to learn the who, what, when, where, and how of their new environment. Requests for information often begin with the porter, bellhop, switchboard operator, front desk clerk, cashier, or concierge, because these employees are the most visible to the guest and are perceived to be the most knowledgeable. These employees are believed to have their finger on the pulse of the organization and the community. Their responses to guests' requests for information on public transportation, location of hotel facilities, special events in the community, and the like indicate how well the hotel has prepared them for this important role. Front office managers must take an active part in gathering information that will be of interest to guests. They must also be active in developing procedures for the front office to disburse this information.

The relationships the front office manager develops with the other department directors and their employees are vital to gathering information for guests. Developing positive personal relationships is part of the communication process, but it cannot be relied on to ensure that accurate and current information is relayed. How does the front office manager encourage effective interdepartmental communication (communication between departments)? This chapter provides relevant background for you as you begin your professional career. It is important to note that this discussion is applicable to intradepart-mental communication (communication inside a department) as well.

The front office is at the center of the diagram to illustrate the many interdepartmental lines of communication that exist. These lines are based on the direction each department is given to provide hospitality in the form of clean rooms, properly operating equipment, safe environment, well-prepared food and beverages, efficient table service, and professional organization and delivery of service for a scheduled function as well as accurate accounting of guest charges and the like. These general objectives help department directors organize their operations and meet the overall goal of delivering professional hospitality. However, in reality, constant effort is required to manage the details of employees, materials, procedures, and communication skills to produce acceptable products and services.

FRONT OFFICE INTERACTION WITH OTHER DEPARTMENTS IN THE HOTEL

The front office staff interacts with all departments of the hotel, including marketing and sales, housekeeping, food and beverage, banquet, controller, maintenance, security, and human resources. These departments view the front office as a communication liaison in providing guest services. Each of the departments has a unique communication link with the front office staff. The front office in any type of lodging property provides the faceand voice of hospitality for the organization around the clock. Guests are most likely to approach the front office staff for connections to staff in other departments. As you review the following lodging facility departments, try to grasp the role of the front office in communication with each. The members of the front office team must know to whom they can direct guest inquiries for assistance. They learn this by means of a thorough training program in in-house policy and procedures and a constant concern for providing hospitality to the guest.

Marketing and Sales Department

The marketing and sales department relies on the front office to provide data on guest histories, or details concerning each guest's visit. Some of the information gathered is based on ZIP code, frequency of visits, corporate affiliation, special needs, and reservations for sleeping rooms. It is also the front office's job to make a good first impression on the public, to relay messages, and to meet the requests of guests who are using the hotel for meetings, seminars, and banquets.

The guest history is a valuable resource for marketing and sales, which uses the guest registration information to target marketing campaigns, develop promotions, prepare mailing labels, and select appropriate advertising media. The front office staff must make every effort to keep this database current and accurate.

The process of completing the booking of a special function (such as a wedding reception, convention, or seminar) depends on the availability of sleeping rooms for guests. The marketing and sales executives may have to check the lists of available rooms three or six months, or even a year in the future to be sure the hotel can accommodate the expected number of guests. A database of available rooms is maintained in the property management system by the front office.

The first guest contact with the marketing and sales department is usually through the hotel's switchboard. A competent switchboard operator who is friendly and knowledgeable about hotel operations and personnel makes a good first impression, conveying to the prospective client that the hotel is competent. When the guest finally arrives for the function, the first actual contact with the hotel is usually through the front office staff. The front office manager who makes the effort to determine which banquet supervisor is in charge and communicates that information to the desk clerk on duty demonstrates to the public that this hotel is dedicated to providing hospitality.

Messages for the marketing and sales department must be relayed completely, accurately, and quickly. The switchboard operator is a vital link in the communication between the prospective client and a salesperson in the marketing and sales department. The front office manager should instruct all new front office personnel about the staff in the marketing and sales department and what each person's job entails. Front office employees should know how to pronounce the names of all marketing and sales employees. To help front office staff become familiar with all these people, managers should show new employees pictures of the department directors and supervisors.

Requests for service at meetings, seminars, banquets, and the like are often made at the front office. The banquet manager, the person responsible for fulfilling the details of service for a banquet or special event, or sales associate, who books the guest's requirements for banquets and other special events, might be busy with another function. If a guest needs an extension cord or if an electrical outlet malfunctions, the front desk staff must be ready to meet the guest's needs. The front office manager should establish standard operating procedures for the front office employees to contact maintenance, housekeeping, marketing and sales, or the food and beverage department to meet other common requests. Knowing how to find a small tool kit, adapters, adhesive materials, extra table covers, or window cleaner will help the guest and save the time involved in tracking down the salesperson in charge.

Housekeeping Department

Housekeeping and the front office communicate about housekeeping room status, the report on the availability of the rooms for immediate guest occupancy. Housekeeping room status can be described in the following communication terms:

- Available Clean, or Ready-room is ready to be occupied
- Occupied-guest or guests are already occupying a room

- Stayover-guest will not be checking out of a room on the current day
- Dirty or On-Change-guest has checked out of the room, but the housekeeping staff has not released the room for occupancy
- Out-of-Order-room is not available for occupancy because of a mechanical malfunction

Housekeeping and the front office also communicate on the details of potential house count (a report of the number of guests registered in the hotel), security concerns, and requests for amenities (personal toiletry items such as shampoo, toothpaste, and mouthwash; electrical equipment). These issues are of immediate concern to the guest as well as to supervisors in the hotel.

Reporting of room status is handled on a face-to-face basis in a hotel that does not use a property management system (PMS). The bihourly or hourly visits of the housekeeper to the front desk clerk are a familiar scene in such a hotel. The official reporting of room status at the end of the day is accomplished with a housekeeper's room report-a report prepared by the housekeeper that lists the guest room occupancy status as vacant, occupied, or out of order. Sometimes even regular reporting of room status is not adequate, as guests may be anxiously awaiting the opportunity to occupy a room. On these occasions, the front desk clerk must telephone the floor supervisor to determine when the servicing of a room will be completed.

The housekeeper relies on the room sales projections-a weekly report prepared and distributed by the front office manager that indicates the number of departures, arrivals, walk-ins, stayovers, and no-shows-to schedule employees. Timely distribution of the room sales projections assists the executive housekeeper in planning employee personal leaves and vacation days.

The front desk also relies on housekeeping personnel to report unusual circumstances that may indicate a violation of security for the guests. For example, if a maid or houseman notices obviously nonregistered guests on a floor, a fire exit that has been propped open, or sounds of a domestic disturbance in a guest room, he or she must report these potential security violations to the front office. The front office staff, in turn, relays the information to the proper in-house or civil authority. The front office manager may want to direct the front desk clerks and switchboard operators to call floor supervisors periodically to check activity on the guest floors.

Guest requests for additional or special amenities and guest room supplies may be initiated at the front desk. The prompt relay of requests for extra blankets, towels, soap, and shampoo to housekeeping is essential. This is hospitality at its best.

Food and Beverage Department

Communication between the food and beverage department and the front office is essential. Transfers, which are forms used to communicate a charge to a guest's account, are used to relay messages and provide accurate information. Communication activities also include reporting predicted house counts, an estimate of the number of guests expected to register based on previous occupancy activities, and processing requests for paid-outs, forms used to indicate the amounts of monies paid out of the cashier's drawer on behalf of a guest or an employee of the hotel. These vital services help an overworked food and beverage manager, restaurant manager, or banquet captain meet the demands of the public.

Incoming messages for the food and beverage manager and executive chef from vendors and other industry representatives are important to the business operation of the food and beverage department. If the switchboard operator is given instructions on screening callers (such as times when the executive chef cannot be disturbed because of a busy workload or staff meetings, or vendors in whom the chef is not interested), the important messages can receive top priority.

In a hotel that has point-of-sale terminals, computerized cash registers that interface with a property management system, information on guest charges is automatically posted to a guest's folio-his or her record of charges and payments. When a hotel does not have such terminals, the desk clerk is responsible for posting accurate charges on the guest folio and relies on transfer slips. The night auditor's job is made easier if the transfer slip is accurately prepared and posted. The front office manager should work with the Milichael DeCaire is the food and beverage manager at the Houston Hilton, Houston, Texas. His previous experience includes positions as executive chef at the Park Hotel in Charlotte, North Carolina; executive and executive sous chef at the Pacific Star Hotel on the Island of Guam; and executive sous chef at the Greenleaf Resort in Haines City, Florida.

Mr. DeCaire relies on the front desk for accurate forecasting of arrivals, notification of VIPs and Hilton Honors Club members, communication of complaints and positive comments concerning food and service, and processing of guest bills. He also works with the front desk to obtain a thorough knowledge of the needs and location of banquet and meeting guests through a ten-day forecast of banquet and meeting events.

The communication emphasis at the Houston Hilton is extended into a nine-week cross-training program, in which all departments (food and beverage, front desk, housekeeping, sales, etc.) participate in learning the basics of each department. This training effort allows the salesperson to appreciate the duties of a cook, the waiter or waitress to understand the duties of a front desk clerk, and the front desk clerk to value the duties of a housekeeper. Another area of cooperative training efforts is fire command post training.

Mr. DeCaire offers the following advice for students wanting to make a career in the hotel industry: Take an entry-level job in the hospitality industry so you can understand the work requirements of weekends, holidays, and nights prior to investing in a college education. This effort will pay big dividends for your career growth.

The supervisors in the food and beverage department rely on the predicted house count prepared by the front office manager to schedule employees and predict sales. For example, the restaurant supervisor working the breakfast shift needs to know how many guests will be in the hotel so he or she can determine how many servers to schedule for breakfast service. Timely and accurate preparation of this communication tool assists in staffing control and sales predictions.

Authorized members of the food and beverage department occasionally ask the front office for cash, in the form of a paid-out, to purchase last-minute items for a banquet, the lounge, or the restaurant or to take advantage of unplanned opportunities to promote hospitality. Specific guidelines concerning cash limits, turnaround time, prior approval, authorized signatures, and purchase receipts are developed by the general manager and front office manager. These guidelines help maintain control of paid-outs.

Banquet Department

The banquet department, which often combines the functions of a marketing and sales department and a food and beverage department, requires the front office to relay information to guests about scheduled events and bill payment.

The front desk staff may also provide labor to prepare the daily announcement board, an inside listing of the daily activities of the hotel (time, group, and room assignment), and marquee, the curbside message board, which includes the logo of the hotel and space for a message. Because the majority of banquet guests may not be registered guests in the hotel, the front office is a logical communications center.

A daily posting on a felt board or an electronic bulletin board provides all guests and employees with information on scheduled group events. The preparation of the marquee may include congratulatory, welcome, sales promotion, or other important messages. In some hotels, an employee in the front office contacts the marketing and sales department for the message.

The banquet guest who is unfamiliar with the hotel property will ask at the front office for directions. This service might seem minor in the overall delivery of service, but it is essential to the lost or confused guest. The front office staff must know both how to direct guests to particular meeting rooms or reception areas and which functions are being held in which rooms. Front desk clerks, as shown in Figure 3-2, must be ready to provide information for all departmental activities in the hotel.

The person responsible for paying the bills for a special event will also find his or her way to the front office to settle the city ledger accounts. If the banquet captain is not available to personally present the bill for the function, the front desk clerk should be informed about the specifics of food and beverage charges, gratuities, rental charges, method of payment, and the like.

Front desk clerks must be able to provide immediate responses to guests' requests for information. Photo courtesy of Radisson Hospitality Worldwide.

Controller

The controller relies on the front office staff to provide a daily summary of financial transactions through a well-prepared night audit. This information is also used to measure management ability to meet budget targets. Because the front office provides the controller with financial data for billing and maintenance of credit card ledgers, these two departments must relay payments and charges through the posting machine or property management system.

The information produced by the front office is a necessary first step in the process of the factual guest accounting process and the financial assembly of data for the controller. Without accurate daily entry by desk clerks and production of a night audit, the controller does not have the figures to produce reports for the owners, general manager, and supervisors. One might expect this communication to be in the form of reports. However, the front office and controller departments often communicate orally. They share a common concern for guest hospitality, and when finances are concerned, oral discussion is inevitable.

Mr. Heale says his relationships with desk clerks, cashiers, and night auditors are important; however, his relationship with their respective managers is more important. He audits the work of the desk clerks, cashiers, and night auditors but does not directly supervise them. If they make mistakes, Mr. Heale tries to show them why. He makes sure they receive proper training, which includes letting them know the results of audits when they occur and making them aware of their individual performance.

Mr. Heale has a good relationship with the front office manager. They work together to forecast room sales and to audit daily cash banks. The front office manager monitors the payroll and may ask for Mr. Heale's assistance. The front office manager is also involved in cash management problems; he and Mr. Heale alert each other to problems and work together to solve them. The front office manager monitors accounts receivable and is required to let Mr. Heale know when a guest has exceeded his or her credit limit.

He adds that everyone in a hotel is a salesperson. Selling is a big part of his job through fostering a good relationship with local vendors. His efforts may encourage vendors to become customers of the hotel.

Maintenance or Engineering Department

The maintenance or engineering department and front office communicate on room status and requests for maintenance service. Maintenance employees must know the occupancy status of a room before attending to plumbing, heating, or air-conditioning problems. If the room is reserved, the two departments work out a time frame so the guest can enter the room on arrival or be assigned to another room. Cooperative efforts produce the best solutions to difficult situations. Figure 3-3 depicts the essential communication and planning by departmental managers to provide guest services at a time that does not interfere with delivering hospitality.

Likewise, the requests from guests for the repair of heating, ventilating, and air-conditioning units, plumbing, televisions, and other room furnishings are directed to the front desk, which relays them to the maintenance department. The front desk clerk must keep track of the repair schedule, as guests want to know when the repair will be made.

Coordination of maintenance service requires cooperation between the maintenance and front office departments. Photo courtesy of Host/Racine Industries, Inc.

Security Department

Communications between the security department and the front office are important in providing hospitality to the guest. These departments work together closely in maintaining guest security. Fire safety measures and emergency communication systems as well as procedures for routine investigation of guest security concerns require the cooperation of these departments. Because of the events of September 11, 2001, the nature of the security hotels offer their guests has changed. All members of the front office team must be on alert for people who don't belong in the lobby and report inconsistencies with the security department. This professional view of security allows the front office to support the security department.

Human Resources Management Department

The human resources management department may rely on the front office staff to act as an initial point of contact for potential employees in all departments. It may even ask the front office to screen job candidates. If so, guidelines for and training in screening methods must be provided.

Some directors of human resources management depend on the front office to distribute application forms and other personnel-related information to job applicants. The potential employee may ask for directions to the personnel office at the front desk. The human resources management department may also develop guidelines for the front desk clerk to use in initially screening candidates. These guidelines may include concerns about personal hygiene, completion of an application, education requirements, experience, and citizenship status. This information helps the executives in the human resources management department interview potential job candidates.

Analyzing the Lines of Communication

This section describes situations in which communications between the front office and other departments play a role. Each situation involves communication problems between departments, traces the source of miscommunication, analyzes the communication system, and presents methods that will help improve communications. The purpose of this method of presentation is to help future professionals develop a systematic way of continually improving communications.

Situation 1: Marketing and Sales Knows It All-But Didn't Tell Us

Mr. and Mrs. Oil Magnate are hosting a private party for 200 people in the Chandelier Room of City Hotel. On arriving at the hotel, they approach the front desk and ask if Mr. Benton, the director of marketing and sales, is available. The desk clerk checks the duty board and sees that Mr. Benton has left for the day. He responds, "Sorry, he's left for the day. What are you here for anyway?" The Magnates immediately feel neglected and ask to see the manager on duty.

Mr. Gerard, the assistant general manager, arrives on the scene and asks what he can do for the Magnates. Mr. Magnate has a number of concerns: Who will be in charge of their party? Will their two favorite servers be serving the cocktails, appetizers, and dinner? Have the flowers that were flown in from Holland arrived? Mr. Gerard says, "Gee, you'll have to speak with André, our banquet captain. He knows everything."

When André arrives, he tells the Magnates that Mr. Benton left no instructions about who will be serving the party, and he has not seen any tulips in the walk-in. Mrs. Magnate declares her party will be a disaster. Mr. Magnate decides to proceed with the party and take up the lack of professional service later.

Later has arrived: Mr. Magnate has complained to the general manager and I. M. Owner-the owner of City Hotel-and both are upset about the situation. Mr. Magnate and I. M. Owner are co-investors in a construction project. Even if the two men were not business associates, the treatment of any guest in such a shabby way spells disaster for future convention and banquet sales.

Analysis

The communications breakdown in this case was the fault of all the employees involved.

Communication is a two-way process, and both senders and receivers must take active roles. As the sender, Mr. Benton, the director of marketing and sales, did not do his homework. Assuming he was aware of I. M. Owner's relationship with Mr. and Mrs. Magnate, he should have adjusted his work schedule so he could be there for the party. He also should have informed the front office manager of the Magnates' scheduled event, explained who they were, and asked that he be summoned immediately on their arrival. Mr. Benton should also have worked more closely with André, the banquet manager, in scheduling employees and receiving and storing the flowers. Although Mr. Gerard, the assistant general manager, would not normally be involved in the details of a party, in this case, the VIP status of the guests would be a reason for him to be aware of the presence of the Magnates in the hotel.

The receivers in the communication process are also at fault. These include the front office staff, the banquet manager, and the assistant general manager. At times, a member of the management team fails to communicate the particulars of an upcoming event. However, the front office staff, the banquet manager, and the assistant general manager are responsible for reviewing the daily function board as well as the weekly function sheet. They are also responsible for learning about the backgrounds of the people, associations, and corporations that stay at and conduct business with the hotel.

Several things can be done to avoid this type of situation. First, the front office manager can ensure that the initial guest contact will be professional by reviewing the function board with each front desk employee on each shift. The manager can then help the front office staff focus on the day's upcoming events. Weekly staff meetings may also provide an opportunity for the director of marketing and sales to give brief synopses of who will be in the hotel in the coming week. At that point, special requests for VIP treatment can be noted.

Situation 2: Peace and Harmony in 507

Veronica is busy at the front desk checking in a busload of guests. Several of the guests ask her for directions to the nearest dining facility because they are hungry. Two of the guests seem restless and want to get into their room right away. One of them is an elderly traveler who needs assistance with his luggage and the other one, his young grandson, had experienced motion sickness on the bus. Although it seemed normal that a couple of guests would be restless and require special attention, something about these two disturbs Veronica. The elderly man's blank look on his face and his uneasy restlessness made her wonder what was on his mind. She checks them into room 507, calls the bell staff and asks for assistance with the elderly guest's luggage, suggests that the elderly guest take a nap so he could rest from the bus trip, and directs the younger guest to do likewise.

The day continues, and several more routine check-ins and check outs occur. Veronica takes a midafternoon break and happens to notice the elderly traveler crossing the lobby of the hotel on her way to the hotel's restaurant. She remarks to herself, "He seems to be walking much straighter and taller than he did when he checked in. It's only been two hours since he got off the bus; that nap must have done him some good!" Likewise, on her return from her break, she sees the younger guest laughing and talking with friends while they listened to their boom box in the lobby. That nap must have helped cure his motion sickness.

Veronica greets her replacement afternoon coworkers, John and Delanney, and checks out. She has to hurry because she had an appointment in the city. Two hours into their shift, John receives a phone call from room 505 complaining of strange, loud noises in the hallway. John alerts Ishmael, the security guard on duty, and Ishmael investigated the situation. When Ishmael approaches room 507, he couldn't believe what he saw. The two guests are hosting a nondenominational religious party complete with live animals, musical instruments, and oh, yes-a bright 1,000-watt lamp. "The people in the room," Ishmael said later. "There must have been at least 45 of them, and they invited me in to share peace and harmony." They are quite taken aback when Ishmael tells them the party will have to break up because state law prohibits more than two people in that particular room. However, they cooperate and abide by the law.

Analysis In this situation, we can see three communication opportunities were overlooked. First, when Veronica had misgivings about the elderly traveler and his grandson who had experienced motion sickness, she should have discussed them with a coworker or supervisor. It may have been nothing, but then again, it may have been a situation that would warrant further investigation. Then, when these misgivings were supported by the quick cures two hours later, this should have alerted her to something questionable-and precipitated a discussion with her supervisor or a call to the director of security. Again, it could have led to nothing, but a polite courtesy call to room 507 could have saved time later on. The third missed opportunity was Veronica's failure to relate her concerns about these two guests to John and Delanney. This shift-change communication is vital for keeping guests safe. All the communication training employees receive does not override the human instinct that should underlie the communication process.

Situation 3: I Know What You Said, and I Think I Know What You Mean

The director of maintenance, Sam Jones, has assigned his crew to start painting the Tower rooms at the hotel. Prior to making this assignment, he checked with the reservations manager, Keith Thomas, for approval to place the Tower rooms out of order for four days. Keith consented because a prior reservation for 150 rooms for Photo Bugs International had been confirmed for 100.

At 1:00 P.M., Sam receives a call from Keith asking if it is possible to reassign the painting crew to some other duty. The Photo Bugs have arrived-all 150 rooms' worth! The lobby is filled with guests for whom there are no available rooms. Sam tells Keith to give them one hour to clean up the mess and air out the south wing. He says the north wing has not been prepared for painting, so those guest rooms are ready for occupancy.

Analysis : What went right? What went wrong? This case demonstrates that cooperation between two staff members can resolve even the most unfortunate of situations. Sam was aware of the need for prior approval to take guest rooms out of service. Keith's decision to grant the request had a legitimate basis. Sam was also able to head off a nasty situation for the guests by being flexible. Then what went wrong?

The words that people use in communicating with hotel staff members must be clarified. In this case, the person who booked the convention said there were confirmations for 100. Was this 100 guests for 50 rooms or 100 guests for 100 rooms? This lack of clarity was at the root of the problem. In some hotels, the reservations manager may require a change in reservations to be written (in the form of a letter); these written instructions are then attached to the convention contract. These examples of day-to-day problems in a hotel underscore the importance of good communication between the front office and other departments. Similar problems will occur again and again as you begin your career in the hospitality industry. You will grow as a professional if you adopt an analytical view of the communication system. Front office managers who actively participate in systematic communications are more effective managers. Training employees in proper procedures for dealing with other employees as well as their own departments helps improve the delivery of professional hospitality.

Justin, the front desk clerk on duty, cannot speak Spanish fluently but knows how to commu-(SfSflS) J nicate pho netically w ith th e S panish-speaking housekeeping staff. Wh en Vic torio, the house-

A man, approaches the front desk to inform Justin which rooms are clean, they use the phonetic pronunciation of numerals and housekeeping status.

The Role of Total Quality Management in Effective Communication

Total quality management (TQM) is a management technique that encourages managers to look with a critical eye at processes used to deliver products and services. Managers must ask front-line employees and supervisors to question each step in the methods they use to provide hospitality for guests. Examples: "Why do guests complain about waiting in line to check out?" "Why do guests say our table service is rushed?" "Why do guests get upset when their rooms aren't ready on check-in?" Managers and their employees must then look for answers to these questions.

Total quality management was developed by W. Edwards Deming, a management theorist, in the early 1950s. His intent was to offer a new way for American manufacturers to improve the quality of their products by reducing defects through worker participation in the planning process. American manufacturers were reluctant at first to embrace total quality management, but Japanese manufacturers were quick to adopt Deming's principles of streamlining methods to manufacture products such as automobiles. He gave managers tools such as flowcharts to analyze production by dividing the manufacturing process into components and then focusing on the segments of processes that produce the end product.

The most important aspect of total quality management in the context of the hotel industry is the interaction between frontline employees and their supervisors. The interaction of employees in a group setting or on a one-on-one basis to determine the root of the problem and how the desired end result can be achieved thrusts them into an atmosphere of cooperation that may not have previously existed. First-shift and second-shift employees, who usually do not understand each other's activities, find they do have common concerns about serving the guest. Housekeeping and front desk employees come to realize that a guest's request for a late checkout plays havoc with the delivery of hospitality. Total quality management practices ensure that the front office checks with housekeeping to determine room availability in such a situation. The bottom line is that interdepartmental communication is enhanced each time a team of members of various departments meets to analyze a challenge to the delivery of hospitality. Figure 3-4 provides a view of the interaction necessary to make total quality management a success.

An Example of Total Quality Management in a Hotel

Total quality management in a hotel may be applied as follows: The general manager has received numerous complaints about the messy appearance of the lobby-furniture and pillows are out of place, ashtrays are overflowing, flowers are wilted, and trash receptacles are overflowing. The front office manager recruits a total quality management team, consisting of a front desk clerk, a maid, a waiter, a cashier, and the director of marketing and sales. The team discusses how the lobby area could be better maintained. The maid says her colleagues are overworked and are allotted only 15 minutes to clean up the public areas on the day shift. The front desk clerk says he would often like to take a few minutes to go out to the lobby to straighten the furniture and pillows, but he is not allowed to leave the front desk unattended. The director of marketing and sales say she is embarrassed when a prospective client comes into the hotel and is greeted with such a mess. She has called housekeeping several times to have the lobby cleaned but is told, "It's not in the budget to have the lobby cleaned six times a day." All of the team members realize the untidy lobby does create a poor impression of the hotel and the situation does have to be remedied.

The team decides to look at the elements in the situation. The furniture is on wheels for ease of moving when the housekeeping staff cleans. The pillows add a decorative touch to the environment, but they are usually scattered about. The waiter jokingly says, "Let's sew them to the back and arms of the sofa!" Might the ashtrays be removed and receptacles added for guests to use in extinguishing a cigarette? Could a larger waste receptacle with a swinging lid be used to avoid misplaced litter? "The fresh flowers are nice," adds one of the team members, "but many hotels use silk flowers and plants. This must save money over the long run."

The team discussion encourages each person to understand why the maid can't straighten the lobby every two or three hours and why the desk clerk can't leave his post to take care of the problem. The employees' comments concerning furniture and appointments foster an atmosphere of understanding. Team members start looking at one another with more empathy and are slower to criticize on other matters. Was the issue of the messy lobby resolved? Yes, but more important, the team members developed a way to look at a challenge in a more constructive manner.

Solution to Opening Dilemma

Upon initial review, the problem seems to be that all employees should be encouraged to assist guests in an emergency. However, in this case, the desk clerk has a perception problem about his job. This shortsightedness probably results from poor training, a lack of opportunities for employees from various departments to exchange ideas and socialize, and an atmosphere for employee motivation. The front office manager should discuss the situation with the convention representative and emphasize the benefits of total quality management. Supervisors must concentrate on the guests' needs and foster employee growth and development so their employees will likewise concentrate on guests' needs. These concepts are at the heart of effective interdepartmental communications.

4

Property Management Systems

At a recent hotel trade show, you noticed a new property management system that seems to produce all the types of reports your current system cannot produce. The vendor at the show said she will set up a meeting with you in a week or two to talk more about this system. How would you prepare for her visit?

The first three chapters of this text provided an overview of the hotel industry, organization of the hotel, organization and management of the front office, and interdepartmental communication, which laid the groundwork for understanding how the front office fits into a network for providing service to the guest. In this chapter, we focus on the operational aspects of the front desk department, which include considering the physical structure and positioning of the front desk, selecting a property management system (PMS), and using PMS applications.

Computer applications are central to front office operations in today's modern hotels. For new properties, computers are standard equipment; for existing hotels, computers are being integrated into everyday operations to assist in providing hospitality to guests. Computer applications include routinely processing reservations as well as handling registrations, guest charges, guest checkout, and the night audit. Interfacing, the electronic sharing of data, of hotel departments such as food and beverage and the gift shop through point-of-sale, an outlet in the hotel that generates income (restaurant, gift shop, spa, garage); maintenance through monitoring of energy and heating and cooling systems; and security through control of guest keys are just a few of the applications that are explored in this chapter.

As you begin your career in the lodging industry, you will want to develop a thorough understanding of front office computer applications. This text does not refer to one particular computer hardware or software system; your training at any lodging property will include specific operating procedures to produce reports or review information from the database. Instead, this chapter provides general information on which you can base your understanding of computer applications at the front desk. These applications are encompassed by the term property management system (PMS), a generic term for applications of computer hardware and software used to manage a hotel.

You will notice that PMS is not confined to the front office; it interfaces with housekeeping, food and beverage, marketing and sales, gift shop, controller, engineering, safety operation at the Marriott in Overland Park, Kansas, is a graduate of the University of Houston in hotel and restaurant management. Mr. Corprew has worked with Marriott Hotels in various places and positions, including the Marriott Medical Center in Houston, Texas, as a desk clerk, rooms controller, and supervisor; the Airport Marriott in Houston, Texas, as a banquet manager; and the Marriott Courtyard in Legacy Park, Dallas, Texas, in rooms care (housekeeping and engineering), front office, and restaurant and bar areas. He also worked at the Hilton Washington and Towers in Washington, D.C., in sales.

Mr. Corprew indicates that the ambience of the front desk requires a simple, elegant appearance. Preliminary discussions of new trends in front desk structure include a walk-through for associates that allows them to pass in front of and behind the desk to accommodate guests. Also, the front desk and lobby should be considered together in design and function.

The organization of the front desk, with its computers and vast amounts of details, revolves around an uncomplicated guideline: Keep it simple. Mr. Corprew provides plenty of key machines (electronic devices to make electronic guest room keys); ensures that all staff follow standard operating procedures, such as keeping faxes and mail in one location; and requires associates to be considerate of guests' needs. His organizational principle is continued at the time of check-in, when a 100 percent automated property management system requires the associate only to swipe a credit card and to prepare and present the room key to the guest.

Kevin Corprew urges young professionals who want to make a career in the hospitality industry to lead by example with high morals and standards. He encourages students to start in entry-level jobs so they have a basis for dealing with employees and security, and other departments, all of which are service departments of a hotel. Each department plays a role, along with the front office, in serving the needs of the guest- before, during, and after the guest's stay. The front office staff coordinates the communications, accounting, security, and safety requirements of the guest. As the nerve center of the hotel, the front office handles most of the recordkeeping and so benefits most from a computerized system.

The first part of this chapter sets the stage for adopting a PMS. Software and hardware are discussed, as are other considerations in choosing a PMS. The final section of the chapter discusses the various computer modules of the PMS as they apply to the lodging industry.

Physical Structure and Positioning of the Front Desk

While manual equipment is still used in some independent properties, the computerized system has become the system of choice, primarily because of the needs of guests, management, and owners.

Guest First Impression

The front desk has always held a pivotal position of importance in the lodging operation. It is one of the first points of contact with the guest, and, as such, its ambience sets the tone for the hotel. Neatness, orderliness, attractiveness, quality, and professionalism are just a few of the impressions the front desk should convey to a guest. The guest wants to feel important, safe, and in the hands of professionals. The impression conveyed by the physical layout of the desk assists the front office in creating a positive image for the operation. Providing hospitality to the guest and promoting in-house sales are of great importance to the continued financial success of the operation. To provide an environment in which these objectives can be met, a well-planned physical arrangement of the front desk is important.

Creating a Balance Between Guest Flow and Employee Work

Equipment

The front desk should be positioned so that it accommodates the guest while enabling employees to work efficiently. Guests who wait in line for ten minutes only to be told they are in the wrong line will have a negative first impression. Likewise, a desk clerk who has to wait to use a printer or share a computer terminal will not be as efficient as possible. As you become familiar with the practice of processing guests at the front desk, you will see how easy it is to plan a layout of the physical equipment needed.

Guest Safety

The position of the front desk is usually determined by the main entrance of the building and the location of the elevator. The front desk clerk and the night auditor must be able to see anyone who enters the hotel; this helps ensure a safe environment for the guest. Positioning the front desk on the same side as the main entrance and the elevator is not recommended. In all three settings, the front desk clerk has a view of who is coming into the hotel from the street entrance and who is coming off the elevator. This view is essential to the night auditor, who assists security in monitoring the activities in the hotel lobby.

In light of the security issues that emerged after 9/11, the positioning of the front desk is even more important, allowing the front desk staff to be the front-line sentinels of the hotel. Although they may not leave their post, they must be trained to be observant and efficient in summoning the right people to investigate a situation. Positioning a hotel front desk facing the main entry and exit allows the desk clerk to more easily monitor who is entering and leaving the building-an important advantage when considering hotel security.

International translation cards, which assist foreign guests in translating travel phrases of their native language into English, are frequently kept at front desks. Foreign visitors and hotel desk clerks find these cue cards helpful.

Selecting a Property Management System

This section focuses on the components that should be included when deciding to adopt a PMS. The decision-making process begins with understanding the importance of a needs analysis performed by a team of front-line staff members. The needs analysis should focus on the flow of the guests through the hotel and interdepartmental communication needs. A review of administrative paperwork produced by management in all areas of the hotel is also a consideration. After management has gathered relevant data concerning operational needs, it must objectively determine whether a computer will help improve guest service. Other important concepts covered here include software selection considerations and computer hardware terminology. A review of how people interact with computers and how a hotel must make provisions while hardware is being installed is also offered. The importance of computer training and planning a backup power source for continued computer operation is reviewed. The often overlooked maintenance agreement and the important financial payback complete the discussion of selecting a PMS.

Importance of a Needs Analysis

Selecting new equipment for a hotel property is best done after a needs analysis is performed. A needs analysis indicates the flow of information and services of a specific property to determine whether the new equipment-in this case, computers-can improve the flow. The bottlenecks that occur at registration or the lack of information from the housekeeping department on the occupancy status of a room can be alleviated by the use of computers at the front desk. Only after the completion of an operational flow analysis can computer applications be developed to improve the situation.

The importance of needs analysis can be most clearly seen when you consider what can go wrong if such an analysis is not made. The first area of concern for property owners and managers is cost, both initially and over the long term. As the technology has evolved and the equipment become more common, the cost of computerizing a hotel has decreased and the payback period has shortened. However, even with these lower costs, installing and operating a PMS is not inexpensive, and the cost of installing and operating a system that does not meet the specific needs of a particular property is exorbitant.

A system that works well for one downtown hotel may not meet the needs of a downtown hotel in another city or of a motel in the same area. All the technological gadgetry in the world will not impress a guest if the equipment fails to deliver service. The system must meet the needs of the staff as well as the guests. An inappropriate PMS will produce control reports that are not useful to management; the functions of such software therefore are limited, and the cost of the system exceeds its value. For example, a hotel owner who believes that a PMS will speed registrations and decides to purchase a system that does not allow housekeeping staff to input room status from the guest room phone will be disappointed.

Procedure for Performing a Needs Analysis

The following list shows the procedure for performing a needs analysis.

1. Select a team to analyze needs.
2. Analyze the flow of guests through the lodging property.
    - Reservations
    - Registration
    - Guest accounting
    - Checkout
    - Night audit
    - Guest history
3. Analyze the flow of information from other departments to the front office.
4. Analyze the administrative paperwork produced in other departments.
5. Review the information gathered in steps 2, 3, and 4.
6. Evaluate the needs that have been identified-such as control reports, communication, and administrative paperwork produced in other departments-in terms of importance.

7. Combine needs to determine desired applications.

Selecting a Team

The first and most important step in performing a needs analysis for adopting a PMS in a hotel is to select a team to determine the reports and information being generated. The analysis team should include employees at both the management and staff levels. Such a team is better able to see all aspects of the operation; management can provide input on the overall objectives, while staff is more aware of day-to-day needs. The front office manager who feels the reservation system is inefficient may find that the desk clerk not only agrees but can offer suggestions for improving the situation. This desk clerk may not know the first thing about flow analysis processes-preparing a schematic drawing of the operations included in a particular function-but the hands-on information provided will assist the front office manager in evaluating the reservation system. In another instance, the general manager may request that certain additional room sales analysis reports be produced by the marketing and sales department only to find the front office manager producing that information.

Analyzing the Flow of Guests Through the Hotel

The second step in the needs analysis is to analyze the flow of guests through the visit to the property, which provides a structure for this detailed analysis process. The guest stay does not start at registration but at the time a reservation is made. (In reality, the guest stay starts even before this, because guests often select a property as a result of marketing efforts.)

Issues that can be analyzed are quite diverse. They include the ease with which the telephone system can be used, the availability of room occupancy status for guests on any specific date, the length of time it takes to complete a reservation request, the method used to confirm a reservation, the procedure used to block rooms, and the means of finding a single reservation. Also subject to analysis are the methods for gathering guest information upon check-in and the processes for ensuring the correct posting of guest charges, the time required for a guest to check out, the procedure used to resolve a guest's dispute of charges, and the process for posting meal and phone charges just before checkout. How are the daily room charges and taxes posted to the rooms? How long does it take to do this? Are any vital statistics not being produced by completion of the night audit report? How is the information assembled in the night audit? How long does it take to produce this information? Also determine if guest information already on hand from reservation, registration, and guest accounting is being applied for additional visits.

Communicating Information

The third step in the needs analysis process is to look at the information flowing from other departments to the front office. How is information concerning occupancy status received from the housekeeping department? How can a guest report an emergency or fire on the property? How do the food and beverage department and gift shop report guest charges? How does the marketing and sales department determine if blocks of rooms are available on certain dates? How does the engineering department monitor energy use in guest rooms? How does the security department ensure the integrity of guest keys? How is email used? A good PMS can embrace all of these lines of communication.

Reviewing Administrative Paperwork

The fourth step is to review the administrative paperwork produced in the hotel that is necessary to assist management. How does the human resources department maintain personnel files and former employee records? How is direct mail advertising generated in the marketing and sales department? How are function books and individual function sheets maintained? How are tickler files (files used to prompt notice of when certain events will be occurring) maintained? How are work orders processed? What method is used to devise daily menu specials?

Management Review of Information

In the fifth step of this analysis, management must take charge of reviewing the information compiled to determine if needs are being met. Is the marketing and sales department making mistakes because incorrect information concerning the inventory of available rooms is provided by the front office staff? Are desk clerks unable to check the occupancy status of a guest room because the housekeeping department is not providing immediate information? Have misquotes on room rates caused lost revenue for the hotel? Is the night auditor unable to retrieve room status information to confirm or guarantee reservations? The significance of each need and the consequences if the need is not met are then established. Customer satisfaction and quality of service as well as financial implications are considered. How often have conventions not been booked because accurate information on room availability was not at hand? How much revenue was lost as a result? How frequently does a general manager receive complaints because a guest was sent to a room that was under repair or not cleaned? How often must the front office manager adjust a guest's room rate because of a misquote? How does the number of guaranteed reservations compare with the number of confirmed reservations? Why are guaranteed reservations not requested by the night auditor?

Evaluate Needs that Have Been Identified

This step requires a discussion between department managers as to the significance of the reports produced as they relate to producing customer service and financial success of the operation. Each module in the PMS will have a related cost, and the justification for that cost can be simplified if all discussions focus on the goals of the operation.

Assessing Needs Based on Findings

The final step in the analysis is to combine operational and administrative needs to determine which computer applications are appropriate for the property. Often the shared use of a room inventory database is well worth the financial investment. A word processing program to produce direct mail letters, regular correspondence, and daily menus may also justify a particular module of a PMS. The needs analysis enables you to know what you need and what you do not need and will help you choose from the many systems available.

Choosing Software

Selecting software, the computer programs or applications that process data such as guest information and aid in financial transactions and report generation, is more important than selecting hardware, or actual computer equipment such as central processing units, keyboards, monitors, and printers. The effectiveness of a PMS depends on selecting software that allows management to increase guest satisfaction and to access financial and informational data for control purposes. The information obtained from the needs analysis provides a framework for evaluating the numerous software packages on the market today.

Each software package offers numerous features; it is important to choose one package that is most appropriate for your needs. Software on the market today includes guest service, accounting, and information options that are standard in the hotel industry. Investigate the guest service features, accounting options, and information applications to determine which PMS is best for your property. Software vendor personnel will discuss with you the options that fit the size of your hotel and the needs of the guests. Hoteliers should also look forward and think of expansion and growth of their property, or perhaps change in the mix of their market. For example, one hotel may plan to add 200 rooms to the same market, while another hotel may not add any rooms but have a shift in guest type from 20 percent family and 80 percent business to 80 percent family and 20 percent business. Now the family market is doing much more dining in the restaurant (indicating a need for a point-of-sale system that interfaces with the PMS), purchasing more in the gift shop, (another need), and indicating more gift purchases for day-trip packages (yet another need).

If you feel the applications of a particular software package will not help you manage your property, that adding a particular guest service will not increase guest satisfaction, that no significant savings will result from producing more sophisticated accounting reports, or that the arrangement of historical information about guests will not be beneficial, then you should not adopt that PMS. You control the software selection; its function is to help you do a better job. Only you can decide which applications are most useful in your facility.

Examples of how the PMS modules can be applied include the following. The marketing and sales department in any size hotel will clearly find that computerization of client files, meeting room information, and guest history is useful. Preparation of direct mail for a smaller property perhaps would best be outsourced, while a larger property may make better use of a PMS module. The travel agent mode for maintaining a database of travel agents and processing their fees is useful to any size property. The night audit is almost a universal necessity to properties of all sizes. The former eight hours of labor over balancing the guest ledger and city ledger are replaced by a few keystrokes, in some cases. The front desk module, with its applications for check-in, check out, room status, postings to guest accounts, advance deposits, and cashier options, are also acceptable at both small and large properties. The call accounting system is an option that found its way into the hotel's front desk (even at smaller hotels because of the deregulation of telecommunication systems in the U.S.) before some of the other modules, such as the point-of-sale in the restaurant. A maintenance module is more appropriate for a large hotel, whereas a small hotel can rely on an in-house email system, telephone, or paper mail system. These examples, as any other technologies that are developed, should always be evaluated against goals of the hotel, the needs of guest, and a budget.

Future hoteliers should maintain a library of current PMS vendors. The Internet provides a useful and immediate resource for most hoteliers. This first step is accomplished by going to your favorite Web browser and typing in such key phrases as "property management system," "hotel pms" "hotel computer," or "HITEC" (Hospitality Industry Technology Exposition and Conference, which features all the latest computer software for the hospitality industry.) Another method of keeping your PMS file up to date is to attend local and regional trade shows. Stopping by a booth at the hotel show and discussing your current needs with a software vendor will assist you in maintaining awareness on the developments in the industry and matching them with the needs analysis of your guests.

Choosing Hardware

Choosing hardware for a PMS is not as difficult as choosing software. Today, most available hardware is compatible with standard computer operating systems (such as The Opera PMS offered by MICROS®FIDELIO, which connects with [Network] Windows NT Server 4.0 or Novell IntraNetware 4.1; [Database] xBase running under DOS 6.22/Windows 3.11; or [Client] Windows NT 4.0 Workstation or Windows 95). This consideration is essential because most software programs are written to run on these standard operating systems. In short, you must choose your hardware based on its ability to handle the software; review this with your hardware vendor.

Other technology factors to consider include the following working concepts:

Processor speed: how fast a central processing unit (CPU) makes calculations per second; expressed in megahertz (MHz)

Disk drive: a place in the computer where data is stored or read; CD or DVD drive or 3 1?2-inch floppy drive

Megabyte: 1,024 kilobytes of formatted capacity

Gigabyte: 1,024 megabytes of formatted capacity

Access time: the amount of time required for a processor to retrieve information from the hard drive; recorded in milliseconds

Internet: a network of computer systems that share information over high-speed electronic connections

Intranet: a computer network for in-house users to share timely operational information to conduct business.

I/O ports (input/output devices): keyboard, monitor, modem, mouse, joystick, light pen, printer, and trackball

Monitor: a television screen with color or monochrome capacity to view input and output data, control column width and line length of display, adjust height of character display, and allow visual control

Keypad: a collection of numeric typewriter keys and function keys that allow the operator to enter numbers or perform math functions in a computer

Keyboard: a standard or Dvorak-type typewriter-style keypad that allows the operator to enter or retrieve data

Printer: computer hardware that produces images on paper Inkjet: produces small dots printed with liquid ink on paper Laser: produces photo images on paper Letter-quality: a better type of dot-matrix print Single-sheet: a type of printer that uses single-sheet paper

Modem: computer hardware that allows for transfer of data through telephone lines; expressed in baud-information transfer-rates CPS (characters per second): measure of the speed with which individual characters are printed Computer supplies: paper, forms, ribbons, ink cartridges, and floppy disks needed to operate the system Megahertz (MHz): one million cycles per second; indicates computer speed PPM (pages per minute): printing speed capability

The front office manager must be aware of the operational capabilities of the PMS. Computer texts and trade journals can help you understand the hardware options available; Personal Computer PC magazine, in particular, is helpful for keeping up to date with hardware configurations and software applications. Visits to hospitality industry trade shows also help keep you informed on state-of-the-art systems.

The basic hardware requirements are organized around the point-of-sale and customer service areas. Keyboards, monitors, disk drives, and printers constitute the basic user setup. The data manipulation and storage area is part of the mainframe, minicomputer, or personal computer.

The ability to interface among computer databases (sharing or networking of information) is very important. This concept must be designed into the PMS for it to contribute to the effective delivery of hospitality to the guest and to generate a return on its investment. As computer applications become more sophisticated, sharing databases is essential. For example, the information secured at the time a reservation is made can be used by the marketing and sales department to generate more business. The point-of-sale data captured in the restaurants can be reviewed by front office staff to check how they can sharpen their hospitality delivery skills for guests on arrival. For example, if the staff knows a guest likes to order a certain Italian pastry as part of his meal, then they can perhaps use that as part of the welcoming chat upon arrival. Or if a review of a guest folio reveals that she played a particular sport during her previous stay, the staff could men-tion the opportunity to set a start time for that sport. All of these ideas help make the guest feel important and help make a positive return on the investment for the PMS.

The positioning of the hardware at workstations should be based on the same workflow analysis used for any new process or equipment. Consider the needs of the guest (who will be the end user), the employee who will operate the equipment, and the other staff who will want access to information. The information you gain from the needs analysis will assist you in explaining your particular needs to the computer consultants who will install your PMS.

The installation of the electronic cables that connect all of the hardware must also be analyzed. Installation and replacement of cables that run through walls and floors can be costly. Proper computer functioning requires an air-conditioned environment; in guest service areas, this may not present a problem, but in other areas, it may pose difficulties.

Ergonomics, the study of how people relate physiologically to machines, is also a consideration for the front office manager. Glare and flicker from the cursor, a flashing point on a monitor that indicates where data can be entered, and movement on screens can cause eyestrain. In fact, it is fairly common for computer operators to require lenses to correct eyestrain. Another common complaint is neck pain due to improper positioning of the monitor. The swivel base provided on most hardware helps eliminate these problems.

Pain in the wrist may also occur if the keyboard is positioned above the waist of the operator. Carpal tunnel syndrome, or compression of a nerve in the wrist and fingers, is another unfortunate result of overuse of computer keyboards. Because carpal tunnel syndrome causes extreme pain for a computer operator, the keyboard should be positioned at or below waist level. Also, pain in fingers and hands can occur with extensive entry of data on a keyboard.

Other PMS Selection Considerations

Other factors to consider in choosing a PMS are vendor claims, installation plans, training, backup power sources, and maintenance.

Vendor Claims

The prospective PMS purchaser should contact current users of the system being considered and ask relevant questions: How easy is it to operate this system? How useful are the reports you obtain? Has the vendor been available to help train staff and provide emergency service? Answers such as "I don't know how the property could manage without it" or "It is difficult to operate, and the reports are awkward" may alert you to potential advantages or problems. (Remember, however, that different properties have different needs and priorities; a rave review because the system provides an option you consider unimportant is meaningless for your purposes.) Consider the amount of time these properties spent on needs analyses. A visit to the hotel property is worth the effort. Learning how different features of the system work, how various departments interact with the PMS, and what kinds of forms are used will help you with part of your decision. You will also develop a feeling for how guest services are affected.

Hardware Installation Plans

A careful plan for hardware installation will help the management maintain guest service and employee morale. First, it is key to determine who will install wiring or cables. Next to be determined is which hardware will be installed and at what times, followed by which departments will receive hardware first and what methods will be required to get all departments of the property online, a term used to indicate that a computer is operational and connected with a central computer. This information should be used to develop a flowchart, which will help departments adapt and interact using online operations.

Computer Training Programs

The training offered by a computer company ranges from classes held at the corporate headquarters to on-the-job training sessions and informal consultant hot lines. The staff that will use the computers must be thoroughly trained if the equipment is to be put to its best use. Training at the terminals should be preceded by an explanation of how the system will help staff members in their work. Some computer companies lend a dummy computer setup to a lodging property so the staff can experiment with the training modules. This allows them to make mistakes in private and to become familiar with the keyboard configuration. Documentation of procedures will also assist the staff in developing an awareness of the system's capabilities, as will individual hotel-developed step-by-step computer application cue cards.

It is also important to note that employee resistance to change can be overcome with an early buy-in to a new concept and a user-friendly training program. The team concept will help employees overcome resistance to change because they are included on the team. Members of the needs analysis team will see an idea develop from concept to fruition. Many employees resist change because they fear they will be unable to perform a new task; a training program that allows adequate time and practice will help introduce the technology and decrease this fear.

Backup Power Sources

What happens if the power goes out? This concern, as well as the possibility of brownouts, partial loss of electricity, and blackouts, total loss of electricity, is addressed by computer dealers. Battery-powered temporary energy units are used when power is lost or cut to ensure that operational data are not lost. Hotel managers who have experienced power losses are well versed in maintaining communication among the departments and posting charges as required. Once the power returns in full, the staff can catch up on posting to the electronic folio.

Maintenance Agreement

One final consideration in adopting a PMS is the maintenance agreement, which should spell out the related costs of repair and replacement of hardware and software. Allowance for emergency service and times available for general service should also be listed. Loaner or backup equipment availability enhances the attractiveness of the agreement.

Financial Considerations

Purchasing or leasing a PMS for hotel use is a major financial decision. Such an investment can tie up cash flow. If the costs and benefits are not realistically projected, profits may be in jeopardy. The first part of this chapter stressed the importance of performing a needs analysis. Hotel properties that match computer applications with needs by going through this process will achieve the most realistic assessment of costs versus benefits when adopting computers.

The controller of a lodging property usually prepares a budget in consultation with the general manager. Sales of room-nights, food and beverages, and other products and services are projected. Considered with these projections are the related costs of producing those goods and services. The controller is usually aware of the specific costs in each department-the amount of overtime pay required at the end of the month to produce the monthly inventory in the food and beverage department, the extra part-time help required to staff the front desk for a busy checkout or check-in, the cost to produce a direct mail piece for the marketing and sales office, and the fee charged by the outside accountant to produce a monthly profit-and-loss statement. This knowledge is helpful in determining how much money can be saved if a PMS were to be introduced. The amount of money that can be saved (along with tax depreciation advantages) must be equal to or greater than the amount spent on the computer system. Sometimes management may feel that less tangible benefits, such as greater service to the guest or improved morale among employees, justify the cost even when dollar savings are not quite equal.

The decision about whether to purchase or lease must also be made. The outright cost of purchase, related finance charges (if applicable), discount for cash, and depreciation are only a few of the points to review if the hotel decides to purchase. These considerations must be weighed against continuance of cash flow, application of lease payments to the purchase price, and tax advantages of leasing.

Determining the payback period-the time required for the hotel to recoup purchase price, installation charges, financing fees, and so forth through cost savings and increased guest satisfaction-will also assist management in deciding whether or not to install computers. If the controller reports a series of financial problems such as the following, the payback period becomes clearer:

- 5 percent of all local phone calls are not posted at the front desk
- 2 percent of sales are lost every month because guest checks are inaccurately totaled in the food and beverage department
- 10 hours of overtime could be saved through internal preparation of paychecks for each pay period

As the department directors go over their respective profit-and-loss statements with the controller, additional areas for cost recovery can be noted. The time invested in preparing an accurate needs analysis will pay off in the long run.

The above concerns of the controller include areas in addition to the front desk. Remember that the adoption of a PMS includes the management of all guest services and accounting functions. While the needs of the front desk alone-for a call-accounting system or the rental of a reservations system-may not justify the expense of a PMS, the needs of all departments can make such a system cost-effective.

PMS Applications

The property management system is organized around the functions needed to assist in delivering service to the guest. The software options listed earlier in this chapter are only a few of the many available to hoteliers. For purposes of this review, assume that the lodging property is equipped with a state-of-the art PMS and that the system is up and running. The software program main menu lists on the screen all the available individual programs (modules) included in the system. Refer to Figure 4-6. These modules lie at the heart of the front office manager and his or her staff's ability to deliver excellent service to the guest because of the underlying role of communication between departments and sharing of financial information. The PMS has become so much an essential part of lodging operations that to operate a hotel without one would be very difficult. The front office manager relies on the reservation module almost hourly to check changes that may affect the day's service and financial operations. The night audit, if completed as it was in previous years-tallying columns or using a mechanical audit machine-would take much training and many labor hours. The posting module is another timesaver that produces a much more accurate and efficient-looking guest ledger.

The front desk clerk can access any of these individual programs by typing the designated keystrokes or following directions on a touchscreen, a type of computer monitor that allows the operator to input data with the touch of a finger. The documentation, which consists of either printed or on-screen (monitor) instructions, explains how to operate the hardware or software that accompanies a specific PMS. This documentation comprises written step-by-step instructions as well as a flowchart of individual programs and subprograms, all of which are valuable in training staff. The flowcharts are comparable to the blueprints of a building. The following discussion of individual modules and subprograms highlights the applications of these software options in a property management system.

Reservations

The reservations module consists of subsystems that can receive individual guest or group data, check a guest's request against a data bank of available rooms, and store this information. The guest data are received through a personal phone call, through another computer in the referral system, or via the Internet. All of the possibilities or room types and locations, room rates, and special requests can be matched with the existing room inventories. This information can be stored for up to 52 weeks (or more) in most systems.

Information concerning guarantees with credit cards or confirmed reservations is captured at this time. Details on deposits, blocking, times of arrival and departure, VIP guest lists, and projected occupancies, and reports on these reservation functions assist the front office manager.

The guest who is checking out of the Limited-Service Inn in Dallas, Texas, and wants to make a reservation at the Limited-Service Inn in Chicago for that evening can have the reservation confirmed within seconds. The guest information is already available in the data bank, and through electronic transmissions, the request is verified (via a check of the existing room inventories held in the data bank for the Limited-Service Inn in Chicago) by a central computer. Other referral agencies follow similar procedures.

Revenue Management

Revenue management, a process of planning to achieve maximum room rates and most profitable guests (guests who will spend money at the hotel's food and beverage outlets, gift shops, etc.), encourages front office managers, general managers, and marketing and sales directors to target sales periods and develop sales programs that will maximize profit for the hotel. This module shares similar databases with the reservations module-room inventory, room rates, reservation status, and guest information. If a hotel is entering a maximum demand sales period, the yield management module allows the reservations manager to block out that period to prevent guest requests for room reservations for less than the minimum time. Also, the computer prompts the reservations clerk on which room rate category to apply. Daily reports on how well the front office achieved maximum yield of rack rates, the highest room rate charged in a hotel, provides feedback to the general manager and owners. A history of guest sales in food and beverage also assists sales and marketing managers in determining if a group reservation has potential for profitability.

Registration

Guest registration modules have greatly improved the check-in process. Because information has already been captured at the time of reservation, less time is required for registration. The front desk clerk need only verify the guest's request for room type, location, and rate with room inventory and room status. Provisions for walk-in guests without reservations are similarly handled. Method of payment is also established. The hard plastic key can be issued after the security module has changed the entrance code for the room. The guest registration procedure can also be completed by the self-check-in process, a procedure that requires the guest to insert a credit card having a magnetic stripe containing personal and financial data into a self-check-in terminal and answer a few simple questions concerning the guest stay. Also note the inclusion of the intranet in this module; it greatly supports the communication process required by the front office staff in delivering hospitality at the time of check-in.

As an example of how this module works, consider the guest who flies to Chicago from Dallas, signs a guest registration form, waits until the desk clerk checks the status of the room, and receives a key-check-in is complete. All guest information was captured when the initial reservation at the Dallas Limited-Service Inn was made. The data bank of room occupancy information provided by the housekeeper is available to the front desk via the computer. The front desk clerk chooses the room the guest will occupy and issues a key. The total time required for registration is less than five minutes.

Room Status

Access to the room status module provides information on availability of entry to a guest room. There are two types of room status: reservation and housekeeping. Reservation status can be open, confirmed, guaranteed, or repair. Housekeeping status can be ready, on change, or out of order. Reservation status is maintained by the reservation department or reservation system, while housekeeping status is provided by the housekeeping department. The room status feature is one of the most valuable features of the PMS.

It streamlines the operation problems of check-in and assists other departments as well. This module, which may share the same room data bank with reservations, provides reports used by the housekeeper, front office manager and staff, maintenance engineer, night auditor, reservations clerk, and marketing and sales department. The housekeeper must know which guest rooms have been occupied and need cleaning; desk clerks must know if the guest room is reserved or open for sale; the maintenance engineer must plan for routine painting and refurbishing; the night auditor must verify which rooms have been sold to complete the night audit; the reservations clerk needs information on the availability of guest rooms; and the marketing and sales department must have current information on room availability for conventions. This is another module that might include the intranet; however, room status information is immediate in nature, and the posting of a message with a delayed response time may not be appropriate. On the other hand, if a series of rooms will be taken out of use for an extended period, the intranet could be the appropriate place to post an advance notice for the marketing and sales department and the front office. Such a notice would prevent taking reservations for unavailable rooms.

The posting module of a PMS often supplies one of the first benefits realized by the front office manager: immediate posting of charges incurred by the guests (Figure 4-11). Not only is the posting operation streamlined but also accuracy is ensured. A PMS allows the posting to occur at the point of sale in the restaurant, lounge, or gift shop. Similarly, room and tax charges or telephone calls can be posted to the electronic folio in a very short time. Transfers and adjustments of guest charges (with approval by management) to folios are easily made. Charges incurred on behalf of the guest can be posted to the electronic folio by entering room number, amount of charge, department, and transaction type. These data are stored in memory and retrieved after an inquiry, during report generation, or at checkout. The accuracy of these charges still depends on the employee operating the point-of-sale terminal in the restaurant. Entering an inaccurate room number (room 412 entered as 712) or a reversed amount ($32.23 entered as $23.32) will still result in an incorrect posting.

Our guest at the Limited-Service Inn in Chicago wants to charge his valet expense of $20.95 to his room account. After the desk clerk has processed the paid-out to the deliv-eryperson, this charge is posted to the electronic folio by entering the room number, amount of charge, department, and type of transaction. The night auditor verifies the integrity of all department totals.

Call Accounting

The call accounting module of a PMS is a system that automatically posts telephone charges and a predetermined markup to a guest's folio. The individual subscriber to the telephone system (the lodging property) can charge a service fee for any local or long-distance call. The hotel can now use the telephone system to generate profit rather than to simply supply service to the guest. The ability to make a profit through adding service charges, combined with the increased frequency and accuracy of electronic posting, has made the call-accounting option a desirable one. However, with the increased use of cell phones, phone cards, and personal digital assistants (PDAs), telephone revenue has declined in some properties. The PMS call-accounting feature retrieves data for time, charges, and service fee and then posts these charges to the electronic folio. The accuracy of processing telephone charges is greatly increased through the use of a PMS call-accounting feature.

Checkout

The inconvenience of guest checkout (long lines, disputes over charges) is greatly reduced with the PMS checkout feature, which prints out an accurate, neat, and complete guest folio in seconds.

Disputes over guest charges still occur at the time of checkout, but not as often. The posting of a long-distance telephone call to room 295 instead of room 296 is less likely to occur with a PMS, because the PMS interfaces with the call-accounting system and the phone charge is automatically posted to the guest's electronic folio.

Efficiency at time of checkout is also improved when the desk clerk retrieves a hard copy of the folio and presents it for review to the guest. The guest has already indicated method of payment at check-in. An imprint of the credit card has been made, or prepayment has occurred. The floor limit, a dollar amount of credit allowed by the credit card agency, and house limit, a dollar amount of credit allowed by the hotel, have been monitored by the PMS. These controls help avoid high debit balances, the amount of money the guest owes the hotel. Last-minute purchases of products or services are automatically posted at the point-of-sale terminals.

The guest completes the checkout process by confirming the method of payment. The desk clerk may suggest making future reservations at this property or other properties in the chain or referral group. Transfers to the city ledger are made electronically at this time. Cashier activity reports are monitored, as is other information about the day's checkouts (such as number of guest departures and time of departures). A PMS can generate a paid in advance (PIA) listing, which monitors guests who paid cash at check-in. The PIA prevents guests from charging products or services to their guest folio.

Guests can avoid checkout lines by using in-room guest checkout, a feature of the property management system that allows the guest to use a guest room television to check out of the hotel. For this process, the night desk staff slips a copy of an updated guest folio under the door the night before checkout. The guest enters a few digits on the television control panel to start the process. After he or she answers questions about multiple guest accounts in the same room, accuracy of charges, and method of payment, for example, the process is complete. The guest can pick up a copy of the folio at the front desk if desired.

Night Audit

The night audit has always been labor-intensive. In addition to acting as a desk clerk and posting the room and tax charges, the night auditor must balance the guest transactions of the day. To extend credit to guests, debits and credits, the amount of money the hotel owes the guests, must be balanced daily. The debits originating from the various departments must be checked against the totals posted to the guest folios. The credits, in the form of guest payments, must be accounted for by reviewing the guests' outstanding balances. Although this sounds like a simple process, the procedure can be very involved.

The PMS simplifies the night audit by producing totals from departments and guest folios. These data are assembled into standard report forms. Financial information is presented in the daily report, used by the management of the lodging property to determine the financial success of a particular day. Note that the intranet can also be included in this module because the night auditor can post emails to departmental employees concerning the final night audit or other operational details from the previous evening.

Inquiries/Reports

The inquiries/reports feature of the PMS allows management

to retrieve operating or financial information at any time. The front office manager may want to check the number of available rooms in the room inventory for a particular night, the number of guests expected to be checked in, the number of guests to be checked out for the day, the current room status from the housekeeping department, or the outstanding balance report, a listing of guests' folio balances. These reports can be produced easily on a PMS. The inquiries/reports feature of the PMS enables management to maintain a current view of operations and finances.

Back Office

The hotel's accounting office, known as the back office, uses the accounting module of a PMS, which assists in the overall financial management of the hotel. The PMS simplifies the accounting processes, which include the labor-intensive posting procedure of accounts payable, which is the amount of money the hotel owes vendors; the transfer of accounts receivable, which is the amount of money owed to the hotel, based on the guest ledger and city ledger; compilation and production of the payroll; budget preparation; the production of the profit-and-loss statement, which is an official financial listing of income and expenses; and the balance sheet, which is an official financial listing of assets, liabilities, and owner's equity at a certain point. For example, financial information concerning a certain vendor is entered once on a terminal located in the back office (also referred to as controller's office). This information is then reflected throughout of the accounting process. Likewise, the financial information produced through the night audit can be accessed for various reports. These and other features assist in streamlining the accounting process. The intranet is another feature on this module that is most useful in communicating to front desk staff about situations where a guest's charges may need clarification after check out or about cost centers that have incurred charges that need clarification.

Housekeeping

Obtaining current information concerning guest room status has always caused problems for the front desk staff. Guests become impatient when they are delayed check-in. Desk clerks who have not received a room release from housekeeping have no choice but to remain calm and try to appease the guests. The process of obtaining ready status is quickly achieved with a PMS. The maid or houseman enters the ready status immediately through a computer terminal on the guest floor instead of waiting to report a block of rooms to the floor supervisor. The housekeeper no longer needs to make several trips per day to the desk clerk to release blocks of rooms. The efficiency of this module depends on the continued efforts of the housekeeping staff in reporting room status.

Assigning room attendants to clean rooms can be done easily. Labor analysis of number of guest rooms cleaned by room attendants and number of labor hours required to clean guest rooms is performed faster, and the daily housekeeper's report is quickly generated. Inventory of equipment and guest room supplies is also readily available.

Maintenance requests for guest rooms can be communicated instantly through the PMS. The maintenance department staff can also check room status information to determine if the housekeeping staff noted repairs to be made. If the maintenance department wants to take a room out of service for a few days to perform repairs, this information can be relayed to the housekeeping and front desk staff through the housekeeping module on the intranet.

Food and Beverage

The food and beverage module reduces paper flow (vouchers) as well as telephone calls from the restaurants and lounges to the front desk. It also facilitates the accounting process, verifying the integrity of the point-of-sale system. Cashier reports (cash, credit, room service) are easily produced. Other features include inventory control and calculation, recipe development, pricing, item profit evaluation, and sales projections. Sales production analysis and labor analysis are also possible with this module.

Maintenance

Using a PMS streamlines the processing of work orders. Repair orders are entered by various department members. Incomplete jobs can be prioritized, and completed jobs can be analyzed for cost. Inventories of equipment and parts can be maintained. The maintenance module is also used to track energy costs and areas of use. In fact, heating and air conditioning in guest rooms can be activated at the front desk. This module enables the management of a hotel to analyze operational information of this vital department.

Security

Electronic key production has enhanced key control. Each guest receives an electronic key that has a unique electronic code, because the PMS changes the key configuration or combination for each new guest room. Blank key cards (plastic or metal) can be coded at the front desk for each new guest.

Continual monitoring is a feature of the security module of the PMS. Fire alarm systems, including sprinklers and smoke detectors in guest rooms, public areas, and operational areas are kept under constant surveillance via a fire safety display terminal. An alarm system or a voice telephone monitoring system alerts guests to a fire anywhere on the property. Elevators return automatically to the main lobby or other designated floor. Burglar alarms are also monitored through this module. The security feature of a PMS monitors security codes in other modules as well.

Marketing and Sales

The marketing and sales department makes extensive use of the PMS. This department can retrieve guest histories-information on guests' previous stays that reveals geographic origin, telephone information, organizational affiliation, credit card usage, room accommodation preferences, and the like-from reservation and registration files. The source of the reservation (secretary, group, travel agent), type of accommodation requested, and ZIP code of business office or personal domicile are only some of the data that can be obtained from the reservation files. Additional marketing data (newspapers read, radio stations listened to, source of recommendation) can be collected at the time of registration to give the marketing and sales department information on advertising media for target markets.

Another PMS application that the marketing and sales department can use is the ability to produce direct mail letters, which are letters sent directly to individuals in a targeted market group. Individual letters advertising certain products and services, together with mailing labels, can be prepared. Weekly function sheets, listings of the daily events in a hotel such as meetings, banquets, and receptions, can be produced by assessing individual banquet sheets, listings of the details of an event at which food and beverages are served. Information on clients can be stored and updated as required. Contracts can also be produced. Tickler files on upcoming events are a great asset in keeping an edge on the competition. In addition, monthly newsletters can be produced through the word processing and desktop publishing applications. This module maintains reserved occupancy status of meeting and banquet rooms-a great organizational feature.

Personnel

The maintenance of personnel files is greatly enhanced by using a PMS. Information concerning job category, date of hire, record of orientation and training, rate of pay, last evaluation date, promotions, pay increases, payroll deductions, and the like assist management in developing a well-operated human resources department. The amount of paper involved in employee recordkeeping can be kept to a minimum. The word processing application is used to generate form letters, job descriptions, reports, employee procedures, and policy manuals. The PMS also permits labor analysis to be performed with ease.

Electronic Mail

The electronic mail feature, often called email, is a communication system that uses an electronic network to send messages via computers. It is helpful in distributing current information on policies and procedures to a large staff as well as communicating with current and former hotel guests. When email is used, security codes are issued to maintain privacy. Staff members are able to check their email at the computer terminal. Copies of email can be printed if needed for future reference.

In a large corporation with many company-owned properties or franchises, email allows for communication among establishments. In a hotel with many operating departments and thus many department heads, this feature is a great asset to the communication process. Regardless of the size of the lodging property, the email function in an intranet configuration is a useful communication tool. Throughout this section, applications highlight its value to the front office manager and his or her staff as well as the other department managers and their staffs.

Solution to Opening Dilemma

Prior to the PMS vendor's visit, it is advisable to perform a needs analysis. Although such an analysis may have been performed five years ago, the needs of hotel guests, management, and operations change over time. Forming a team of frontline employees and supervisors allows for a good decision. This team should analyze the flow of guests through the duration of their stay to establish a list of guest needs that could be enhanced through PMS technology. Because the team is composed of employees from different departments, other departmental requirements, including administrative paperwork, must also be discussed. These discussions enable the team to prepare a list of ways to enhance the guest's stay, assist departments in preparing reports, and improve communications among departments. The final step is to prioritize the needs and measure them against the budget. Other considerations include verifying vendor claims, developing installation plans, discussing training programs provided by the computer company, finding out about the availability of backup power sources, and securing a reasonable maintenance agreement. Financial considerations include cost-benefit analysis, the decision to purchase or lease, and working out a realistic payback period.

5

Systemwide Reservations

Two days remain before the first guest checks in for the Forest Conservation Conference. A quick review of the reservation module report indicates that several of the new desk clerks took guaranteed reservations (35 rooms) for that convention that account for 10 percent more rooms than are available.

Making reservations is a necessity for travelers and an important marketing tool for lodging establishments. Travelers in various market segments depend on a well-organized reservation system that is easily accessible through toll-free numbers, the Internet, or at a few hours' notice. Lodging establishments want to provide a continuous flow of guests, which will bring profits. A reservation system must ensure efficient means of accessing, processing, and confirming information. Without an efficient reservation system, all aspects of managing a hotel are negatively affected. For example, while overbooking reservations may guarantee a full house for the hotel, it also leaves the guest who is turned away with a negative impression. This not only decreases the hope of repeat business but also ensures that the dissatisfied customer will tell others of the negative experience. This chapter examines the reservation system as an integral part of progressive front office management and discusses the operation of a well-run system.

- Importance of guest reservations to travelers and lodging establishments
- Overview of reservation system
- Sources of reservations
- Forecasting reservations

- Overbooking (occupancy management)
- Processing guest reservations

A reservation clerk is ready to process a guest's request for a room reservation. Photo courtesy of Radisson Hospitality Worldwide.

Importance of a Reservation System

Profitable business ventures rely on effective marketing principles, which include reviewing people who require hotel products and services, determining their specific needs, developing products and services that meet these needs, and making a profit on the sale of those products and services.

A well-organized reservation system allows hotels to ensure a steady flow of guests into their properties. Hotel chains, through their central reservation system, offer their members the ability to fill 30 percent or more of available rooms nightly. Independent hoteliers, in contrast, must create exciting marketing programs to capture room business. Easy access to a hotel's data bank of rooms helps in fulfilling the customers' needs as well as in reaching a targeted daily occupancy rate, average daily rate, yield percentage, and RevPAR. A reservation system is the primary means of producing positive cash flow and a favorable income statement.

Overview of the Reservation System

The hotel industry is powered by sales derived from the use of computerized reservations systems. The systems used to fill rooms consist of the hotel's primary efforts (via marketing and sales and use of their own brand reservation system), their toll-free number, global distribution systems (GDS), travel agents, and third-party sources such as wholesalers who buy rooms from the hotel and resell them on the Internet. The following information shows how hotels rely on a combination of these well-organized systems to produce a profit.

Choice Hotels International

The following information on Choice Hotels International, Intercontinental Hotel Group (Six formerly Continents Hotels) (formerly Bass Hotels &C Resorts), Carlson Hospitality Worldwide, and Pegasus Solutions provides a concise view of the importance of computerized reservation systems to the hospitality industry.

Choice Hotels International, with 5,000 franchisees in 42 countries, operates under the Comfort, Quality, Clarion, Sleep Inn, Econo Lodge, MainStay Suites, and Rodeway Inn brands. In a press release, Choice Hotels International announced its capability of offering guests reservation services through handheld computers:

Owners of the Palm VII or Palm VIIx handheld computer can download Choice's web clipping application to their handheld by visiting www.choicehotels.com, then clicking on "wireless" on the options menu. After following the download instructions, Palm VII or Palm VIIx handheld owners with Palm.Net service are able to reserve rooms, check room availability, check on existing reservations and more. "Essentially, the application provides all of the booking capabilities available through our web site," said Gary Thomson [senior vice president and chief information officer at Choice].

At one of its two reservations call centers, they received 32,000 calls per day, which accounted for 40 percent of all Choice worldwide reservations.

InterContinental Hotels Group

Intercontinental Hotels Group (formerly Six Continents) operates 3,500 hotels and 535,000 guest rooms in nearly 100 countries and territories around the world. Holidex Plus is the hotel's reservation system. The company states, IHG (Intercontinental Hotels Group) experiences over 7 million visits to its Web site each month. Plus, Internet revenues have increased by 50 percent since the launch of the industry leading Lowest Internet Rate Guarantee (LIRG) more than one year ago. IHG was the world's first hotel company to offer the LIRG. This is a consumer promise that states every hotel reservation booked directly through an InterContinental Hotels Group Web site is guaranteed to have the lowest rate publicly available on the Internet for that hotel. HOLIDEX(R) Plus links hotels directly to various Global Distribution Systems (GDS) and travel Web sites. HOLIDEX Plus is far more than an inventory and rate system; it is a strategic revenue system. This includes the ability to set and fence rates giving your hotels business and market requirements. It will allow a hotel to create programs that will compete in your unique market like tailor-driven promotions-resulting in increased revenue and a wider choice of personalized packages for guests.

Carlson Hospitality Worldwide

Carlson Hospitality Worldwide's central reservation system is called Curtis-C (pronounced "courtesy").

Carlson Hospitality Worldwide Reservations Services today (December 18, 2003) announced it has completed its enhanced "Next Generation" seamless interface with three Global Distribution Systems (GDS), providing travel agents and those booking through the GDS direct access to real-time rates and availability at Carlson hotel brands. Regent International Hotels; Radisson Hotels &C Resorts; Park Plaza Hotels & Resorts; Country Inns &C Suites By Carlson; and Park Inn, now offer hotel shopping via the company's central reservations system, Curtis-C, through Sabre (Direct Connect Shop), Galileo (Inside Shopper), and Amadeus (Dynamic Access).

The Carlson system services approximately 730 hotel locations and six cruise ships operating on all seven continents. For the year 2000, it processed approximately 8,900 reservations per day, with a total of 3,242,031 for that year. Brands include Regent International Hotels, Radisson Hotels &C Resorts, Country Inns &C Suites by Carlson, Park Plaza and Park Inn hotels in North America, and Radisson Seven Seas Cruises. It is connected to 455,000 travel agents via the global distribution system (GDS). Curtis-C interfaces with the company's hotels via HARMONY, the company's property management system, and the CustomerKARE (or Customer Knowledge and Relationship Enabling) system. It also interfaces with the HARMONY Database Manager, which provides access to hotel inventory (updated rates and availability) along with the ability to deliver reservations through several distribution systems; the Guest Communication Manager, a system that manages guest satisfaction information (providing a history of service problems per guest per hotel and scanning for trends and patterns); and Knowl-edgeNet, which provides hotels with easy access to valuable company information (corporate policies, forms, reports, hotel procedures, and newsletters) and eliminates monthly printing of hotel reports and distribution to the properties. The benefits of this interfacing of data include creating and distributing products worldwide in seconds, making information easily accessible to customize the customer experience, allowing for synergies among applications and reducing resource requirements, and adapting to changing markets and technologies.

Global Distribution Systems (GDS) in Securing Reservations

Global Distribution Systems (GDS) are distributors of hotel rooms to corporations such as travel agents that buy rooms in large volume. GDSs that play a prominent role in securing guest reservations include Amadeus, Galileo, SABRE, and Worldspan. The following details the scale of their operation.

TravelCLICK, the source of hotel industry electronic distribution for many GDSs, reported the following based on GDS bookings and Internet travel sites. Electronic bookings for European hotel rooms in the second quarter of 2004 were up by almost 17 percent relative to the same period in 2003. The average daily rate (ADR) improved by about 9 percent.

Role of the Internet in Securing Reservations

The business and pleasure traveler have entered the marketplace with a great degree of sophistication. Armed with information from advertising television promotions, direct mail promotions from credit cards, airline frequent flyer incentive plans, and other promotional sources, they want to secure the best rates and value for their accommodations. They search the Internet for the best price and make sure they are satisfied with their hit. How did this free marketplace come about? How did it seem to become a buyer's marketplace? Why do the hoteliers grimace at the thought of the Internet rate? The following discussions on the background of room rates offered via the Internet, the effect of the Internet on pricing rooms, and consumers' response to use of the Internet in making reservations shows how technology has changed the way hoteliers do business.

Background on Room Rates Offered Via the Internet

Sharon H. McAuliffe outlines thoughts for you to consider on room rates offered via the Internet.6 Prior to the Internet entrance into the marketing of rooms, the only public rates available for consumers were those published on brochures or obtained by means of phone calls to the hotel property or a travel agent. Any discounts were offered to wholesalers and corporate clients based on their volume of business or length of stay. When the dot.com mania hit consumers, the wholesalers decided to advertise free offers to entice consumers to use the Internet. This has left a lasting impression on the consumer's purchasing manner. An initial wholesaler offered to take empty hotel rooms into their inventory on the Internet, and hoteliers were grateful to sell the rooms at low sale prices. Internet volume was light and everything seemed fine. Then other Internet sites offered similar models with their discounts and with a guaranteed lowest price. The result is a transparency of rates. Guests can check room rates before check-in to see if their guar-anteed room rate has been offered lower on the Internet.

Effect of Internet on Pricing Rooms

Imtiaz Muqbil,7 reports on Pricewaterhouse Coopers' study, "Effect of the Internet on Pricing," which was to estimate of the effect of the Internet on lodging room rates, focusing on what room rates in 2003 would have been without the effects of the Internet. He mentions that the Travel Industry of America figures quoted in the study indicated that approximately 35 percent of Americans used the Internet to research travel. The real-time rate information availability causes business and group consumers to rebook reservations if lower rates are posted. He says these posted rates are now becoming negotiated maximum rates. Another feature of the Internet search yields reduced search costs for leisure travelers because they can compare room rates in their destination areas.

So what is the net effect of this Internet search? The study estimated the net effect to be minus $1.27 billion. This loss is caused by the combination of lower average daily room rate (ADR) because of increased transparency and price competition and increased revenues due to increased bookings stimulated by the lower rate. It is interesting to note that the study found that the average rate for Internet bookings was 17 percent below the rate for non-Internet bookings. Furthermore, Internet reservations consisted of about 13 percent of all U.S. hotel reservations in 2003. The study estimated that about 7 percent of these online bookings were incremental reservations, made by travelers who would not have reserved without the existence of low Internet rates. The study estimates that the net Internet effect on the U.S. lodging industry in 2005 will have increased by about 30 percent.

What type of person goes online to make a reservation? The report indicated that in 2003, 75 percent were discount seekers and 25 percent were convenience bookers. The study estimates that in 2005 Internet bookings will come equally from people seeking convenience and people seeking discounts.

Another point Muqbil makes is that price transparency, or the ability of the consumer to determine room rates, will continue to affect the ability of hotels to increase room rates during low seasons. However, during peak seasons, the Internet may enable hotels to increase rates more rapidly than was possible before the Internet.

Consumers Response to Use of the Internet-Third-Party Websites

Third-party websites such as Expedia and Travelocity provide the consumer an opportunity to view hotel room availability and rate with a few keystrokes on the computer. The consumer response to the opportunity to book room reservations online has been overwhelming. TravelCLICK, a Chicago-based electronic provider of reservations for consumers, serves over 7,500 customers in more than 140 countries around the world. It indicated the continued consumers' reliance on the Internet to process reservations.

"Internet (consumer online) room nights displayed growth of 18.7% above the second quarter of 2003 [in 2004]." Year-to-date performance figures [second quarter 2004] reveal total GDS [Global Distribution System] and Pegasus Hotel e-Commerce room night sales at 57,131,438. Of that total, 46,510,434 were sold by travel agents and 10,621,004 originated by the consumer off the Internet.

This overwhelming response to the Internet continues. Price and Starkov9 report that "in 2004 twenty percent of hotel bookings will be influenced by the Internet, but done offline (call center, walk-ins). In 2004, for the first time Internet hotel bookings will surpass GDS hotel bookings. Two years from now the Internet will contribute over 27% of all hotel bookings (PhoCusWright)." This trend began in 2003, when The Hospitality Sales &C Marketing Association International (HSMAI) and Smith Travel Research reported10 that branded hotel sites accounted for 75 percent (14.8 million) of Internet reservations. Third-party (Expedia, Hotels.com) and GDS Internet sites accounted for 25 percent.

Financial Effects of Third-Party Reservations

The financial effects of this consumer response should be evaluated. The chapter on revenue management considers the job of the revenue manager, which includes evaluating channels of room reservations. For example, a reservation completed via a travel agent may incur a 10 percent commission, while a third-party reservation may incur a commission as high as 18 percent. If you do the math on a room that sells for $100, the commission equals $10 for the 10 percent and $18 for the 18 percent. If you extend that example of an $8 difference to just 10 rooms per night for 365 nights per year, the result is $29,200 ($8 x 10 x 365 = $29,200). However, there is another side to that argument. What if you didn't place those extra rooms for sale on the third-party reservation site? Would they have remained unsold? Would you have lost all income, let alone the differential of $29,200? It is indeed a struggle of wits and experience to compete in the revenue management venue.

Types of Reservation Systems

Franchisee

A franchisee is a hotel owner who has access to a national reservation system and receives the benefits of the corporation's management expertise, financial backing, national advertising, and group purchasing. A franchise member of a reservation system or a member of a referral system gains significant advantages from interhotel property referrals, a system in which one member-property recommends another member-property to a guest, and national advertising.

Referral Member

A referral member of a reservation referral system, a worldwide organization that processes requests for room reservations at a particular member-hotel, is a hotel developer/owner who has access to the national reservation system. Hotels that are members of the reservation system are more than able to justify these costs; for example, a chain property may obtain 15 to 30 percent of its daily room rentals from the national reservation system, depending on local economic and market conditions. Compared to the costs incurred by an independent property that must generate every single room sale with individual marketing and sales efforts, franchise referral costs seem minimal.

Use of the reservation system by franchises and referral properties incurs fees such as royalty, marketing, and reservations. For example, in 2005, Hilton requires an initial fee of $85,000 for the first 275 guest rooms or suites plus $300 for each additional guest room or suite, with a minimum fee of $75,000. A 5 percent of monthly gross rooms revenue is considered the franchise fee. The monthly program fee is 4 percent of monthly gross rooms revenue. Hilton requires installation of their OnQ proprietary business software and hardware system; the costs for these systems range from $40,000 to $150,000. Hilton notes that the franchisee doesn't need to purchase the hardware or software components (except for the up-front costs of installation), or pay for ongoing maintenance and technical support, because these are provided by Hilton Hotels Corporation and paid through the franchisee's monthly fee of 0.75 percent of the hotel's monthly gross room revenue. There are other fees for participation in the Frequent Traveler/Guest Reward program, training, and computer system.

Marriott charges similar franchise fees for an investor seeking a Fairfield Inn franchisee. A $40,000 or $400/room (which ever is greater) application fee is charged. The royalty fee is based on 4.5 percent of the gross room revenues. Marriott assesses 2.5 percent of gross room revenues fee for marketing. Reservation fees include 1.00% of gross room revenues, $2.95 per non-property reservation, and a communication support fee of $412.00 per accounting period. Marriott lists $52,500 to $76,500 pre-opening fees and property management system costs depending on the size of the property, the training required, and where the property management system hardware and software is purchased.12

If you do the math on the cost of operating a hotel under the auspices of either of these franchises, you can determine that a franchise is a very expensive business option. However, the benefits (reservation system, advertising, management development, etc.) of operating a hotel with a franchise are numerous and far outweigh those costs.

Sources of Reservations

Guest reservations come from a variety of market segments. Some of the more common groups are corporate clients, social/military/educational/religious/fraternal (SMERF) organizations, group travelers, leisure travelers, and current guests who want to return to the same hotel. This is only one way of classifying guest reservations. The purpose of analyzing these segments is to understand the needs of each group and provide reservation systems to meet their needs. Keep in mind that reviewing their needs will assist you in gaining insight into guests' methods of communication. The more you learn about those methods, the better you will be able to monitor and improve current reservation communication systems.

Corporate Clients

The corporate client is a hotel guest who is employed by a business or is a guest of that business. Corporate clients provide a hotel with an opportunity to establish a regular flow of business during sales periods that would otherwise be flat. For example, a hotel located in an area popular with weekend tourists would operate at a loss if an aggressive marketing effort were not made to secure corporate clients from Sunday through Thursday nights. Corporate clients are usually in town to visit corporate headquarters or to attend business meetings or conventions. Visits are usually structured in advance, with detailed agendas and itineraries. Such structured schedules suggest the corporate guest needs reservations to ensure a productive business visit. The reservation for the corporate guest may be initiated by a secretary or an administrative assistant. These office personnel are vital to the marketing efforts of a hotel. Many hotels offer a secretaries club, which is a powerful marketing and public relations effort aimed at this group. The program encourages the secretary or administrative assistant to make room reservations with the hotel for visiting business clients by providing incentives such as gift certificates for the person who books the most reservations, free meals for being a member, and free special-interest seminars. This system provides the basis for a loyal contingent of secretaries and administrative assistants who think of the club's hotel first. This marketing program helps the front office manager and the reservationist get to know the leaders in the business community in an indirect way. If such people need a quick reservation on a busy night, they feel they will receive special consideration from the hotel's management.

A toll-free phone number assists the cost-conscious corporate client by giving corporate guests calling from outside the property's area code an opportunity to save on phone bills. The independent lodging property that has installed a toll-free phone number gives itself a marketing advantage. If the person making the reservation wants to check out rates, location, amenities, related hotel services, and the like, he or she can do so without incurring expense. The corporate client can then match travel needs with available lodging properties.

The corporate client can also place the reservation through the reservation/referral system of the chain organization. The large chains, which advertise by radio, television, billboard, and print, allow the corporate client to make reservations easily through a toll-free number.

The number connects the caller to a reservationist who has access to a data bank of available rooms at lodging properties that are members of the chain or referral system. The reservation can be completed in minutes. The use of a single phone number to access all properties offers the corporate client an easy, standard way to make reservations for stays in several cities with one call. In the lodging industry, this opportunity to gain repeat business is very important.

The travel agent also makes reservations for corporate clients. The travel agent who is booking air or other transportation for clients usually books room reservations as well.

The corporate client can also visit a hotel's website to obtain information and make a room reservation.

Social/Military/Educational/Religious/Fraternal (SMERF)

The SMERF market provides a good opportunity to fill vacancies in odd times of the business of the cycle, because this market will travel at off-peak times to save money. For example, educators may hold meetings during the Christmas vacation or summer recess so they can secure a lower room rate. SMERF groups may number just 50 to 100, but there are many such groups to be courted. They can be mined through the combined efforts of a local travel and tourism board, Internet searches to determine when they schedule their annual, semiannual, or quarterly meetings, and a review of local newspapers to identify the leaders of local chapters.

Meetings/Incentive/Conference/Event (MICE)

The lucrative MICE market requires a devoted hotel marketing and sales team or agency to locate large groups of conference attendees who want to schedule their meeting at a conference hotel. Many details are involved in encouraging a group to book an event, including airfares, supply of hotel rooms, room rates, and area cultural activities. The support of a local tourism and travel association is a major asset.

Group Travelers

Group travelers are persons traveling as a group either on business or for leisure. Convention guests and seminar attendees are examples of groups that travel on business. Participants in organized tours who pursue recreation, education, and hobbies, and special interests constitute some of the leisure segment. The key to marketing reservations to this group is providing an efficient access method for planning details of a tour. The group planner is the person responsible for securing guest room accommodations, food and beverage program transportation reservations, meeting facilities, registration procedures, tours, and information on sightseeing, as well as maintaining a budget for group travelers. The group planner must satisfy the needs of the group in an efficient, orderly, and professional manner. The details involved in organizing a three-day convention in a large city for 700 attendees or a seven-day tour of points of interest for 44 people are quite extensive. How does the group planner begin?

Options available for the tour or meeting planner include tapping into the bus association network, an organization of bus owners and tour operators who offer transportation and travel information to groups, using directories listing lodging properties, communicating with hotel representatives of lodging properties, and contacting hotel brokers. Hoteliers provide information concerning lodging facilities and tourism through these sources.

Bus associations are professional organizations on the national and state levels that provide their members with organized destination information needed for planning tours and conventions. Usually these associations organize conventions of their own by working with hotels, tourist attractions, and travel and promotion associations in the public sector that supply facilities and points of interest to the group traveler. Through the monthly publications of these associations, members can remain current on the travel industry. The lodging operation that advertises in these publications will reach a market that is looking to add variety to a group tour.

Travel directories, organized listings of hotel reservation access methods and hotel geographic and accommodations information, also help the group travel planner match facilities with the needs of the group. The most common of these directories is the Hotel and Travel Index. Other directories include Travel Books & Guides from AAA, Miche-lin Guide, Mobil Travel Guides, Official Hotel Guide, Official Meeting Facilities Guide North America, The Hotel Guide, and Weissmann Travel Reports. However, the ease of access to information on a hotel's products and services via the Internet is highlighted by Starkov and Price,13 who indicate that "over 162 million Americans are active Internet users (Nielsen)." Beatty14 urges hotel operators to use websites to attract online customers: "A recent survey of 1,100 Internet users conducted for Genex, an Internet design company based in Atlanta, found that 65 percent of respondents will not patronize a poorly designed site-even if it is a favorite brand."

Working with a hotel representative, a member of the hotel's marketing and sales department who actively seeks group activities planners, is another method the group planner may find quite useful. Armed with details about the lodging facility, points of interest in the area, and community background, the hotel representative can prepare a package deal for the planner. The active solicitation of group business can prove profitable for a hotel.

Another type of active solicitation for group travelers is done by the hotel broker. This is the person who sells hotel room prize packages to corporations, sweepstakes promoters, game shows, and other sponsors. By booking reservations in volume, a hotel broker obtains a discount for the organization that wants to offer a hotel visit as a prize. Chain and referral organizations usually have people in their corporate marketing and sales divisions who contact organized groups or brokers to sell the hotel rooms and facilities.

As mentioned earlier, the key to securing the business of group travelers is to develop a structured access system that assists the planner in meeting the needs of the group. The more readily available the information concerning the lodging property, tourist attractions, and the community, the easier it is for the planner to choose a property. (Please note that hotel brokers also solicit room blocks from hoteliers on certain dates for resale on their third-party website.)

Leisure Travelers

Leisure travelers are people who travel alone or with others to visit points of interest or relatives, or for other personal reasons. These travelers, who are often unrestricted by deadlines or schedules, are more flexible in their travel plans than are corporate clients and group travelers. They are more willing to seek someplace to stay along the way; however, some of the people in this group may want to obtain guaranteed reservations to ensure a trip with no surprises. This fragmented group consists of many subgroups, including singles, married couples, young families, senior citizens, and students. Some of the methods the leisure traveler can use to secure room reservations are travel agencies, toll-free numbers, reservation/referral systems, and the Internet.

Although using travel agents to place reservations may not be as common with leisure travelers as it is with businesspeople, the ease of one-stop shopping that travel agents offer encourages hotels to develop strong business relationships with them. The fee a lodging facility pays for accepting a reservation placed by a travel agent is usually 10 percent or more of the room rate, a minimal sum compared to the increase in volume and subsequent profits that an agent can generate for a property. Another method used by the traveler to make reservations is the toll-free phone number. Calling these numbers, which are listed in travel guides and the phone book, provides travelers with up-to-the-minute room rates and reservation availability status.

The third method available for the traveler is the reservation/referral system. This option offers the traveler a quick way to contact a particular hotel via a national or an international reservation/referral system. Travelers planning long trips or visits to unfamiliar areas usually prefer some assurance that accommodations will be available, clean, safe, and comfortable. The name recognition built up over time by a chain provides that assurance and convinces the traveler to place room reservations through its reservation/referral system.

A fourth method used by the market segment to make reservations is via the Internet. Travelers can visit the website of participating hotels to investigate accommodations and pricing as well as to make reservations. The leisure market has embraced this method, via their home computers and widespread Internet connection.

Current Guests

An often overlooked way to attract room reservations is through current guests, guests who are registered in the hotel. (Although this topic is covered in more detail in chapter 13, it is important to mention it here as a source of reservations.) This potential market is a promising source of repeat business. The people in this group have already experienced the services and facilities of a lodging property and may be willing to make an immediate commitment to more hospitality from the same hotel or another hotel in the same chain or referral group.

The opportunity to book additional reservations occurs during the check-in and checkout phases of the guests stay. After registering the guest, the front desk clerk may ask if he or she will be continuing to travel after leaving the hotel. If the guest mentions plans to travel to another city, the desk clerk may inquire if a reservation is needed. Likewise, the desk clerk may ask the guest on checkout if additional reservations are needed for continuation of this trip or for future trips. The hotel that promotes its facilities to current guests in this way will be rewarded with an increase in room occupancy.

Forecasting Reservations

Forecasting, or rooms forecasts, which involves projecting room sales for a specific period, is a natural next step after collecting the data from the reservation process. This step includes previewing the effects of reservations on the income statement, scheduling labor, and planning for the use of facilities. In addition to presenting a practical method for preparing a rooms forecast (sometimes referred to as a projection of room sales), this section also explains how such a forecast can be used as a means of communication with other departments.

One of the purposes of a rooms forecast is to preview the income statement. It enables hotel managers to determine projected income and related expenses for a certain period. The front office manager who has estimated total room occupancy to be 100 rooms with an average room rate of $90 for a seven-day period can project a revenue of $63,000 (100 x $90 x 7) from room sales. Budgeted cost control policies allow the front office managerto allocate a certain amount of that income for front office staff. This process of projecting sales and related expenses is important to the successful management of the front office.

The front office is not the only department that depends on a well-constructed rooms forecast. The food and beverage department, housekeeping department, and maintenance department rely on the house count, or the number of persons registered in a hotel on a specific night. This is important for scheduling labor, using facilities, planning improvements or renovating facilities, ordering supplies, and the like. For example, if a full house, 100 percent hotel occupancy, is predicted and there are no scheduled banquet-breakfasts, extra waitstaff must be scheduled in the dining room. Employees in the housekeeping department may be refused vacation when a full house is expected. Other contingencies include a maintenance department's need to schedule major repairs and preventive maintenance, annual cleaning, and remodeling of guest rooms when occupancy is low; a controller's need to prepare a cash flow estimate; an executive housekeeper's need to schedule adequate staff based on guest room occupancy; a security department's requirement to be aware of activity projected for the hotel; and a parking garage manager's need to know if the garage can meet the auto/van space requirements for the anticipated guests. These are just a few of the uses of the rooms forecast.

The front office manager determines the revenues projected by this rooms forecast. To do this, the average room rate or the specific room rate for a group may be applied. This information is important to the controller, general manager, and owner of the hotel, who use it in managing the hotel's finances. This system can also be used to prepare quarterly or yearly forecasts.

Overbooking (Occupancy Management)

The practice of overbooking-accepting reservations for more rooms than are available by forecasting the number of no-show reservations, stayovers, understays, and walk-ins, with the goal of attaining 100 percent occupancy-is viewed by the general public with skepticism. As a future hotelier, you should prepare for the onerous task of developing a policy on overbooking. The front office manager is responsible for administering this policy.

American courts seem to agree that "in many instances, overbooking to overcome the problem of no-shows and late cancellations may produce advantages by way of operating efficiencies that far outweigh the occasional inconveniences to guests and travellers." They have held hotel overbooking to be customary and justifiable practice for offsetting the losses from no-shows. Writing in February 1980, Gould et al. could find no direct statutory or administrative law governing hotel overbooking with the exception of one Florida regulation.15 Hoteliers and front office managers who practice overbooking do so to meet an organization's financial objectives. They do not intentionally overbook to cause problems for the traveler. Rex S. Toh reports "the no-show rate is anywhere between 5 and 15% in most markets."

The financial loss due to no-shows may be substantial. In a hotel that typically has 100 confirmed reservations (not guaranteed with a credit card) and experiences a 5 percent no-show rate, five rooms per night would remain unsold. With an average room rate of $70, these five rooms would cost the hotel $350 in revenue. Over a year, this amounts to $127,750. Lost revenues of this volume force the hotelier to develop an aggressive occupancy management policy. This policy is based on management of the occupancy categories into which guests are placed: those with confirmed reservations, those with guaranteed reservations, stayovers, understays, and walk-ins. However, most hoteliers require a guest guarantee his or her stay with a credit card number to ensure their intent of arrival and thus guarantee payment for product and services on the part of the guest and hotel.

Confirmed reservations, prospective guests who have a reservation for accommodations that is honored until a specified time, represent the critical element in no-shows. After that time (usually 4:00 P.M. or 6:00 P.M.), the hotel is under no obligation to hold the reservation. The front office manager must keep accurate records of no-shows in this group. Various types of travelers with confirmed reservations-corporate, group, leisure-have different no-show rates. For example, corporate confirmed reservations may have a 1 percent overall no-show rate. Group travelers may have a 0.5 percent no-show rate, with no-shows all coming from one or two particular bus companies. Leisure travelers may have a 10 percent no-show rate. A detailed investigation of each of these categories will suggest methods for minimizing no-show rates.

Guaranteed reservations, prospective guests who have made a contract with the hotel for a guest room, represent a less volatile group because the guest provides a credit card number to hold a room reservation. Rex S. Toh reports that the no-show rate for guaranteed reservations was 2 percent, compared to 10 percent for confirmed reservations.17 The front office manager should investigate these no-shows to determine their sources and plan accordingly.

Stayovers are currently registered guests who wish to extend their stay beyond the time for which they made reservations. Accurate records by traveler category (corporate, group, leisure) reveal the stayover rate of each. For example, employees of a corporation who travel with spouses may extend a Thursday and Friday business trip to include a Saturday. Similarly, a group conference scheduled from Monday through Thursday may encourage the attendees to stay longer to sightsee.

Understays are guests who arrive on time but decide to leave before their predicted date of departure. Leisure travelers may find their tourist attraction less interesting than anticipated. Urgent business may require the corporate client to return to the office sooner than expected. Maintaining accurate records helps the front office manager predict understays.

A welcome sector of the hotel market, walk-in guests, can enhance daily occupancy percentages when effectively managed. The front office manager must be aware of activity in the local area. Heavy tourist seasons, special tourist events, conventions, and the like will increase the number of potential guests. Awareness of such possibilities helps the front office manager plan. Walk-in numbers are often higher if the front office manager maintains good relations with the front office managers of nearby hotels, who may refer guests to the property when their own are fully booked. Sending guests who cannot be accommodated to nearby hotels is a win-win situation for guests and hotels.

When these occupancy categories are tracked, the front office manager can more accurately predict occupancy. The front office manager can obtain the data for this formula by reviewing the property management system (PMS) reservation module, which lists the groups, corporate clients, and individual guests who have made reservations for a specific period. Also, the front office manager should check tourist activity in the area, business events planned in other hotels, and other local special events.

The following occupancy management formula considers confirmed reservations, guaranteed reservations, no-show factors for these two types of reservations, predicted stayovers, predicted understays, and predicted walk-ins to determine the number of additional room reservations needed to achieve 100 percent occupancy. No-show factors are based on prior experience with people with confirmed or guaranteed reservations who did not show up.

Total number of rooms available

- .confirmed reservations x no-show factor based on historical data
- guaranteed reservations x no-show factor based on historical data
- predicted stayovers + predicted understays
- predicted walk-ins

= number of additional room reservations needed to achieve 100 percent occupancy

Here is an example of how to use this formula:

1. If a 200-room lodging property has 75 confirmed reservations with a 5 percent no-show factor in that category, 71 rooms can be predicted to be occupied by guests with confirmed reservations. The no-show factor is based on historical records of this category for this property maintained and reviewed by the front office manager.
2. There are 100 guaranteed reservations with a historical no-show rate of 2 percent. This means that 2 rooms have probably been reserved by no-show guests and may be available for sale. The policy of the hotel may or may not allow the sale of these 2 rooms. If the hotel knows of other hotels in the immediate area that have available rooms for that particular night, the front office manager might be willing to walk a guest with a guaranteed reservation to another hotel if all the guests with guaranteed reservations arrive. It is important to be extremely cautious in this category. An unpleasant scene can occur if an exhausted guest arrives at 3:00 A.M. with a guaranteed reservation and finds no vacancies.

3. The predicted number of stayovers at this given time-based on historical records, with considerations for the season of the year, tourist attractions, nature of the current guests (convention, tourist, or business traveler)-is 4 rooms. This number of rooms must be subtracted from the number of rooms available for sale.
4. The predicted number of understays at this given time, considering factors similar to those applied to stayovers, is 5. This number of rooms is added to the number of rooms available for sale.
5. The predicted number of walk-ins for this given period-using historical records and available information concerning tourist events, activity at other hotels, attractions in nearby communities, and the like-is 8.

The arithmetic for this example works out as follows:

- 200 rooms available
- 71 confirmed reservations (75-[75x0.05])
- 98 guaranteed reservations (100 -[100 x 0.02])
- 4 stayovers + 5 understays

  The occupancy management formula indicates to the front office manager that 24 additional rooms must be rented to achieve 100 percent occupancy. By predicting this number, the front office manager has reasonable flexibility in accepting 24 additional reservations for the evening.

Revenue Management

Revenue management is the technique of planning to achieve maximum room rates and most profitable guests. This practice encourages front office managers, general managers, and marketing and sales directors to target sales periods and to develop sales programs that will maximize profit for the hotel. This topic is fully explored in chapter 6. Revenue management is part of the successful administration of a reservation system because it forces the front office manager to make a realistic attempt to produce a favorable income statement. Applying rate categories to specific periods with minimum length of reservations and reviewing potential markets and their spending habits assist the front office manager not only in meeting the goal of 100 percent occupancy but also in achieving maximum profitability.

Processing Guest Reservations

Means of communication with the client; room inventory data banks; systems for reservation, confirmation, deposits, and cancellations; and blocking procedures, a process of reserving a room on a specific day, are the major components of a well-organized guest reservation processing system.

The guest who wants to secure overnight lodging accommodations must have an efficient means of communicating the room reservation to the hotel, such as a toll-free phone number, fax number, or personal computer. In turn, the hotel must have a way to check reservation requests against a data bank of available rooms. To ensure the reliability of the room reservation, the hotel establishes a deposit or guarantee system that commits the guest to the purchase of the accommodation. A cancellation process allows the guest and the hotel the flexibility necessary to function in a complex society. A blocking procedure that balances future commitments with present room requirements also helps the front office manager provide an effective room reservation processing system.

Systemwide Reservation Systems

The lodging property associated with a systemwide reservation service is connected to the system via a nationwide toll-free telephone number. The telephone number is widely distributed by the marketing and sales departments of the corporation. The potential guest who dials this toll-free number is greeted by an operator located at the central reservation headquarters. This operator has access to the computerized data bank of available rooms at each participating lodging property, so that, for example, a request for a certain type of room for three consecutive nights (February 15, 16, and 17) at a property in Boston can be matched through the data bank. If the participating property has rooms available for those nights, the request can be processed. If it does not have space available, the operator can suggest properties in the reservation/referral system that do have rooms available.

After the operator determines that the guest's room request can be satisfied, he or she asks for the arrival time. The many lodging properties in the industry have different policies on how long they will hold a reserved room; some will hold the room until 6:00 P.M., for example, while others will hold the reservation only until 4:00 P.M. In any case, the time of arrival is extremely important to the hotel's income. Rooms held for guests who do not show and that cannot be resold adversely affect the front office manager's ability to produce income. The maxim that "a room unsold is an opportunity lost forever" has profound implications for the profit-and-loss statement.

Because the hotel must have lead time to resell a no-show reservation and because guests want to ensure that their accommodations will not be resold before they arrive, a system must be in place to meet the needs of each. Both computerized and traditional reservations systems can offer various levels of reservation assurance to accomplish this goal via advanced, confirmed, and guaranteed reservations.

Outsourcing Reservations

In addition to central reservation systems (CRS) operated by hotels, outsourcing providers of central reservation systems are available for hotel managers.

This new breed of CRS and service provider processes voice, Internet and Global Distribution System-based reservations on behalf of hotels. This hybrid group provides reservation systems to clients that want to manage closely their reservation processing, while also offering all the services of a traditional representation company. In addition, these companies offer their services through Web-enabled application-service provider [ASP] models.

SynXis Agent, a suite of reservation-management and distribution products, consists of four main components-a CRS; GDS connectivity; alternate-distribution-system connectivity; and Book-A-Rez, an Internet-booking tool. Through its suite of Internet-based applications, SynXis enables hotel operators to consolidate and control hotel inventory from all booking sources. It also provides direct access to the four major GDSs and enables consumers to book hotel reservations online through the hotel's

Web site. Sally Payze, former vice president of operations at SynXis, indicates, "It consolidates inventory across all booking channels into a single image of inventory. That allows all channels to have access to the last room available and there is no managing of allotments by channel. Its interface allows hotels to define and manage group profiles, administer room blocks and manage rooming lists. In addition, travel planners can enter their own rooming lists directly from the Web, which saves hotel labor, provides immediate confirmation numbers and reduces data-entry errors."

Another provider of reservations outsourcing is Pegasus Solutions. The services they offer include real-time availability and pricing for property and room types, a Web-based property access tool for rate and inventory management, property information and electronic report distribution, connectivity to electronic distribution systems, interfaces with key industry property management systems, revenue systems, and loyalty program systems to approximately 7500 hotels.

Types of Reservations

Confirmed

The confirmed reservation is comparable to a contract that becomes void at a certain hour of a certain day. The confirmed reservation allows the hotel to project the number of guests that will check in by the deadline hour. After that deadline, the hotel is free to sell unclaimed room to walk-in guests or to accept overflow guests from another property. The hotel usually keeps track of the number of no-shows and compares them to the total number of confirmed reservations that were made; these historical records help in predicting occupancy-and revenue-accurately.

Guaranteed

Guaranteed reservations enable lodging establishments to predict revenue even more accurately. They commit the guest to pay for a room night and the hotel to provide accommodations regardless of arrival time. If the guest does not show up (without prior cancellation), the hotel may process a credit card voucher for payment. Likewise, no matter when the guest arrives on the reserved night, the hotel must have the reserved accommodation available. The guaranteed reservation requires the hotel to determine the method of guest payment. The guest may secure the method of payment with a valid credit card, an advance payment, or a preauthorized line of credit.

Reservation Codes

Reservation codes are a sequential series of alphanumeric combinations that provide the guest with a reference for a confirmed or guaranteed reservation. (Reservation codes are also referred to as confirmation numbers.) Such a code indicates that accommodations have been secured for a specific date with a commitment to pay for at least the first room-night. The code, which usually consists of several letters and digits that do not necessarily have any meaning to the guest, may identify the hotel in the chain/referral group, the person who processed the reservation, the date of arrival, the date of departure, the type of credit card, the credit card number, the room rate, the type of room, and/or the sequential number of the reservation. The organization that develops the code includes in it information appropriate for the efficient management of a particular reservation system. A guaranteed reservation code may look like this:

122-JB-0309-0311-MC-75-K-98765R

- 122: the identification number of the property in the chain
- JB: the initials of the reservationist or desk clerk who accepted the reservation
- 0309: the date of arrival
  - 0311: the date of departure
  - MC: the type of credit card (MasterCard)
  - 75: the nightly room rate of $75
  - K: indication that the reserved room has a king-size bed
  - 98765R: the sequential reservation number

A few things should be kept in mind when establishing a reservation code system. The amount of memory available to store the code information in a computer data bank may be limited. Therefore, a short code that provides less information may be necessary. The reservation code should be designed to give adequate information to the hotel property that must provide accommodations for the guest. The purpose of the code is to communicate the details of a guaranteed accommodation to the host property. The guest data have already been entered into the central computer and usually can be easily retrieved. However, there are times when these data may not be available, or they may be misplaced.

When this happens, a reservation code allows the host property to provide appropriate accommodations.

The method of paying for a guaranteed reservation is established when the reservation is made. Credit cards or previously approved direct billing are the most common methods. Sometimes the guest sends a bank check or delivers cash to secure a reservation. A bank check is acceptable, as long as adequate time is available to process it. The cash advance payment and bank check, however, should alert the front office manager that this guest has not established a line of credit with a credit card organization or with the hotel. Determining how the guest will pay the final bill is essential. The folios of guests who pay cash in advance must be monitored.

Cancellations

Cancellations due to a guest's change in plans are easily handled by a computerized reservations system. The guest calls the central reservation system or the hotel where the reservation was made. Some lodging organizations stipulate a period for canceling reservations. Twenty-four, 48, or 72 hours' notice may be required for the guest to be exempt from paying the first night's room rate. Policies vary among reservation systems, based on the historical frequency of cancellations (and the subsequent effect on the profit-and-loss statement) and the public relations policy (the potential of lost repeat business) of the organization.

Cancellation Codes

A cancellation code is a sequential series of alphanumeric combinations that provides the guest with a reference for a cancellation of a guaranteed reservation. (Cancellation codes are also referred to as cancellation numbers.) Such a code verifies that the cancellation has been communicated to the hotel property and assures the guest that he or she is not liable for the canceled reservation. For example, if the front office staff mistakenly processes a charge for a guaranteed reservation that had been canceled, the guest could refute the credit card billing with the cancellation code.

A cancellation code is composed like a reservation code and consists of letters and digits that may identify the hotel property, the person who processed the cancellation, the date of arrival, the date of departure, and/or the sequential number of the cancellation. This and other information is included to ensure efficient management of room cancellations. If the guest had applied a cash deposit to the room, a credit balance on the guest folio would have to be processed. A cancellation code may look like this:

122-RB-0309-1001X

- 122: the identification number of the property in the chain
- RB: the initials of the reservationist or desk clerk who accepted the cancellation
- 0309: the date of arrival
- 1001X: the sequential number of the cancellation

Blocking Procedure

After a reservation is received, the reserved room is blocked in the room inventory. In a computerized reservation system, the room is automatically removed from the available-room data bank for the dates involved. For example, if each of the participating 75 hotels in the reservation/referral system has 200 rooms available, the room bank would have 15,000 rooms available to be sold on any one night. As a reservation request is processed, the room or rooms involved are blocked out of the available-room inventory. Reservation requests for 4,000 rooms on a particular night at the participating properties require the computer to block (or reserve) those rooms at the appropriate hotels. If additional reservation requests are received for that night at a particular property and that hotel is already filled to capacity, the computer will not process the requests. It may, however, tell the computer terminal operator that a hotel in the same geographic area has vacancies. This is undoubtedly one of the major advantages of participating in a reservation/referral system. This type of blocking is usually referred to as blocking on the horizon-that is, in the distant future. Another type of blocking, referred to as daily blocking, involves assigning guests to their particular rooms on a daily basis.

Process of Completing Reservations Through a PMS

The previous discussion focused on processing guest reservations through a central reservation headquarters. However, the individual PMS at a member hotel of a reservation/referral system is also able to process a reservation request. Chapter 4 discusses the reservation module and includes the list of applications available to the reservationist or desk clerk. The clerk enters the data into the PMS as requested. That data is then cleared through the rooms reservations bank to confirm the availability of the room requested.

Other options in the menu are accessed as needed. For example, option 2, Room Inventory, lists the reservation status, or the availability of a guest room to be rented on a particular night-that is, open (room is available for renting), confirmed (room is reserved until 4:00 P.M. or 6:00 P.M.), guaranteed (room is reserved until guest arrives), and repair (room is not available for guest rental). Option 3, Deposits, is accessed when the clerk must determine whether the guest had a deposit on file. The information for this option is compiled from the Guest Data option, where the clerk indicates the guest wanted to guarantee a reservation with a credit card or send a cash (bank check) deposit. Option 4, Special Requests, assists the reservationist or desk clerk in determining if rooms are available to meet the specific needs of a guest. Facilities for handicapped guests, smoking/no smoking options, particular views, and locations near other hotel facilities are some of the features listed here. This option helps the new desk clerk provide hospitality to guests.

Option 5, Blocking, provides reports to the front office manager on which rooms are to be reserved for incoming guests on a particular day or on the horizon. This option assigns a guest or guests to a specific room. Option 6, Arrivals, lists the individuals or groups expected to arrive on a specific date. Option 7,

Departures, indicates which guests are expected to check out on a particular date. This option is used by the front office manager or desk clerk to determine room availability for guests who wish to overstay their reserved time as well as to sell future visits. Option 8, VIP, provides the desk clerk with information on guests with VIP status. Even though all guests are very important persons, VIP status is granted to persons who may be regular guests and expect special treatment, or celebrities or officials who need to spend minimal time checking in. If this information is obtained with the reservation request, it will assist the desk clerk at registration.

Option 9, Projected Occupancy, provides the various departments in the hotel with information concerning the number of guests who will be in the hotel on a certain day. Option 10, Travel Agents, allows the reservationist to maintain data on the travel agent or travel agency that initiated a reservation. This option allows speedy processing of the agent's or agency's fee for placing a reservation with the hotel. This option interfaces with the accounts payable module. Option 11, Guest Messages, allows the front desk clerk to relay important information to the guests on registration. This feature is another way the hotel can convey hospitality to the guest by demonstrating attention to details. Reports concerning reservations can be obtained by the front office manager by selecting option 12, Reports.

These examples provide only a brief overview of the capabilities of the reservation module of a PMS. Your hands-on experience will provide you with real-life applications of a valuable management tool. Managing reservation data allow the front office manager to organize hundreds of details into usable information-information that helps provide hospitality to guests and bring financial success to the lodging property.

Database Interfaces

To plan their work, department managers rely on information captured at the time a reservation is made. Database interfaces, which transfer shared information among computers, allow managers to retrieve this information at will. Marketing directors need current data to monitor projected sales, while sales representatives in the marketing department need immediate information on room availability for specific periods. Housekeeping staff members plan routine care and maintenance activities depending on projected occupancy. Maintenance crews plan refurbishing and repairs when projected occupancy is low. Food and beverage directors can promote a positive cash flow by increasing food and beverage marketing programs during slow room sales periods. The controller also needs to access the reservation database when planning fiscal budgets.

True Integration

The term true integration denotes a hotel's central reservations system and property management sharing a database. Rebecca Oliva reports the term true integration, in which the CRS and PMS use the same database for processing reservations. This allows for realtime reservations, which are a perceived benefit for consumers, as well as less technology investment for the storage of data, which is a benefit for hotel investors. Hotels can access reservation data via the Internet.

Solution to Opening Dilemma

The override feature on a reservation module for a property management system allows individual employees to book reservations beyond the number of rooms available and beyond the occupancy management limit. This feature must be controlled by the reservations manager, front office manager, or manager on duty. The front office staff must check out the room availability in nearby hotels and notify guests that their room reservations will be handled at another hotel. In some cases, guests can't be notified prior to their arrival, and the front desk staff must be prepared to deliver customer service with utmost composure.

6

Managing the Financial Matters

The lodging industry has always prided itself on its ability to maintain up-to-date records of outstanding guest balances. The front office processes a multitude of charges and payments every day, requiring a well-organized bookkeeping system. This chapter addresses how those guest charges are processed.

Common Bookkeeping Practices

Debits and Credits

Knowledge of basic bookkeeping methods enables the front office manager to understand the reasons for following particular procedures when handling financial transactions. This ability greatly assists the front office manager in training front desk clerks and night auditors. Instead of teaching the staff which keys to press on the keyboard to process a transaction, the manager explains why a charge must be posted in a certain way; this facilitates bookkeeping procedures. Many of you have already taken a basic accounting course or have had experience with a bookkeeping system. However, this chapter does not assume any previous knowledge of accounting procedures.

Assets are items that have monetary value. Liabilities are financial or other contractual obligations or debts. These two concepts provide the basics for a bookkeeping system. Examples of assets include ownership of a cell phone, a textbook, or two tickets to a concert. Examples of liabilities include a contract to pay for the cell phone on a monthly basis, a contract to pay for a car, or a promise to pay a friend for word processing a term paper. Guest charges are financial obligations that are owed to a hotel; these are considered an asset for the hotel. If a guest prepays an account, this is a liability to the hotel because the hotel must return the money to the guest at checkout.

Assets and liabilities are increased and decreased by an organized set of accounting practices. These are called debits, which refer to an increase in an asset or a decrease in a liability, and credits, which refer to a decrease in an asset or an increase in a liability. Debits and credits provide a basis for the hotel bookkeeping system. They provide the power (mechanical means) to increase and decrease assets and liabilities for the guest and the hotel.

While this definition may be easy to remember, it is sometimes difficult to apply. However, if you apply it with regard to the type of account, you should have no problem. The following examples demonstrate how to apply debits and credits.

If a guest charges $100 on a credit card for goods and services in the hotel on any one day, the individual charges are processed as a debit (an increase) to the guest account and an asset to the hotel's accounts receivables. A credit (an increase) of an equal value is applied to the respective departmental sales accounts (a revenue account, part of owner's equity).

If a guest pays $100 in advance to reserve a room, this amount is processed as a credit (an increase) to the guest account (the hotel's advance payments, a liability). A debit (an increase) of an equal amount is applied to the hotel's cash account (an asset).

Forms Used to Process Guest Charges and Payments

Folio, Transfers, and Paid-out Slips

The folio, transfers, and paid-out slips are documents that allow for the documentation and transfer of charges and payments to a guest's account. In a property management system, the electronic folio is stored in the computer memory until a hard copy is required. The hard copy of the electronic folio is a standard folio that lists the date of transaction, item, transfer slip number for referral, debit or credit amount, and updated balance. The transfer slip allows the desk clerk to transfer an amount of money from one account to another while creating a paper trail. A paid-out slip (a numbered form that authorizes cash disbursement from the front desk clerk's bank for products on behalf of a guest or an employee of the hotel) documents the authorized payment of cash to a vendor or an employee for a quick purchase of materials for the hotel. In a hotel with a PMS that interfaces with point-of-sale departments, the transfer of charges incurred by the guest or the transfer of a portion of one guest's bill to another guest's folio is done automatically.

The front desk clerk uses these forms in posting charges and payments, which is the process of debiting and crediting charges and payments to a guest folio. The night auditor then tracks the procedures the front desk clerk used in posting. These forms assist in maintaining control of bookkeeping activities in the front office.

Account Ledgers

Guest Ledger and City Ledger

The guest ledger is a collection of folios (records of guests' charges and payments) of current guests of the hotel. The city ledger is a collection of folios of unregistered hotel guests who maintain accounts with the hotel. These guests may submit cash advances for a future purchase of the hotel's goods and services, such as a deposit on a banquet or on a reservation. The hotel may also offer personal billing accounts to local businesspeople; these are also part of the city ledger. Unregistered hotel guests may keep open accounts for entertaining clients, for example. All of the folios are held in a folio well, a device that holds the individual printed hard-copy guest folios and city ledger folios, or bucket that provides the physical dimensions of the guest ledger and city ledger. The accurate and timely processing of all these accounts assists the front office manager in maintaining hard copies of guests' financial transactions with the hotel. These accounts are collectively referred to as the hotel's accounts receivable-what guests owe the hotel. The accounts receivable consist of two categories, the guest ledger and the city ledger.

Tracking a guest stay from initial reservation through checkout provides examples of the many charges and payments that affect the guest ledger. Likewise, following the activities of the unregistered guest shows how city ledger accounts are affected.

Posting Guest Charges and Payments

As mentioned earlier, processing guest charges and payments is referred to as posting (increasing and decreasing assets and liabilities). Posting adds or subtracts guest charges and payments to the guest's individual account.

Again, the accurate and timely posting of guest charges and payments is important to maintaining accurate financial records, as the guest may decide to check out at any time during the day and will require an accurate statement of transactions at that time.

Posting charges and payments in a hotel with a PMS greatly increases the accuracy of the posting. Each of the PMS posting module options, allows the front desk clerk to post the charges and payments that a guest incurs during his or her stay. With relative ease, the guest's electronic folio can be updated at the time of purchase of goods and services. Figure 8-3 is an example of an electronic folio to which charges and payments have been posted with a PMS.

Point-of-Sale

The point-of-sale option allows the front office computer to interface with the computers in other departments. In a hotel, when the front office interfaces with the restaurant, the front office computer terminal accepts and automatically posts charges made in the restaurant (the point of sale) to a guest's folio. Any department (gift shop, recreational facilities, room service, and telephone) in the hotel that can serve as a point of sale (the place where a product or service is purchased) must be able to interface with the front office to post charges to the guest's account.

This electronic transfer ensures that the charge is posted to the guest folio in a timely manner and increases the accuracy of the posting.

When guests incur charges in the dining room, these are immediately posted electronically to the guest folios via the point-of-sale terminal. Photo courtesy of Omron Systems, Inc.

Room and Tax

The room option of the posting module has been described as a "blessing" by front office employees who used to work with a mechanical posting machine. In a mechanical front office system, the desk clerk or night auditor physically removed each guest folio from its file, placed the folio into the posting machine, depressed the correct keys, removed the folio from the posting machine, and then refiled it. In a hotel with a PMS, the desk clerk automatically posts charges to individual electronic folios by activating the room option. While the PMS is posting room charges, the clerk is free to do other tasks. The tax option is often activated with the room option because most properties are required by state or local laws to charge and collect sales and occupancy taxes from guests. The tax option posts the appropriate taxes to the guest folio when the room charge is posted.

Transfers and Adjustments

The transfer and adjustment options enable front office personnel to correct errors in and make requested changes to the guest folio. The charges posted to a guest's electronic folio at times must be transferred to another folio, or adjustments to the amounts must be made. For example, a guest may discover that his or her hotel bill will be picked up by a corporation in the city. The bill had been guaranteed with the guest's credit card. The front desk clerk must transfer the guest's charges from the folio in the guest ledger to the corporation's house account in the city ledger. Another guest may claim that a charge from room service should have been charged to the person who was sharing the room. In this case, the front desk clerk adjusts (removes) the charge from one guest folio and transfers it to the other guest folio.

A guest may question charges for a phone call, movie viewing, or other services. The desk clerk can immediately adjust the account, depending on the authorized financial correction flexibility policy. This policy spells out the guidelines for a desk clerk to follow in adjusting a guest's account. For example, a guest may refuse to pay for a telephone call because it should have been posted to the folio of the guest who was sharing the room. Otherwise, the front office shift supervisor or front office manager will authorize the adjustment. It is important to remember that immediate correction of errors may influence a guest's perception of a hotel's service. The policy on authorized financial correction flexibility reflects the quality of service the hotel wants to deliver.

All of these transfers and adjustments can be made easily with a PMS. Also, the adjustments are at once reflected in all the guest and departmental accounts affected by the change, with very little paperwork. This system makes the night auditor's job of verifying the integrity of accounts much easier.

Paid-Out

The paid-out option is used to track authorized requests for cash paid out of the desk clerk's cash drawer. Desk clerks may be required to pay immediately for goods and services on behalf of guests, such as delivery of flowers, valet services, and COD (cash on delivery) packages.

These charges are usually preauthorized by the hotel on behalf of the guest. The amount paid out can be charged to the guest's folio and reflected in the desk clerk's cash balance and the departmental account in one process. This saves the tedious effort of initiating a paper trail and also avoids the possibility of human error.

Miscellaneous Charges

The miscellaneous charges option is included in a PMS to allow the desk clerk to post charges that are atypical of the majority of hotel properties. If a hotel has, for example, a recreational facility that lacks a point-of-sale terminal, this option may be engaged. This feature can also be used to post miscellaneous charges to the city ledger accounts.

Phone

The phone option is included in a PMS for properties that do not have an interface with the call-accounting system. With the call-accounting interface, the charges for local and long-distance phone calls, plus surcharges, are posted automatically. Without the interface, the desk clerk must manually post the phone charge on the electronic folio.

Display Folio

The display folio option permits the front desk clerk or other authorized members of the management staff to view a guest's electronic folio at any time. If a guest requests the current balance on his or her folio, the desk clerk can produce a hard copy of the folio with a few keystrokes. After the guest reviews the hard copy, he or she may indicate that a certain charge is in error. This discrepancy can be resolved prior to checkout.

Reports

The reports option allows the front office manager to organize data in a way that is useful to the controller and the management team. The night auditor can cross-check departmental totals from the restaurant, phone service, gift shop, or recreational facility with the amounts charged to the guest folios. These data can be shared with department managers to provide feedback for evaluating marketing programs and cost-control efforts.

Transferring Guest and City Ledgers to Accounts Receivable

The debits and credits incurred by guests and future guests of the hotel are maintained as back office accounts receivable (monies owed to the hotel). Once the guest has received the goods and enjoyed the services of the hotel, then this financial record must be transferred to the master accounts receivable for the hotel. If a guest's folio shows a debit balance (an amount the guest owes to the hotel) of $291 and the guest wants to pay that off by charging $291 to his MasterCard, then the amount is transferred to the MasterCard accounts receivable.

Another type of transaction involves the back office accounts payable, amounts of money prepaid on behalf of the guest for future consumption of goods or services (sometimes referred to as back office cash accounts), such as when a guest deposits a sum of money for a future stay. For example, the personal check a guest sends to the hotel, dated February 5, for a stay on the following December 21 must be credited first to the hotel's back office accounts payable or back office cash account and then to the guest's folio. This amount of money is held for the guest's arrival on December

21. When the guest arrives on December 21, the guest folio is brought to the front of the folio well and activated upon registration.

These examples demonstrate that the activities in the guest ledger and city ledger are not isolated. They are reflected in the back office account. The guest ledger and city ledger are temporary holding facilities for the guest's account. The back office accounts are the permanent arenas for financial processing.

Importance of Standard Operating Procedures for Posting and the Night Audit

Standard operating procedures for processing charges and payments are used for the night audit, which is performed to balance the day's financial transactions. The financial activities recorded in the guest ledger, city ledger, and various departments within the hotel must be processed accurately. It is not uncommon for a night auditor to spend many hours looking for a small or large dollar amount to correct a discrepancy in the accounts. Errors can often be traced to a front desk clerk who transposed a dollar amount ($35.87 entered as $53.87) or transferred a charge to an incorrect account ($20.50 valet charge as a $20.50 restaurant charge). However, it is difficult to detect if a desk clerk used an incorrect folio (room 626 instead of room 625). An experienced night auditor can usually pinpoint the error and resolve discrepancies caused by transposing figures or picking up incorrect accounts.

Because of the tedious effort required to resolve such errors, front office managers must thoroughly train front office personnel to process guest charges and payments correctly. This training program must include a statement of behavioral objectives, preparation and demonstration of detailed written procedures to follow when posting charges and payments, preparation and discussion of theoretical material that explains debits and credits, explanation of all related backup paperwork, clarification of the relationship of front office accounting procedures to back office accounting procedures, and delivery of hands-on training on the PMS. Such training efforts pay off in reduced bookkeeping errors and better customer service.

7

Guest Checkout

The general manager of the hotel indicated at the staff meeting today that the budget allows for the purchase of an additional module in the property management system. She suggests the guest history module might be just what the hotel needs to increase room sales. The general manager has scheduled a visit from the PMS vendor tomorrow and wants you (the front office manager), the director of marketing and sales, and the revenue manager to prepare a list of questions for the vendor that will help determine whether the purchase of the guest history module for the hotel is justified.

Guest checkout can be a time of confusion, short tempers, and long lines, a test of the patience of both the guest and the cashier. Think of the last time you checked out of a hotel. How did it go? Was the cashier courteous and hospitable? If not, were you angry because of his or her indifference? Always remember what it is like to be a guest. This simple approach will serve you well throughout your career in the hospitality industry.

This chapter assists you in developing a thorough understanding of the guest checkout process. It is not a difficult procedure to understand and implement; however, it does require planning in order to organize the details of this part of the guest's stay.

Organizing Late Charges to Ensure Accuracy

As you learned in earlier chapters, when a hotel utilizes all modules in the PMS throughout the guest's stay, charges for room, tax, food and beverages, valet, and other services are posted to the guest folio as they are incurred. At the time of checkout, late charges, or guest charges that might not be included on the guest folio because of a delay in posting by other departments, can result in substantial loss of income.

Failure to post telephone charges for local or long-distance calls made by the guest prior to checkout is another area where revenue may be lost. For example, a lodging property that fails to post 20 phone calls per day, at an average cost of 50 cents each, would lose $3,650 per year.

Front offices with a property management system that can interface the posting module with the point-of-sale departments and the call-accounting system can post late charges easily. As soon as the charge is incurred at the point of sale or through the call-accounting system, it is posted to the electronic folio. Without this interface, the point-of-sale cashier must telephone the front desk clerk prior to the guest's checkout. The telephone operator and front desk clerk must have a good reporting system to record all phone calls. When a PMS is not used, the front office manager and other department managers should initiate a communication program for their employees that ensures the quick and accurate relay of last-minute charges.

Guest Checkout Procedure

If front office personnel collect and post guest late charges in an appropriate and timely manner, then the guest checkout can proceed without bottlenecks. However, when the cashier or front desk clerk must make phone calls to the restaurant, gift shop, and switchboard to verify charges, delays and disputes can occur. The guest checkout involves the following steps:

1. Guest requests checkout.
2. Desk clerk inquires about quality of products and services.
3. Guest returns key to desk clerk.
4. Desk clerk retrieves hard copy of electronic folio.
5. Desk clerk reviews folio for completeness.
6. Guest reviews charges and payments.
7. Guest determines method of payment.
8. Guest makes payment.

9. Desk clerk inquires about additional reservations.
10. Desk clerk files folio and related documents for the night audit.
11. Desk clerk communicates guest departure to housekeeping and other departments in the hotel if necessary.

The objective of the checkout process is to process the guest's request for settlement of his or her account as quickly and efficiently as possible. The lodging establishment also wants to maintain a quality control system for both the guest and the hotel; posting errors can mean erroneous charges for the guest and lost money for the lodging establishment.

Throughout your career in lodging management, you will be called on to develop operational procedures. First, set your objectives and keep them simple. Accommodate guests and maintain necessary data to provide the lodging establishment with information for the income statement. The steps outlined for guest checkout show how easy it is to establish operational procedures when you keep these goals in mind. The narratives that follow elaborate on each step in the guest checkout.

Inquiring about Quality of Products and Services

When the guest arrives at the front desk to check out, the cashier should inquire about the guest's satisfaction with the accommodations, food and beverages, and miscellaneous services provided by the hotel. Cashiers should be alert to possible problems.

Incidental comments about a cold room, low water pressure, leaky plumbing, or damaged furniture should be noted and passed along to the appropriate department heads.

Because guests often do not verbalize complaints or compliments, all lodging properties should have guest comment cards available as an optional source of communication. In many leading lodging chains, the chief executive officer answers these cards personally. The general manager of an independent lodging property can provide a similar personal touch by acknowledging negative comments. A good public relations program can be enhanced by addressing minor problems experienced by the guest that might indicate lack of concern. Also, concern for guest satisfaction affects the financial success of the hotel.

Retrieving the Room Key

Lodging properties that use a hard-key system must request the return of the hard key. The security of the guest as well as the financial investment in the hard-key system mandates that this procedure be a part of the guest checkout. Guest security is jeopardized if keys are lost or not returned. A 200-room property with approximately five keys per room that must be constantly replaced finds that a great deal of money is spent to maintain the key supply. Some properties require a key deposit, returnable on guest checkout. The hotel with a PMS and/or an electronic key system can easily change the electronic code on a key for future entrance to the guest room. Although the initial financial investment in such a system is substantial, security is the ultimate objective in adopting this technology.

In checkout, a front desk clerk asks a guest if his accommodations were acceptable. The guest says the heater in the room didn't work last night. Because the hotel has a 100 percent satisfaction guarantee, the desk clerk is obliged to comp the room. If you were the front office manager, what would you do to follow up on this incident?

Retrieving and Reviewing the Folio

In a front office with a PMS, the cashier uses the folio option of the checkout module to retrieve the electronic folio by entering the guest's name or room number. A hard copy is printed for the guest.

The guest and the cashier should both review the folio. The cashier reviews the obvious charges: room fee and tax for the number of nights spent in the hotel (day of arrival through last night), incidentals (such as movie rental, personal phone calls, and purchases at the gift shop) paid for by the individual rather than a corporation, and the like. The cashier must inquire if late charges were incurred at the restaurant or other hotel department or if last-minute phone calls were made.

The guest must also be shown a copy of the folio for a final review. The front office manager should develop an empowerment procedure based on a list of tasks in which to follow if charges are questioned. Typical questions concern charges for phone calls that were not made, meals not eaten, gifts not purchased, flowers not received, laundry not sent out, or in-room movies not viewed. Using the list provided by the front office manager, the front desk clerk or cashier may adjust these charges up to a certain dollar amount. A thorough cost control procedure to track the total adjustments by each employee can help keep such adjustments in line. Large dollar amounts that are questioned by the guest should be referred to the front office manager. The adjustments option of the checkout module in a property management system can be used to make changes.

This empowerment concept is important to develop in staff members because many guests do question postings made to their accounts. Employees must learn listening skills that will enable them to discern just what form of satisfaction the guest is asking for. Employees should be encouraged to try several techniques to determine which will meet the needs of the guest within the financial and service limitations.

In-Room Guest Checkout

Before proceeding with the guest checkout procedure, it is important to note the guest's option to use in-room guest checkout, a computerized procedure that allows guests to settle their accounts from their rooms. In some PMSs that feature in-room guest checkout, the guest can initiate the guest checkout the night before departing by following instructions located near the television set in the guest room. The guest can view a final version of the folio on the television screen on the morning of checkout. This expedites the process by alerting the front office to have a hard copy ready for payment. If the guest indicates that he or she will pay by credit card or direct billing (bill-to-account), the guest does not have to stop by the front desk to check out. A control procedure is built into the PMS to prevent cash customers from using in-room checkout. A guest who is going to pay with cash has not established a line of credit with the hotel.

Determining Method of Payment and Collection

During registration, the guest indicates the method of payment he or she plans to use. Possibilities include credit cards, direct billing (bill-to-account), cash or personal check, traveler's checks, or debit cards. During checkout, the guest confirms the method of payment.

Credit Cards

Today's business and leisure travelers usually pay with a credit card. "Plastic money" has advantages for the cardholder as well as for the hotel. The cardholder is assured instant credit to satisfy debts incurred. The extensive travel required of some businesspeople would make the almost constant requests for cash advances by corporate employees difficult to manage. The advantage for the lodging establishment is that payment is assured (less a discount paid to the corporation issuing the credit card). It is important to note that with the increased use and advances of computers in the business world, the reimbursement period can be reduced to none-the hotel is immediately credited with payment. As these advances occur, the ready acceptance of various credit cards will change. The front office, in cooperation with the controller, usually establishes a priority system for accepting credit cards based on cash flow requirements and the effect of the discount rate offered. The average guest is probably not aware of the discount rate and may be willing to use whatever credit card the front desk clerk requests.

Processing a credit card in an automated hotel follows a standard procedure. The objectives of the procedure include accurate recording of the amounts of charges and tax, name (address and phone number of cardholder are optional), verification of the credit card dollar limit, and capture of fraudulent credit cards. The procedure includes the following steps:

1. Note the credit card expiration date.
2. Enter the approval of the amount of the charge on the PMS checkout screen.
3. Verify the credit limit available by using the credit card validator.
4. Allow the guest to review folio and sign.
5. Check the guest signature on the folio against the signature on the card.
6. Give the card and the guest copy of the folio to the guest.

Once the procedure is developed, it must be followed to the letter, without exception. The fraudulent use of credit cards takes a great toll on the profits of the hotel. An incentive system for cashiers and front desk clerks can be built into the procedure for processing credit cards to encourage the capture of fraudulent cards. The small monetary reward is nominal compared to the cost of a hotel bill that may never be recovered. In addition, hotels should develop a procedure for retrieval of fraudulent credit cards. The safety of front desk staff is extremely important in this procedure.

Bill-to-Account (Direct Billing)

Hotel guests, both corporate representatives and private guests, may also use the bill-to-account, a preauthorized account that allows guests to have their charges processed on a regular billing cycle without the use of a credit card (sometimes referred to as direct billing) to settle an account. Direct billing requires prior approval of the credit limit of an organization (corporate representatives) or an individual (private guest). Usually the corporation requesting direct billing completes an application for credit approval. The controller in the lodging establishment then performs a credit check to determine a credit rating and a credit limit. This house limit of credit, a credit limit set by an individual hotel, varies depending on the amount of projected charges and the length of time allowed for charges to be paid. The credit rating of the corporation in question plays a large part in assigning a credit limit.

The application usually lists people who are authorized to use the account as well as authorized positions within the corporation. Identification cards with an authorization number are issued by the hotel. It is the responsibility of the corporation applying for credit to monitor the authorized use of the credit. The cashier must verify identification of the corporate guest.

The bill-to-account option should be reviewed with an eye toward cost-effectiveness. Although the hotel does not have to pay a 3-8 percent discount rate to the credit card agency, the cost incurred by the controller's office (credit checks, billing, postage, collection of bad debts) must be considered. The question of cash flow-almost immediate payment from the credit card agency versus a four- to eight-week waiting period for corporate accounts-should also be considered. The marketing implications of direct billing deserve attention as well. The status conferred by this option may be desirable to corporate representatives and private guests.

The following procedure is used to process a bill-to-account payment:

1. Request corporate or personal identification.
2. Check to be sure the individual is authorized by the account holder to bill to the account.
3. Note credit limit per employee.
4. Note red flags on the credit file due to nonpayment of bills.
5. Note authorized signature.
6. Enter charges into the point-of-sale terminal along with bill-to-account identification. When this information is entered into the POS, it is also entered into an electronic folio in the city ledger of the PMS.

Cash and Personal Checks

When guests indicate during registration that they will pay their bills with cash or a personal check, the front desk clerk should immediately be on the alert. Such a guest may well charge everything during his or her stay (perhaps only one day in length) at the hotel and then exit without paying. Consequently, most hotels require cash in advance from guests who choose this method of payment, as the guest has not established a credit rating with the hotel.

In addition, close monitoring by the night auditor and front desk clerks of the guest's charge activity is in order. Such guests are not allowed charge privileges at other departments in the hotel. In properties with a PMS, the guest name and room number are entered to block charges at point-of-sale areas. In a hotel without food and beverage, gift shop, and health club POS terminals, the front office must alert those departments that this guest has not been extended charge privileges. To process a cash payment, the following procedure can be used:

1. Check the daily currency conversion rate when converting foreign into national currency. Take time to ensure the math is accurate.
2. Retain the amount tendered outside the cash drawer until the transaction is completed.
3. Maintain an orderly cash drawer, with bills separated by denomination.
4. Develop an orderly procedure to make change from the amount tendered.
5. Count the change out loud when giving it to the guest.
6. Perform only one procedure at a time. Refuse to make change for another bill of a different denomination if a previous transaction has not been completed.
7. Issue a receipt for the transaction.

Most lodging properties simply do not accept personal checks; the opportunity for fraud is too great. This policy often comes as a surprise to guests, who may protest that this is the only means of payment they have.

However, the hotel can use commercial check authorization companies and credit card companies that guarantee a guest's personal check.

The procedure for processing personal checks is as follows:

1. Request a personal check-cashing card.
2. Refer to the list of persons who are not allowed to present checks as legal tender.
3. Compare the written amount of the check with the figures to be sure they match.
4. Note low-numbered checks. Low numbers may indicate a newly opened, unestablished account, and the check will require a supervisor's approval.
5. Request identification (a valid driver's license and a major credit card) and record the numbers on the back of the check. Compare the name and address imprinted on the check with a valid driver's license.
6. Compare the signature on the check with the requested identification.

7. Validate the amount of the check and the credit rating of the guest with a commercial check authorization company or credit card company.

Traveler's Checks

Traveler's checks are prepaid checks issued by a bank or financial organization; they have been an acceptable form of legal tender for many years. These checks are a welcome method of payment in the lodging industry. Traveler's checks are processed like cash. Proof of credit is already established, and the hotel pays no percentage of the sale to a credit card agency, as the guest paid a percentage of the face amount of the traveler's check to the issuing agency. However, checking proof of identification (a valid driver's license or major credit card) should be a standard traveler's check-cashing policy. The guest should sign the traveler's check in the cashier's presence, and that signature should be compared with the signature already on the check. The list of traveler's check numbers that are not acceptable, supplied regularly by the check-issuing agency, must be consulted to ensure that the checks are valid.

Debit Cards

Debit cards, or check cards, are embossed plastic cards with a magnetic strip on the reverse side that authorize direct transfer of funds from a customer's bank account to the commercial organization's bank account for purchase of goods and services. Some examples of debit cards are MAC, NYCE, STAR, and PLUS. These are similar to credit cards in that they guarantee creditworthiness, against which the hotel charges the bill; however, the payment is deducted directly and immediately from the guest's personal savings or checking account and transferred to the hotel's account rather than being billed to the guest on a monthly basis. Debit cards continue to gain in popularity as the use of credit cards becomes more costly to the guest. However, the concept of float, the delay in payment after using a credit card, may remain a more attractive benefit for some guests. Some debit cards have a credit-card logo embossed on the plastic card, which indicates they are acceptable at places that accept that particular credit card and are processed through a credit card financial organization.

Debit cards are processed similarly to credit cards. To process a debit card payment, the following procedure is used:

1. Insert debit card into validation machine.
2. Have guest enter personal identification number.
3. Process debit-card voucher as a cash payment on the guest folio.

Assisting the Guest with Method of Payment

Guests may find they are short on cash or are otherwise unable to pay their bill due to an expensive emergency, overextension of credit card limits, or theft. When these situations occur, the front desk clerk or cashier should be ready to offer the following services.

Money Wire

Western Union provides money wire, an electronic message that authorizes money from one person to be issued to another person; this service has been available to travelers for many years, with a fee charged by Western Union. This convenient service should be established as an option for a guest. The front office manager should develop and communicate a procedure that includes the phone number and address of the nearest money wire center.

Travelers Aid Society

The Travelers Aid Society was founded for the purpose of aiding the down-and-out traveler beset by an unexpected emergency in an unfamiliar city. The phone number and address of this organization must also be communicated to the front office staff as an option of payment.

Auto Clubs

The auto clubs-AAA (American Automobile Association) being the best known-and private gasoline companies offer their members immediate cash advances in case of an emergency. Again, a listing of phone numbers of auto clubs for guest use not only helps the guest but ensures that the lodging establishment will be paid.

The method of payment, in the end, can affect the hotel's bottom line. The preap-proval criterion for credit card and debit card holders is an important requirement when a hotel is extending credit to a guest from check-in to checkout. The discount rate charged by the issuing agency, which takes a percentage of the gross charges, affects the income statement as well. It is important, however, to show concern for the guest whose circumstances have taken a turn for the worse (serious accident, theft, unexpected illness, etc.). The front office should be equipped to offer information on alternatives such as auto clubs and money wires; this can be perceived as a display of genuine hospitality.

International Currency Exchange

When an international guest presents a credit card for payment at checkout, the credit card issuing agency processes the payment according to the current exchange rate between countries. If a guest wants to pay in his or her national currency, the cashier must compute the exchange. The daily international exchange rate can be found by calling a bank or other financial institution or reviewing the international exchange rates published in the Wall Street Journal in the Currency Trading section. Exchange rates for the U.S. dollar, pound, euro, peso, yen, and Canadian dollar are listed.

On January 1, 1999, the euro became the accepted currency for the following 11 member-states of the European Community: Belgium, Germany, Spain, France, Ireland, Italy, Luxembourg, the Netherlands, Austria, Portugal, and Finland. In January 2001, Greece adopted the euro, and in January 2002, euro coins and bills were introduced. The euro provides ease in traveling throughout Europe, as travelers need not exchange currency at each participating country.

It is important to consider the float time of the international currency collected and presented to a bank for deposit in a hotel's account; that is, it will take several days or weeks before the currency is credited to the hotel's account. Also, a different rate of exchange may be in effect at the time of the currency exchange transaction. For example, a U.S. hotel may deposit £10,000 from an English tour group thinking it will receive US$20,000 (US$2.00 for each English pound), but three weeks later, when the transaction occurs, the exchange rate may be US$1.90 for £1. In this case, the U.S. hotel would receive approximately US$19,000 (10,000 x 1.9 = 19,000) instead of the US$20,000 originally computed at the time of deposit.

To compensate for this, the hotel must consider adding a surcharge to the rate used that day as well as to cover a transaction fee charge by banks. For example, in the case in which a U.S. hotel anticipates receiving US$20,000 for a deposit of £10,000 based on an exchange rate of £1 for each US$2, it may be better for the hotel to use £1 for each $1.90 to cover a volatile exchange rate and a banking fee. The U.S. hotel would collect £10,526 ($20,000 ÷ 1.90 = £10,526) at the time of checkout to compensate for the float time of the international currency.

Obtaining Future Reservations

Checkout, the last contact point with the guest, is the best opportunity for securing additional reservations. It is at this time that the cashier or front desk clerk can best assist the marketing and sales department. The front office manager should develop a standard procedure for the front office staff to follow, which may include these steps:

1. At the beginning of the checkout procedure, inquire about the guest's stay. Maintain good eye contact and listen closely.
2. Ask if the guest will be returning to the area in the near future or if he or she will need a reservation for a property in the hotel's chain or referral group. If so, ask whether he or she would like to make a reservation for that visit. Because all the guest data are already on file, a confirmation of the reservation can be sent later. If the guest is in a hurry, the reservation staff can follow up later. Your role is to plant the seed of a future sale as well as to accommodate a guest.
3. Continue to check out the guest. Again, make eye contact. If the guest does not respond positively to the first inquiry, offer a departure brochure or directory that includes information about making additional reservations at the hotel's property or properties within the chain or referral group.

4. Bid the guest farewell.
5. Report to the shift supervisor any negative comments from the guest concerning his or her stay.
6. Process future reservations or alert the reservation clerk to these requests.

This standard procedure should be part of the desk clerk's training program. As with other sales efforts at the front office, selling additional reservations at checkout should be rewarded through an employee incentive program. This procedure gives the front office personnel a basic structure to use in pitching the sale and accommodating the guest. The employee still has the opportunity to adapt the pitch to his or her own style.

Filing Documents

The paperwork documenting the day's transactions must be in place when the night auditor's shift begins. Guest folios, transfers, paid-out slips, and the like must be filed according to a standard system. This may seem like a simple task, but at a busy front desk with many checkouts and check-ins, it is easy to misplace documents. Care must be taken to provide the night auditor with all the necessary proof of origination of charges and trail of payment options.

Relaying Guest Departures to Other Departments

It is essential that other departments be notified that a guest has checked out to ensure smooth operation of the hotel. The PMS allows the front desk clerk and the housekeeping employees to inform one another of guest departures, stayovers, room availability status, and other occupancy details as they occur. As mentioned earlier, once the electronic folio is cleared from active memory after checkout, the guest departure is indicated on all other modules of the system. The front desk clerk need not telephone the housekeeper to say that room 203 is vacant; the housekeeper need not spend hours reporting room availability status to the front desk clerks. Backup phone calls are still made for situations for which current information is needed from the maintenance department. The maid or houseman can inform the front desk clerk electronically of room availability status.

In addition to informing the food and beverage department of guests who have checked out, other departments where guests can incur charges must be notified as well to prevent acceptance of unauthorized guest charges. Other departments, such as gift shops, recreational activity centers, and valet service, are also notified so a guest who has already checked out is no longer able to charge a closed account. A system for notifying other departments, perhaps not interfaced in the PMS, of guest checkouts should be a basic operating procedure of the front office.

The entire communication system between the front office and other departments is enhanced when employees care about doing their jobs right. Desk clerks should ensure that rooms showing a ready status are indeed available. Housekeeping personnel must report when rooms are ready to be occupied. Careful screening of job candidates and proper training, which includes an explanation of the importance of maintaining communication with other departments, are vital to smooth operations. When everyone works together, the guest is satisfied, the lodging establishment receives a fair return on its investment, and the employee's career opportunities are enhanced.

Removing Guest Information from the System

In hotels with a PMS, removing guest information requires closing the electronic folio. This deletes the guest name and room number from the electronic guest database and the call-accounting system. These data are stored for future processing by the accounting office (see the following section) as well as the marketing and sales department for developing guest histories (discussed later in the chapter).

Transfer of Guest Accounts to the Back Office

Some methods of payment require transferring folio balances to the back office for further processing. Credit card payments are processed and added to the master credit card account according to type (such as Visa or JCB). The controller maintains this account as accounts receivable. Bill-to-account charges must also be transferred to the back office accounts receivable. The controller processes the account according to standard operating procedures, which are handled electronically in a property management system. The back office transfer option enables the controller or front office staff to transfer accounts that require special handling or adjustments.

Checkout Reports Available with a Property Management System

The front office manager should review and analyze data produced during checkout. Most of this information is financial. The data can be grouped into categories as the front office manager desires; method of payment and the respective amounts, total room sales, total room count, and total room sales by type are some sorting options. Room status and occupancy availability can also be tracked. The number of guests who actually checked out versus the number who should have checked out can be compared. An analysis of guests who understayed or overstayed their reservations can be made. The reports option of the checkout module in the PMS allows the front office manager, director of marketing and sales, controller, and other department heads to review these statistics.

Guest Histories

Guest histories are marketing analyses of guests' geographic and demographic information that also provide information about guest activities while staying at the hotel. This analysis is simplified by the use of a PMS. The guest history option of the checkout module assists the front office manager in preparing reports of such data for the director of marketing and sales. The particulars of guest histories can also be obtained from regis-tration cards, if the hotel still uses them, the electronic folio and the data from the reservation system in the PMS, or the Internet.

ZIP Code or Postal Code

The most useful part of the marketing data is the ZIP or postal code, an individual local postal designation assigned by a country. It provides the person who is developing marketing strategies with geographic indicators of populations who have tried the products and services of a particular lodging establishment. This geographic information can be matched with communications media, such as website, radio, television, and newspapers, that are available in that area and with demographic (age, sex, income, occupation, marital status, etc.) and psychograpic (lifestyle) data. Matching website, radio stations, television stations, and newspapers to a group that constitutes the hotel's prime market as well as developing well-structured direct-mail campaigns can be a profitable marketing strategy. Defining the market for continued business is part of a sound business plan.

Developing Conventions and Conferences

The front office manager who reviews the registration cards and reservation cards for group affiliations finds data for potential development of guests by the marketing and sales department. Follow-up by the marketing and sales department to representatives of organizations that have stayed in the hotel may lead to the booking of future conventions and conferences.

The constant demand for meeting facilities does not just happen. Corporate clients that book facility space want to be assured that all details will be handled professionally. Trust in a hotel begins with the hotel's establishing a good track record in handling the small details of hospitality-efficiency in processing reservations, registrations, checkout procedures, and in the maintenance of clean and attractive facilities. This trust (along with a good room rate and adequate meeting space) increases room sales to small conferences.

FAM Tours

The guest history also provides information about the method of advertising that helped to secure the reservation and registration. If guest histories reveal that a large number of reservations originated with a particular travel or tour agency, then the marketing and sales department should maintain a strong relationship with that agency and develop relationships with other agencies within that particular point of origin as well. FAM (familiarization) tours-complimentary visits sponsored by the lodging property that host representatives of travel organizations, bus associations, social and nonprofit organizations, and local corporate traffic managers-can produce an increase in future room revenue. During these tours, representatives can see firsthand what the property has to offer.

Origination of Reservation

A lodging property that has a 70 percent corporate client market might also want to review who makes the reservations for these business professionals at the corporate client's office. The administrative assistant, traffic manager, or executive secretary is probably the person who makes the reservations. If this is the case, the lodging establishment should put in place a program that encourages these people to call the lodging establishment for the reservation. Incentive programs that reward those who make a certain number of reservations over a specified period are an example.

Walk-in guests can also provide valuable marketing data. If guests indicate that "the billboard on Route 777N" was the means by which they learned about your hotel, you will have an idea about the cost-effectiveness of this type of advertising. If guests are being referred by the local gasoline station or convenience store, consider providing brochures and other information to these businesses. Perhaps complimentary dinners or escape weekends for the referral source personnel would be effective.

Frequency of Guest Visit

Data from the guest histories concerning frequency of visits also reveals areas for follow-up. The frequent guest, defined as a person who stays at the establishment more than a specified number of times per month or year, might be offered a free accommodation as either a business or a personal guest. This person and his or her company should be entered into the database for follow-up with advertising promotions designed to attract that market segment.

Types of Room Requested

The guest history is useful in determining the types of rooms requested. Are rooms with two double beds requested more often than rooms with one king-size bed? Are rooms designated as nonsmoking being requested more often than rooms designated as smoking? Are suites with cooking facilities requested by corporate clients for long-term guests? Such hard, quantifiable data are what hotel owners use to make construction and purchasing decisions.

Room Rates Versus Occupancy Patterns

Reviewing room rates can assist the controller and director of marketing and sales in forecasting profit-and-loss statements. The frequency with which certain price categories of rooms are rented indicates the price sensitivity of certain market segments. If price sensitivity is an indicator of room occupancy, then marketing programs that maximize profits in that area must be implemented.

Examining occupancy patterns helps the front office manager schedule personnel. In certain corporate market properties, the hotel may be full from Sunday through Thursday nights but nearly empty on Friday and Saturday. A lodging establishment with a large volume of tourist business on weekends experiences the opposite situation. The front office manager should schedule staff accordingly.

The guest history of the PMS checkout module gives the front office manager a sophisticated method of drawing on these data from a database of reservations and registrations. It is easy to group marketing patterns. The concepts already discussed help in developing the data that are readily available.

Last Impressions of the Hotel

The front desk staff has the vital responsibility in the hospitality industry to create the guests' last impression of the hotel. All the great service opportunities afforded the guest throughout his or her stay can be shattered or further advanced at the point of departure. Kind words, a speedy check out, an offer for directions to the airport, etc., all let the guest know you care. For example, Marriott International, Inc., offers At Your Ser-vice®, which includes Internet resources of local weather reports, information on airport shuttle, and prior downloading of a future guest's email. All of these services allow guests to prepare for their visit and, when the time comes for check out, a good opportunity exists for the front office staff to create that last impression that continues the display of hospitality.

The Travel Industry Association of America indicates (2004) that travelers to the United States from China, India, Russia, and Poland will increase. The implications of this type of prediction are that students preparing for a career in the hotel industry must become familiar with the needs of international visitors during checkout. Studying foreign languages, common cultural concerns, and differences in legal tender help students become valuable members of the hotel team. A hotel employee who can assist an international guest in understanding the guest folio and determining the rates of currency exchange greatly improves the chances that this guest will return.

8

Preparation and Review of the Night Audit

The hotel's financial management starts in the front office. Of course, this responsibility is shared with the controller's office, but it begins with the accurate and timely processing of guest accounts. This chapter addresses the assembling and balancing of all financial transactions in the guest accounts and hotel departments for each day of the year. This can be a time-consuming process for the night auditor, but it provides a balance of debit and credit entries to guest and departmental accounts, which include income- and expense-generating areas of the hotel (e.g., restaurants, gift shop, banquets).

The night audit is the control process whereby the financial activity of guests' accounts is maintained and balanced. This process tracks charges and payments (debits and credits) and the departmental receipts and charges on a daily basis. This working definition encompasses not only the mechanical proofing of totals of charges and payments but the further review of account activity by management. The front office manager monitors the credit activity of guests, projects daily cash flow from room sales, and monitors projected and actual sales for the various departments.

Learning the process of the night audit can provide valuable information for someone who plans to continue in the hotel industry. It also gives the necessary objective overview to evaluate the hotel's financial activity. Students will become aware of the role of the general manager, as the night audit allows a review of all the financial activity that takes places in a hotel in one day.

Based on that review, the general manager must determine how the night audit should be adapted to meet the expenses and profit goals for the accounting period. It also allows the general manager to see if marketing plans and operational activities have accomplished their stated profit goals. The night audit provides insight into how each department must be monitored to produce an acceptable income statement. It pulls together the plans and operations of a hotel on a daily basis, not just at the end of an accounting period. Ultimately, the night audit allows general managers to make good financial decisions based on current and cumulative data.

The Night Auditor

The night auditor has many responsibilities in addition to preparing the night audit report. This person also must check in and check out guests who arrive or depart after 11:00 P.M., process reservations, perform the duties of security guard, monitor fire safety systems, act as cashier for banquet functions, and perform the work of manager on duty. The night auditor acts as a communication link between the guest and hotel operations during the 11:00 P.M. to 7:00 A.M. shift. This is an important position.

The Night Audit Process

The night audit is not one of those reports that is put on the shelf and forgotten. Management uses it to verify the integrity of the guest accounts and to review operational effectiveness, which is the ability of a manager to control costs and meet profit goals. Therefore, accuracy is extremely important. Future hoteliers who want to comprehend the significance of the night audit should participate in the preparation of one. The following discussion of the preparation of the night audit will give you insight into the details of "where the numbers come from."

The six basic steps involved in preparing a night audit are:

1. Posting room and tax charges
2. Assembling guest charges and payments
3. Reconciling departmental financial activities
4. Reconciling the accounts receivable
5. Running the trial balance

6. Preparing the night audit report

This listing will guide you through the seemingly endless proofing of totals and crosschecking of entries, and expedite the completion of the process.

The process presented in this chapter describes performing the night audit with a property management system. Learning the mechanical or hand method of doing the night audit, however, will assist the front office manager in understanding the intricacies of following a paper trail of guest and departmental transactions. Undoubtedly, the modern method of performing the night audit on a PMS will be used, but you should also be familiar with the components up close and personal.

Posting Room and Tax Charges

After the night auditor reviews any messages from other front office staff, reviews guests who checked out of the hotel, extends any guest stays, reviews all room rates, and prints a variance report, his or her first task is to post room and tax charges to all accounts. The PMS can easily post these charges to the electronic folios.

Assembling Guest Charges and Payments

The modules in a PMS (food and beverage, call accounting, gift shop, etc.) allow for ease in assembling guest charges and payments. The following is a typical list of point-of-sale departments for which income is reported:

- Restaurant 1 (breakfast)
- Restaurant 2 (lunch)
- Restaurant 3 (dinner)
- Room service 1 (breakfast)
- Room service 2 (lunch)
- Room service 3 (dinner)
- Lounge 1 (lunch)
- Lounge 2 (happy hour)
- Lounge 3 (dinner)
- Lounge 4 (entertainment)

- Valet
- Telephone
- Gift shop
- Spa and pool
- Parking
- Miscellaneous

Note how the restaurant, room service, and lounge paperwork is further classified by meal or function, to facilitate recordkeeping. General managers can review the income-generation activity of each of these departments when they are reported separately.

The guest charges option of the night audit module in a property management system can sort and total all departmental charges and payments posted to the electronic folios from the point-of-sale systems that interface with the PMS. These data are accurate as long as the person entering the charges at the point-of-sale terminal keys them in accurately.

Reconciling Departmental Financial Activities

These totals are compared to posting information received from the point-of-sale system.

Another departmental total that must be verified is the cash tendered by guests at the front office. Hotels vary in their cash-processing policies. Some front offices process restaurant guest checks from cash customers or other departments in the hotel because management wants to centralize the cash transactions. In other hotels, this policy would be a great inconvenience because of the distance of the restaurants, lounges, and gift shops from the front office. It also requires additional personnel to carry the guest checks with the cash or credit cards to the front office.

The cashier option of the night audit module in the PMS reports the amount of cash, credit cards, and coupons received and discounts processed during the shift. The total amount of cash received by each cashier issued a cash drawer must be verified against the total money deposited for that shift.

Reconciling Accounts Receivable

The city ledger is an accounts receivable held at the front

office. As noted in chapter 2, the city ledger is a collection of guest accounts of persons who are not registered with the hotel. They have either received approval for direct billing privileges or paid a deposit on a future banquet, meeting, or reception. The night auditor treats these accounts just like the accounts on the guest ledger for registered guests. He or she must assemble the charges and verify their accuracy. The cash received from these accounts is reflected in the cashier's report.

The figures in a city ledger can be quite large. A hotel that promotes direct billing as a customer service may have outstanding guest debit charges of $10,000 to $50,000. The hotel may hold a credit balance, amounts of money it owes guests in future services, of $25,000 to $150,000 or more from deposits on future receptions and meeting room rentals. The controller of the hotel must closely watch the balances of these accounts to ensure effective cash flow management.

The master credit card account-an account receivable that tracks bank, commercial, private label, and intersell credit cards such as Visa, MasterCard, and JCB-is held at the front office. Depending on the size of the hotel, the services offered to the guest, and the speed of reimbursement from the credit card agency, this figure may also be quite large. It is not uncommon for a medium-size hotel to have an outstanding credit balance of $30,000 to $50,000 at any one time. As checks are received from the credit card agency, this figure is reduced. It rises again when new charges are posted to a guest's folio. When the checks from the credit-card agency are received, they are posted to the respective credit card's account receivable, and a current balance is calculated.

The city ledger and accounts receivable options of the night audit module of a PMS produces a report of the activity on the city ledger and master credit card accounts.

Running the Trial Balance

A trial balance is a first run on a set of debits to determine their accuracy compared to a corresponding set of credits. The trial balance helps the night auditor focus on accounts in which charges may have been posted or reported incorrectly. For that reason, it is important that the night auditor compare the departmental totals against transfers and paid-out slips for each department processed by desk clerks and cashiers.

Goal of Preparing the Night Audit Report

OK, so now that all the financial data have been assembled, what do we do with the numbers? Students studying hotel front office management may ask, "Why should the night audit report be prepared?" It generates a massive amount of daily operational financial feedback that provides an immediate opportunity for managers to react and respond. General managers and supervisors must use the information to improve the situations that have resulted from their efforts. The night audit report is key in maximizing the efficiency of a hotel. The daily figures regarding room occupancy, yield percentage, average daily rate, and revenue per available room (RevPAR) suggest opportunities to improve a slow sales period. Guests who demand an accurate folio complete with guest charges can be helped more efficiently as a result of this process.

As you begin your career in the hotel industry, take the opportunity to review the financial statistics generated by the night audit report. The result will be a capsule review of the importance of departmental financial activities and their role in delivering hospitality. This background will also provide you with insight into the decision-making process, which, in turn, helps hotel departments adhere to their budgets.

Preparing the Night Audit Report

The night audit report is usually organized to meet the needs of a specific lodging establishment. Some general managers might require more financial data than others. Figure 10-5 is a sample of a night audit report of all financial activities of the day. You may want to note the columns headed "Budget" and "Goal." The budget figure is the target amount of sales planned for that day. The goal figure shows what percentage of the budgeted figure was actually achieved. If a larger amount was budgeted than was realized, then some part of the operation is not functioning as expected. Some hotel managers want a cumulative figure reported each day, to gain a more comprehensive overview of the achievement of financial goals.

It is important that managers approach this report as a functional tool that provides daily operational financial data. Its major components may seem overwhelming when perceived as a whole. With experience, you learn to view this seemingly complicated document in separate parts, each of which provides feedback on daily operational performance. Daily review of the reported figures allows management the opportunity to be flexible in meeting financial goals.

Departmental Totals

Each department in the hotel is required to provide a daily sales report to the front office. These figures are listed and compared to the budget goal. General managers of hotels use these figures to determine the profitability of income-generating departments and the success of marketing programs.

Bank Deposit

Bank deposits are also part of the night audit. In large hotels, bank deposits are made several times a day to satisfy security concerns. The bank deposit includes both cash and credit card deposits. It is important to note that cash, business checks, and checks from credit card companies are received several times throughout the business day. After these are received and recorded, they are turned over to a cashier at the front desk to post them to the corresponding guest or city ledger account.

Accounts Receivable

The accounts receivable is an ongoing listing of outstanding amounts owed to the hotel. As mentioned in chapter 8, these potential sources of revenue are essential to positive cash flow. Managing and updating these accounts by reviewing them daily is a primary responsibility of the controller and general manager.

Cashier's Report

Some hotels run the traditional three shifts (7:00 A.M.-3:00 P.M., 3:00 P.M.-11:00 P.M., and 11:00 P.M.-7:00 A.M.) for cashiers. In larger hotels, several cashiers may work each shift. No matter how many cashiers there are per shift, each is responsible for actual cash and credit cards received, which are compared to PMS totals. The cashier's report, discussed earlier in the chapter, lists cashier activity of cash and credit cards and PMS totals and is an important part of the financial control system of a hotel. The front office manager and the controller reviews this part of the night audit and looks for discrepancies between the actual amount received and the PMS total. They also assess the cashier's accuracy.

Manager's Report

The manager's report is a listing of occupancy statistics from the previous day, such as occupancy percentage, yield percentage, average daily rate, RevPAR, and number of guests. Data such as these are necessary for monitoring the operation of a financially viable business. The general manager, controller, front office manager, and director of marketing and sales review these statistics daily.

Room and Tax

The room sales figure represents the total of posted daily guest room charges. The night auditor obtains this figure from the PMS by activating the cumulative total feature, an electronic feature that adds all posted room rate amounts previously entered into one grand total. This figure is only as accurate as the posting of daily room rates. If a desk clerk transposes figures, then the total room sales amount will be incorrect. Because a large portion of room income is considered profit, management watches this figure closely. The room sales figure is verified by the housekeeping report, which lists the occupancy status of each room according to the housekeeping department. The corresponding tax total is obtained by activating the tax cumulative total feature, an electronic feature of a PMS that adds all posted room tax amounts previously entered into one grand total. This figure is necessary for tax collecting and reporting.

Total Restaurant Sales and Sales Tax

The total restaurant sales figure comprises all sales incurred at restaurants or food outlets in the hotel. Restaurant 1 may represent breakfast sales; 2, lunch sales; and 3, dinner sales. Or Restaurant 1 may represent all food sales from Restaurant A; 2, food sales from the pool snack bar; and 3, sales from Restaurant

B. These figures are verified against the daily sales report, a financial activity report produced by a department in a hotel that reflects daily sales activities with accompanying cash register tapes or point-of-sale audit tapes from each of the restaurants or food outlets. The sales tax figure is also obtained from the daily sales reports.

Tips for Restaurant, Room Service, Banquet, and Lounge Employees

Tips paid out to service employees represent an important control feature. Not only is management required to report this amount to state and federal agencies, but the tips may be paid out from the desk clerk's cash drawer or the restaurant cash drawer. In any case, tips charged to the guest's account on restaurant guest checks, tips paid immediately to service employees from the desk clerk's cash drawer on paid-out slips, room service guest checks, and charged tips on credit card vouchers are used to verify this total.

Room Service

Some hotels report room service sales as a separate figure from total restaurant sales. If a hotel has organized a special marketing and merchandising campaign to increase room service sales or feels that careful monitoring of this potentially profitable service is necessary, then the night auditor reports this figure. Room service 1 may represent breakfast sales only; 2, lunch sales; and 3, dinner sales.

Banquet Sales

Hotels with large banquet operations report the banquet sales figure separately from restaurant sales. These figures are a total of the guest checks, which tally the individual banquet charges. The night auditor also checks the daily function sheet to ensure that all scheduled functions have been billed.

The general manager can use banquet sales figures to determine how effective the food and beverage manager is in controlling related expenses for this division. Banquet sales also indicate how effective the director of marketing and sales is in generating business. Banquet breakfast, banquet lunch, and banquet dinner figures are reported separately because they provide marketing information on which areas are successful and which could be more successful.

The banquet sales figures (and the room sales figure) also provide information on the cash flow activity of the hotel. If the hotel has scheduled $25,000 of banquet business and $25,000 of rooms business for a weekend, it can meet various financial obligations due on Monday, depending on method of payment. The controller in a hotel therefore watches room and banquet sales closely.

Banquet Bar and Total Lounge Sales

The sales figures for the banquet bar and lounge areas originate from the point-of-sale cash registers. The total sales figures from the outlets that serve alcoholic beverages are reported to the front office on a daily sales report after each shift. Each report is accompanied by the cash register tapes or audit tapes.

Sales figures from the various lounges and banquets are reported separately because the food and beverage manager must determine how well cost-control efforts are maintained for that department, and the director of marketing and sales may want to research the success of certain marketing and merchandising campaigns.

Room Rental

The charges for room rental-these are not guest rooms but meeting and function rooms-are reported on special room rental guest checks. The night auditor cross-checks these guest checks against the daily function sheet to be sure the banquet manager charged room rentals to the appropriate guests.

This figure is reported separately at hotels that charge fees for the rental of facilities when no food or beverage is ordered. For example, banquet rooms may be rented for seminars, meetings, demonstrations, and shows. Because room rental represents a potentially large profit area (especially during slow banquet sales periods), general managers want to know how effective the marketing and sales department is in maximizing this profit center.

Valet

One of the services a hotel offers is dry cleaning and laundry. This feature must be closely monitored because the hotel pays cash to the off-premises dry cleaner or laundry service when the clothing is returned. These costs, plus a markup for hotel handling charges, are posted to the guests' folios. Some hotels maintain a valet or dry cleaning/laundry journal indicating valet tags, control numbers, processing dates, vendor charges, handling charges, posting activity, daily totals, and the like. Transfer slips are prepared to indicate the charges for valet service. The charges on these transfer slips are then posted to the guests' folios. The total of the transfer slips comprises the valet total for the night audit.

Telephone Charges

After the telephone industry was deregulated in the early 1980s, call accounting became a standard practice in hotels. This allowed hotels to set individual surcharge rates, or rates for adding service charges for out-of-state long-distance telephone service. The telephone department became a profitable area in the hotel business. Because all phone calls are charged to the guest folio, an accurate accounting of the charges is necessary. In a hotel with a call-accounting system that interfaces with a property management system, this tally is electronically obtained.

Gift Shop Sales and Tax

The gift shop in a hotel prepares a daily sales report for the front office. Cash register tapes or point-of-sale audit tapes accompany the report. The general manager examines the financial activity of this profit center-another area in which cash flow potential is monitored. Recording the tax collected on gift shop sales and reporting this figure is a necessary accounting procedure.

Vending

Hotels that maintain their own vending machines monitor the daily collection of cash. If a facility has a large number of vending machines, the food and beverage manager assigns one person to collect and count the money and prepare a daily sales report. These reports provide the total sales figure for vending.

Spa

The use of health facilities at a hotel may be provided free to guests. However, other products and services-such as swimsuits, health-related products and equipment, the services of a masseur or masseuse, sports lessons, and rental equipment-are sold to the guest. These costs are usually charged to the guest folio. A daily sales report is prepared at each of the health/recreation facilities. Some hotels offer their health/recreation facilities for a fee to the general public. Transfer slips for charges to the guest accounts for future billing in the city ledger provide a total against which total spa charges are verified.

Parking

A hotel that offers valet parking or parking spaces to guests and the general public acquires large amounts of cash during a business day. Cash, business checks, and debit and credit card payments are collected throughout the day for general parking, long-term business parking, and parking valet services. Guests in the hotel who are charged for parking services have this amount charged to their accounts.

The parking garage manager prepares a daily report of the cash and charge activities for each shift. Supporting documentation, including parking tickets, cash register tapes, transfer slips, and monthly parking permit renewals, accompany the daily report. The night auditor prepares a summary total of this account from these reports.

Total Revenue and Total Write-Offs

The total revenue and total write-off figures represent all the cash and charge transactions for the day, reflecting all the previously reported figures. General managers compare the actual and budgeted figures to determine how well operations have met the financial goals of the hotel.

Throughout the business day, the front office manager authorizes paid-out slips (for valet service, tips, supplies, and the like), discounts (for rooms or restaurant charges, for example), and adjustments (room, telephone, and restaurant, for example) in the form of write-offs to guest accounts. The general manager maintains strict control over these figures. These amounts are verified with authorized paid-out slips and transfer slips.

Cash Sales and Accounts Receivable Balance

The total revenue represents both cash and charge guest sales. A separate figure is reported for total cash sales for the day. This figure represents the totals reported and received from the departmental daily reports and is also required to justify the daily bank deposit.

Charge sales are reflected in the outstanding accounts receivable (Today's Outstd A/R). This is the amount that remains to be received from the guests. Total paid-outs, total discounts, and total write-offs are subtracted from that figure. Today's outstanding accounts receivable figure is added to yesterday's outstanding accounts receivable (Yesterday's Outstd A/R) to obtain a cumulative balance of outstanding accounts receivable (Total Outstd A/R).

Credit Cards and Cash Applied to Accounts Receivable

Throughout the business day, the controller of the hotel requests front desk clerks or cashiers to post business checks and cash received from credit card companies, direct billing accounts, and city ledger accounts. The charges from these groups were previously moved to accounts receivable. These checks and cash payments represent charges from previously held banquets, guest room rentals, and the like. The general manager of the hotel watches this figure to determine cash flow activity. Again, the outstanding balance of accounts receivable is updated.

Analysis of Accounts Receivable

The front office manager maintains an analysis of the accounts receivable balance that indicates the source of each account receivable-city ledger, direct billing, or various credit cards. (It is important to note here that city ledger accounts may have a credit balance but are maintained as an account receivable. For example, if a guest pays a $500 deposit on a future banquet, a credit balance is maintained on the account. When this credit balance is computed with other debit balances, a debit balance is realized.) The controller uses this information to track the aging of accounts, determining the stage of the payment cycle-such as 10 days old, 30 days overdue, 60 days overdue-and to operate an overdue payment collection program.

Bank Deposit and Amount Transferred to Accounts Receivable

The cash, credit card vouchers, and charges received during the business day from cash, charge, and accounts receivable transactions must be deposited in the hotel's bank accounts or transferred to the hotel's internal accounts receivable. The night auditor provides a summary of the components of the bank deposit. Bank deposits are made throughout the business day. Those individual totals make up the total bank deposit (TTL BANK DEP). Credit card totals are listed here because, in some circumstances, the credit card voucher is considered cash at the time of deposit. The cash and credit card totals deposited must match the total cash sales plus the cash received and applied to outstanding accounts receivable (Cash Rec'd A/R) minus total paid-outs. The total actual cash and credit card payments received, which are reported on the cashier's report, match the total bank deposit figure. The amount transferred to accounts receivable (AMT TR A/R) corresponds to today's outstanding accounts receivable (Today's Outstd A/R).

Cashier's Report

In some hotels, the front desk clerk or cashier is responsible for proofing and collecting the departmental daily reports. In those situations, the cash and credit card vouchers are added to the individual cashier's shift report. Also included in that report are the amounts of cash and credit card checks received for application to accounts receivable. Each cashier's shift report is verified by departmental daily reports, cash and credit card vouchers, and accounts receivable cash and credit card check transactions. These figures must be verified in the daily bank deposit.

The cashier's report also notes variances in actual totals and PMS totals. Usually, the hotel sets a policy regarding the liability of the front desk clerk or cashier for these variances. For example, if the actual amount collected is one cent to one dollar less than the amount obtained in the cashier's report, the front desk clerk or cashier is not liable for the difference. The front office manager should investigate amounts significantly larger than one dollar to see if such losses are regular occurrences. When the actual amount collected is more than the amount obtained in the cashier's report, the extra money is maintained in a house fund to compensate for undercollections. These amounts should also be investigated as to regularity and source. Substantial overages and shortages must be investigated for proper debiting and crediting of a guest's account.

Operating Statistics

The night auditor prepares the daily operating statistics for the general manager and the department directors. This quick summary reviews the day's activities and the hotel's success in meeting financial budget targets. Hotel general managers rely on these statistics as operational feedback mechanisms because they provide information on the need to modify existing operational procedures and offer insight into budgeting for future operational procedures. These figures become part of the hotel's historical operations record.

The rooms sold, rooms vacant, and rooms out of order are determined by assessing the housekeeping module and the housekeeper's report. The number of complimentary rooms (rooms comp) is determined by reviewing guest reservations, registration cards, and electronic folios. Room income for the day is obtained from the total room charges posted after a certain time in the evening (between 11:00 P.M. and midnight) and any half-day rate charges. The number of guests is provided by the PMS registration module. The number of no-shows is compiled by tallying the number of reservations with a confirmed status that did not show. Not included in this figure are guaranteed reservations, which are processed with a credit card number regardless of whether the guest showed.

The preparation of a night audit report can be time-consuming. However, with a great deal of cooperation, planning, and organization, combined with the use of a PMS that interfaces with point-of-sale systems, the time can be greatly reduced. The accurate preparation of the night audit report provides an essential control and communication tool for management.

Daily Flash Report

The daily flash report, a PMS listing of departmental totals by day, period to date, and year to date, is useful to general managers and department managers and supervisors. This report is reviewed daily to indicate how successful a department manager was the previous day in achieving sales. This tool is important in discussing strategies for the successful achievement of financial goals.

Reading the Flash Report

Here are some insights into reading the Flash Report.

Room Sales-The general manager tracks these figures because they are the major source of income for the hotel. Because room sales provide the most profit, this is an important figure to watch daily. Marketing and sales also wants to know this figure, as does the front office manager.

Selected Departmental Totals for Food and Beverage-These figures are a primary concern for the general manager as he or she evaluates the effectiveness of the food and beverage manager and his or her staff. It is important to do this daily rather than weekly or monthly.

Occupancy Totals-These figures provide the general manager, front office manager, and marketing and sales with feedback on the effectiveness of advertising in influencing patronage to the hotel. They provide bottom-line financial details of what works and what doesn't with regard to online and print-based ads, cold calls, etc. When the daily totals fall below the projected figures, a group effort is needed to determine what steps should be taken to revitalize marketing.

Here are some reasons that could lead to low occupancy and that should be researched: Why are O-O-O (out-of-order rooms) at such a high number? Did that have an effect on the low occupancy? Did the low arrival figure occur because of airline problems? Was the low yield caused by a failure of a group not meeting its room quota? Are we not asking for credit cards to guarantee a room reservation? Experience in the hotel industry provides many opportunities for future hoteliers to gain insight into asking questions such as these.

When these questions arise, the general manager follows up with inquiries to the relevant departmental supervisor, such as the director of maintenance (rooms O-O-O); front office manager (airlines); marketing and sales manager (group room quota); and front office manager (reservations without credit card).

Reading the Night Audit

Here are insights into reading the night audit.

Room Sales-Check the budgeted and actual figures to determine if the sales efforts for the previous day were fruitful. If not, hold a brief meeting with the marketing and sales department to determine which strategies worked and which did not work. Include the revenue manager in the discussion to provide feedback on rates and channels.

Restaurant Sales-Review the individual meal periods and determine if they met their goals. If the numbers are not up to the goal, ask the supervisor what factors (weather, quality of food, quality of service, competition, etc.) could have caused these results.

Room Service-Because this is a profitable area for the hotel, it should be reviewed carefully. Review the actual and budgeted numbers and determine what could have caused the difference. Perhaps room service should be actively marketed, compared to the silent marketing of a menu placed in the guest's room.

Banquet Sales-Again, this is a large profit producer for the hotel. However, this type of activity is planned many days and weeks in advance and should be reviewed accordingly. Sometimes unexpected events such as weather or mishap can occur that cause a cancellation. Management should also look at which type of meal is producing or not producing income. For example, if all the banquet income is coming from lunches, then there are opportunities for banquet sales in breakfast and dinner.

Banquet Bar Sales-Bar sales for lunch and dinner also provide additional profit for the hotel. These too should be monitored as an opportunity for their inclusion in the meal occasion.

Room Rental-Room rental provides income for the hotel to pay heating, lighting, air conditioning, and other utilities. Therefore, every opportunity should be made to charge and collect this fee.

Lounge Sales-Lounges throughout the hotel are assigned a goal for the night, depending on their market. The general manager compares the actual with budget to determine if the staff at the lounge has done its job. If not, then a discussion should be held with the supervisor of the lounge and director of food and beverage.

Valet-This service is handled outside the hotel, and a fee is added to the guest's bill. This fee is basically profit for the hotel. The general manager should work with the front office manager to develop a marketing plan that ensures that front desk staff promotes this service to the guest.

Telephone-Telephone charges are usually electronically posted to the guest's folio with the call-accounting module of the PMS. This figure allows the general manager to see how many dollars are collected. With the increased use of high-speed Internet access in guest rooms, this dollar figure is worth watching because of the dollar investment in technology.

Gift Shop-Sometimes the gift shop is outsourced by the hotel to a third party. In that situation, the hotel collects a certain percentage of the total gross sales. The general manager wants to know what gross sales are on this report. If the gift shop is operated by the hotel, the general manager wants to compare actual and budgeted sales and discuss marketing efforts with gift shop manager.

Vending-Vending can also be an outsourced effort for the hotel. If it is outsourced, then the sales agreement that covers a daily, semi-weekly, or weekly deposit is listed here. If the vending is operated by the hotel, then the daily cash deposit is listed here. This is an easy target for theft, so the general manager must keep a close eye on the total that was produced by the few or many vending machines in the hotel.

Spa-Some hotels outsource their spa to a third party. In that situation, the hotel collects a certain percentage of the total gross sales. The general manager tracks those gross sales on this report. If the spa is operated by the hotel, then the general manager compares actual and budgeted sales and discusses marketing efforts with the spa's manager.

Parking-When the parking lot or parking deck is outsourced by the hotel to a third party, the hotel collects a certain percentage of the total gross sales. The general manager tracks those gross sales on this report. If the parking garage is operated by the hotel, then the general manager compares actual and budgeted sales and discusses marketing efforts with the parking garage manager. Parking lots are expensive to operate, but they can also bring in money to the hotel.

Total Paid-Outs-This figure is usually low because not many people are authorized to receive money from the front desk clerk for emergency cash. Large amounts listed here on the night audit would indicate a problem!

Total Discounts-Some hotels have a 100 percent satisfaction pledge, and if this is the policy, you can see where this would be evident. If the restaurant had to credit a guest's check for food, that too would show up here. Mistakes do occur, and they have to be justified to provide feedback.

Total Write-Offs-This section of the night audit is reserved for writing off accounts (rooms and food) that are not being paid for by guests for the evening. These are usually guests of the hotel.

Total Paid-Out and Noncollect Sales-This is a total of total paid-outs, total discounts, and total write-offs; it is a figure that general managers need to control so it doesn't get out of line.

Total Cash Sales-This figure represents non-credit sales. Usually it is low because the hotel operates in credit sales. A high cash figure suggests possible concern for several guests who are paying cash and have not established creditworthiness, and the potential for security problems for the hotel.

Today's Outstanding Accounts Receivable-This is the amount charged by guests on their folio from all departments.

Total Revenue-This figure is a total of all cash sales and charge sales for the day.

Yesterday's Outstanding Accounts Receivable-This number is very large because of the delay in receiving actual funds from credit card companies. For example, when a guest charges a room-night on a credit card, there may be a five-day delay before the actual check or electronic payment clears the hotel's bank account. Until the time of the clearing, the controller maintains the balance of that guest's folio as outstanding. As a note of precaution, it needs monitoring by the controller's staff to be sure the accounts are aged, especially those house accounts tended by in-house staff.

Total Outstanding Accounts Receivable-This is the total of (Today's) and (Yesterday's) Outstanding Accounting Receivable. Again, this is a large number.

Credit Card Received Accounts Receivable-This figure tells the general manager how much money was applied to credit card balances and received in checks from credit card companies. Farther down on the page (Bank Deposit), an analysis indicates to which credit cards this total was applied. As a control procedure, received checks are logged in by one person, then forwarded to another staff person for deposit.

Cash Received Accounts Receivable-This figure represents cash received for application to credit card balances, etc.

Balance Accounts Receivable-This figure is the total of outstanding accounts receivable to the hotel-city ledger, direct bill, and credit cards. This figure is analyzed under Analysis of Accounts Receivable. These two totals must match.

Bank Deposit-This is a listing of the cash and credit card deposits. The figure must match the Credit Card Received Accounts Receivable. This is a control feature. The accompanying Analysis of Bank Deposit provides the general manager with an overview of the sources of the funds deposited. Keep in mind that credit card sales do carry a discount fee and that this adds up over time.

Cashier's Report-This control report is included in the night audit to verify the totals of each cashier for cash sales, credit card sales, and sales applied to accounts receivable. The accompanying Analysis Cash Report provides a summary of these three areas. The totals must match the totals of each shift.

Manager's Report-This is a very useful report for the general manger because it provides an overview of the staff's financial efforts of the previous day. This quick look or comparison of actual versus budgeted figures is extremely helpful for the general manager as well as departmental managers.

9

Managing Hospitality

Upon check-in, a guest indicates that the national reservation agent misquoted his room rate at $95 when it should have been $85 per night. The front desk clerk responds, "Sir, you will have to discuss that with the cashier when you check out in three days. I can only register you with the rate that was entered into the computer. What's $30 to a businessperson on a budget?"

The concept of hospitality, the generous and cordial provision of services to a guest, is at the heart of our industry. These services can include room accommodations, food and beverages, meeting facilities, reservations, information on hotel services, information on local attractions, and the like. Hospitality is a subjective concept, and the degree of hospitality a guest perceives has implications for the overall financial success of the hotel. Guests who feel they are not treated with respect or have not received full value for their dollar will seek out other hotels they believe will provide hospitality. This chapter is intended to instill in you, the future professional in the hospitality industry, a sense of responsibility for providing professional hospitality. As you prepare for a career in an industry that may differentiate its product by continual and efficient delivery of professional hospitality service, this material will serve as a primer for your development.

This chapter was inspired by a book entitled Service America! (Dow Jones-Irwin, 1985) by Karl Albrecht and Ron Zemke. These management consultants were early proponents of the service concept in business. Their writings, as well as my own professional experience in hotels and restaurants, are the basis of this chapter. A chapter devoted to hospitality seems essential because the staff of the front office is often the only direct contact the guest has with the hotel. A recent job advertisement for a total quality manager was offered by the InterContinental Hotels Group. This emphasizes the continued importance this concepts plays in the hotel industry.

Importance of Hospitality

Hospitality is an important consideration for both the guest and the hotel entrepreneur. Every guest expects and deserves hospitable treatment. Providing hospitality to meet guests' needs involves not only a positive attitude but an array of services that make the guest's stay enjoyable. If the market being served by a hotel is composed of business travelers, a hotel staff will find that their needs revolve around schedules and flexible delivery of hotel services. The business traveler may arrive late and leave early. The hotel restaurant must be organized to provide a healthy and quick breakfast. Wake-up services must be located within the room or provided by an efficient staff. The hotel should also offer office services, such as word processing capabilities, advanced telephone systems, fax and photocopying facilities, and computers. The guest who is associated with a convention may want early check-in, late checkout, and a full range of hotel services. If the convention starts at noon on Tuesday, the guest may arrive at 9 A.M., wanting to unload and set up before the noon starting time. If the convention ends on Thursday at 3 P.M., the guest may want to retain occupancy of the room beyond the normal checkout time. While the guest is in the hotel, he or she may require flexible scheduling hours of the swimming pool, health club facilities, lounge and live entertainment, gift shops, coffee shop, and other hotel services. International guests may require assistance with using electrical appliances, converting their national currency into local currency, or interpreting geographic directions.

Success or failure in providing hospitality often determines the success or failure of the hotel. Capitalizing on opportunities to provide hospitality is essential. The failure to make the most of these chances directly affects the hotel's financial success, as Albrecht and Zemke indicate in Service America!:

The average business never hears from 96% of its unhappy customers. For every complaint received the average company in fact has 26 customers with problems, 6 of which are "serious" problems. Complainers are more likely than noncomplainers to do business again with the company that upset them, even if the problem isn't satisfactorily resolved. Of the customers who register a complaint, between 54 and 70% will do business again with the organization if their complaint is resolved. That figure goes up to a staggering 95% if the customer feels that the complaint was resolved quickly. The average customer who has had a problem with an organization recounts the incident to more than 20 people. Customers who have complained to an organization and had their complaints satisfactorily resolved tell an average of five people about the treatment they received.2

What do these issues of delivering hospitality to the guest mean to the entrepreneur? They emphasize that the guest who is not treated with hospitality (remember that the definition of hospitality is subjective) will choose to do business with a competitor and may also influence others not to try your hotel for the first time or not to continue to do business with you. The entrepreneur who is aware of the competition realizes that this negative advertising will severely affect the profit-and-loss statement. Albrecht and Zemke extended their concept mathematically. Let's examine the cumulative effects of poor service in the following example.

If a hotel does not provide the desired level of service to 10 guests on any given day, only 1 of the guests will bring the complaint to the attention of the hotel staff. If the complaint is resolved quickly, this person will almost surely do business again with the hotel. He or she will also have occasion to influence 5 people to use your hotel. On the other hand, the 9 guests who did not bring their complaints to the attention of the hotel staff will probably not do business with the hotel again, and each of them may tell approximately 20 people-a total of 180 people will hear their negative account of the hotel. If this model is extended to cover a whole year of dissatisfied guests, 68,985 people will have a negative impression of the hotel ([180 people told + 9 original dissatisfied cus tomers] x 365 days in a year), and 2,190 will have a positive impression ([5 people told + 1 original satisfied customer] x 365 days in a year).

The financial ramifications of so many people negatively impressed with your hotel are clearly disastrous. Hospitable treatment of guests must be more than just an option; it must be standard operating procedure. It is a concept that must be adopted as a corporate tenet and organized for effective delivery.

Managing the Delivery of Hospitality

It is not enough for the front office manager to decide that the members of the front office staff should provide good service and display hospitality to guests. To provide satisfactory hospitality to all guests at all times, front office managers must develop and administer a service management program, which highlights a company's focus on meeting customers' needs and allows a hotel to achieve its financial goals. This program must be based on sound management principles and the hotel's commitment to meeting those needs.

Management's Role

This may seem an odd place to start a discussion of delivering hospitality. After all, aren't the front desk clerks, switchboard operators, and bellhops the people who meet and greet guests and fulfill their needs at the front desk? Yes, these employees do provide hospitality directly, but management must work behind the scenes to develop a plan that ensures that the employees' efforts are continuous and professional.

For example, management may decide to implement one or two specific, immediate changes on learning that a guest's needs were overlooked. Management may feel that the negative impact of the rude, lazy, or careless employee has unnecessarily caused bad public relations. If a group of employees is not performing to management's standards, the cumulative effects of the group are perceived negatively by guests. This negative impression takes a toll in the long run. Although one or two directives may correct an individual guest's problems, that hotel will reap only short-lived gains. A comprehensive program aimed at meeting the needs of a hotel's prime market-guests who continue to do business with the hotel- provides the foundation for long-term successful delivery of hospitality. This is what makes a hotel profitable.

Management's commitment to a service management program must be as integral to the organization as effective market planning, cost control programs, budgeting, and human resources management. In fact, service management is the most visible responsibility because it affects all the other objectives of the hotel. Often the people in staff positions in hotels become so involved with their day-to-day paper shuffling and deadlines that they forget why they are in business. They may not mean to forget, but it happens all too often. Service management ensures a commitment to long-range effort by appointing someone within the organization to be responsible for developing, organizing, and delivering it.

John W. Young, retired executive vice president of human resources at the Four Seasons Hotels and Resorts, tells us:

> We expect our general managers to respect the dignity of every employee, to understand their needs and recognize their contributions, and to work to maintain their job satisfaction with us-and to encourage their growth to the maximum extent their ability and desire allows. General measurement is based on detailed employee attitude surveys, conducted by an outside firm, as well as such factors as employee turnover [and] employee promotions, both within the hotel and to other hotels. Also specific people-related goals are set according to the hotel's needs or the manager's personal needs, and measured, e.g., implementing a planned change in response to concerns in an attitude survey.

The front office manager usually supervises service management efforts. Other key department heads who supervise employees who deal with guests, such as the food and beverage manager and director of marketing and sales, rely on the organizational leadership of the front office manager. It is important to note that responsibility for delivering hospitality to the guest is always a part of the job of each department's supervisor or shift leader, the person responsible for directing the efforts of a particular work shift. The organizational efforts provided by the front office manager serve as the basis for a homogeneous plan for the hotel.

The owner and general manager must make a financial commitment to ensure the success of the program. An important component is motivating employees to deliver hospitality on a continual basis through incentive programs. Incentive programs are management's organized efforts to determine employees' needs and develop programs to help employees meet their needs and the needs of the hotel. Such programs reward employees for providing constant and satisfactory guest service and often involve money, in the form of bonuses, which must be budgeted in the annual projected budget. These incentives may involve the employees' choice of a monetary bonus, higher hourly rates, shift preference, or additional holiday or vacation days.

Mark Heymann, chairman and CEO of UniFocus, based in Carrollton, Texas, indicates that customer satisfaction and employee satisfaction (in hotels) should be considered simultaneously. He says, "Given today's extraordinarily tough labor market, dissatisfied workers don't stick around. So a happy staff is the key to happy campers."

The goal of every lodging establishment should be to extend the same degree of hospitality to a guest who arrives on a busy Monday morning and to a guest who arrives on a slow Saturday night. Management's ideological and financial commitment, along with the organizational efforts of the front office manager, will ensure that both of these guests are treated equally.

The Service Strategy Statement

To produce an effective service management program, management must devise a service strategy statement, a formal recognition by management that the hotel will strive to deliver the products and services desired by the guest in a professional manner. To accomplish this, management must first identify the guest's needs.

Those of you who have entry-level jobs in a hotel as a bellhop, desk clerk, switchboard operator, table attendant, housekeeping attendant, or gift shop clerk may have some feel for what guests want. They want quick and efficient service. They want to avoid long lines. They want to find their way easily around the hotel and the immediate vicinity. They want the products and services in the hotel to work. They want to feel safe and secure while residing in the hotel. If you use these observations as a basis for understanding guests' needs while they are away from home, you will be able to better satisfy their needs.

John Young reports, "Market research, internal guest comments and our regular employee attitude surveys all confirm that what has set and will continue to set Four Seasons apart from our competitors is personal service."

As Eric Johnson and William Layton note, "It is only through the eyes of a customer that a definition of service quality can be obtained. Senior management cannot adequately determine what is desired at the customer level until a comprehensive evaluation of customer preference is established through a systematic consumer research study."6 Thus, in addition to identifying generally what guests want, management should survey guests about the particular property to determine what services they expect and how they want these services delivered. The general manager of the hotel may assign this task to the marketing and sales director, who may start by reviewing and summarizing customer comment cards, which are usually held on file for six months to a year.

The survey may be administered by a member of the marketing and sales department at various times during the day. This information, as well as that gleaned from the comment cards, gives a general indication of what the guest wants. Sometimes pinpointing guest needs is not easy, because they change over time. These areas, then, should be the focus of the service strategy statement, as they appear to be the primary guest concerns.

Ernest Cadotte and Normand Turgeon analyzed a survey concerning the frequency and types of complaints and compliments received from guests of members of the National Restaurant Association and the American Hotel &C Motel Association (now the American Hotel &C Lodging Association). They report:

The data seem to fall into a four-fold topology that compares how likely an attribute is to garner compliments versus the frequency of complaints.

1. Dissatisfiers-complaints for low performance, e.g., parking.
2. Satisfiers-unusual performance apparently elicits compliments, but average performance or even the absence of the feature will probably not cause dissatisfaction or complaints, e.g., atrium-type lobbies.

3. Critical variables-capable of eliciting both positive and negative feelings, depending on the situation, e.g., cleanliness, quality of service, employee knowledge and service, and quietness of surroundings.
4. Neutrals-factors that received neither a great number of compliments nor many complaints are probably either not salient to guests or easily brought up to guest standards.7

Albrecht and Zemke also identify general guest expectations as follows:

? Care and concern from service providers

" Spontaneity-people are authorized to think

" Problem solving-people can work out the intricacies of problems

" Recovery-will anybody make a special effort to set a problem right?

Their conclusions add another dimension to the service strategy statement. In addition to certain recognizable products and services delivered at a certain speed and level of quality, guests expect employees to accept the responsibility for resolving problems. The guest should not encounter unconcerned staff or be bounced from employee to employee in order to have a problem solved. Management must develop a staff whose members can think and solve problems. This dimension to the service strategy statement makes the delivery of professional hospitality a challenge!

Statement

- A commitment to make service from top-level ownership and management a top priority in the company
- A commitment to develop and administer a service management program
- A commitment to train employees to deliver service efficiently
- A commitment of financial resources to develop incentives for the employees who deliver the services

These directives serve as guidelines in the development of a service management program. More important, they force management to think of service as a long-range effort and not as a quick fix. John W. Young states that the service strategy of the Four Seasons Hotels and Resorts centers on offering . . . exceptional levels of personal service. People are our most important asset. Each person has dignity and wants a sense of pride in what they do and where they work. Success in delivering excellent service depends on working together as a team and understanding the needs and contributions of our fellow employees. [We must] train and stimulate ourselves and our colleagues. [We must] deal with others as we would have them deal with us. [We must] avoid compromising long-term goals in the interest of short term profit.

Here is one example of a service strategy statement:

The owners of fictitious The Times Hotel, management, and staff will combine forces to establish a Service to Our Guests program, administered by management and delivered by staff. Delivery of service to our guests is crucial to the economic viability of our hotel. The owners of the hotel will provide financial support to the people who deliver hospitality on a daily basis.

Another version of the service strategy statement is as follows:

The hotel, in its continual efforts to maintain a leadership position in the hotel industry, will develop a VIP Guest Service program. The administration and delivery of this program are essential to the financial success of the hotel. This program will include incentives and has received a priority budget line for this fiscal year.

These statements, however worded, convey the message from owners and management that a successful service management program depends on the support of all levels of management and staff.

Financial Commitment

Throughout the preceding discussion on service management, financial commitment from management was stressed. Managers who want to develop and deliver a successful service management program must provide adequate staff time to think through a plan and to develop methods to motivate their employees. Scheduling time for planning and strategy sessions can increase the labor budget. Determining and offering motivational opportunities also increases the financial investment. Often, lack of planning for these financial considerations impedes the desire to implement a service management program.

Total Quality Management Applications

The previous discussion of developing a background for managing the delivery of hospitality is essential for adopting total quality management (TQM) practices, as discussed in chapter 2. Hotel owners and managers who fail to develop a clear service strategy statement and make a financial commitment to delivering hospitality experience extreme difficulty in applying TQM. TQM requires an immense commitment of labor to analyze guest and employee interaction, the reallocation of responsibilities and authority to foster an improvement in services, and a long-term commitment to learning a new method of management. Preparation for adopting TQM is a requisite for success.

Patrick Mene is vice president of quality for The Ritz-Carlton Hotel Company, L.L.C. His organization is the winner of the 1992 and 1999 Malcolm Baldrige Award, a prestigious recognition of excellence in overall performance, leadership, profitability, and competitiveness. After he gradu-ated from college, Mr. Mene went to work as a management trainee at Hilton. He has also worked in management positions at Hyatt, Westin International, Omni, Portman Hotel in San Francisco, and L'Ermitage Hotels. He has performed a great deal of research, particularly on the teachings of Joseph Juran, a management specialist in quality planning, improvement, and control.

Mr. Mene states that competing for the Baldrige Award provided great feedback for the hotel. He explains that the hotel was organized vertically; it is now organized horizontally to concentrate more on the critical processes that drive the company and to provide more employee empowerment. For example, a traditional hotel may have 30 departments, while the Ritz-Carlton has only four; each one is run by a horizontally organized team. One team focuses on the prear-rival process (customer contact with the sales office; making reservations; planning meetings, conferences, and banquets), one team focuses on arrival (laundry, housekeeping, front desk), one team runs the restaurant, and one team is responsible for banqueting. This horizontal structure creates a "leaner, linked, empowered organization." Mr. Mene describes the managers in this type of organization as "coaches and advisers," while managers in traditional organizations are more "chief technicians and problem solvers."

Mr. Mene reports that customer dissatisfaction has decreased. The new structure has resulted in fewer breakdowns and less need for rework. In the past, the hotel experienced problems with incorrect or late honor bar billings; guest rooms were always clean but were sometimes missing supplies; and, at times, when guests called for information or assistance, agents were not available and calls went unanswered. These problems have been dramatically reduced.

He states that quality management science is a new branch of knowledge. Traditional methods of management that concentrate on selling hard, raising prices, and forcing a profit cannot identify and eliminate waste. He adds that, in any hotel, 30 percent of expenditures are the result of quality failures and are unnecessary. He feels that TQM is the most effective way to achieve revolutionary results.

W. Edwards Deming's principles of TQM10 can be applied to front office management practices. Managers must focus on a distinct level of service at the front office. Managers and frontline employees must view the interaction between customers and service providers. A front office team develops a flowchart, an analysis of the delivery of a particular product or service, to illustrate what occurs after a customer has verbalized a request for a product or service. Analysis of this interaction by the group of people who deliver the product or service allows for suggestions for improvement. A key component of TQM is a commitment to continuous analysis of the delivery of guest services and plans for improvement.

Developing a Service Management Program

Employee involvement in planning a service management program is as important as obtaining a financial commitment from owners in establishing such a program. Too often, when the employees are not included in the planning stages, they look at the final plan and remark, "This is ridiculous; not for me. Let the people in marketing and sales worry about it." In many cases, service is perceived as just another fancy concept pro-posed by management. Management must address this attitude from the outset. When employees are involved early, they are much more likely to buy into the program because they are already a part of it.

This TQM team is analyzing the delivery of a particular service to a guest. Managers and front-line employees provide an objective review. Photo courtesy of Radisson Hospitality Worldwide.

Guest Cycle

The front office manager responsible for developing an effective service management program, along with other department directors, should first look at the employees they supervise. Representatives from all job categories and shifts should be included on the planning committee. Planning by committee can be cumbersome (scheduling, planning meetings, incurring additional payroll, etc.), but it can ensure that an effective program is developed. It allows a drafted plan to be altered in the planning stages by those who must implement it and ensures clear, workable operational methods. It gives the employees time to adjust to the new concept while allowing time to develop adoption procedures. At each planning phase, employees learn how they will benefit from the program. This is a realistic way to focus management's efforts to promote this important concept. Once the members of the planning committee are chosen, their first step is to analyze the guest's perception of the hospitality system:

Visualize your organization as dealing with the customer in terms of a cycle of service, a repeatable sequence of events in which various people try to meet the customer's needs and expectations at each point. It may be the instant at which the customer sees your advertisement, gets a call from your sales person, or initiates a telephone inquiry. It ends only temporarily, when the customer considers the service complete, and it begins anew when he or she decides to come back for more.

Another benefit of analyzing the cycle of service is that the analysis may reveal inefficiencies built into the system. Rectifying these will assist in delivering first-rate hospitality, as the following example, reported by Nancy J. Allin and Kelly Halpine of the quality assurance and training department at the Waldorf-Astoria in New York, indicates:

While there can be many reasons to combine the positions of registration clerk and cashier, and many aspects were considered at the Waldorf=Astoria, the decision was driven by a desire to improve guest service where its impact is most obvious-at the front desk. Cross-trained employees speed the check-in and checkout process by performing both functions, as the traffic at the desk dictates. Registration clerks can cash checks and cashiers can issue duplicate room keys, in many cases eliminating the necessity of having the guest wait in two lines.

Moments of Truth in Hotel Service Management

Central to the development of a guest service program is the management of what Albrecht and Zemke call moments of truth: "episode[s] in which a customer comes into contact with any aspect of the company, however remote, and thereby has an opportunity to form an impression."13 Every time the hotel guest encounters some aspect of the hotel, he or she judges its hospitaiity. Guests who are told by a reservationist that they must "take this room at this rate or stay elsewhere" will not feel that hospitality is a primary consideration at this hotel. When a potential guest calls and asks to speak with Ms. General Manager and the switchboard operator answers, "Who is that?" the guest will expect the same kind of careless, impersonal treatment when (or if) he or she decides to stay at the hotel. The guest who is crammed into an elevator with half the housekeeping crew, their vacuum cleaners, and bins of soiled laundry will not feel welcomed. All these impressions make the guest feel that service at this hotel is mismanaged.

These examples are only some of the moments of truth that can be identified from an analysis of the guest service cycle. Whether a guest considers an event a moment of truth or barely notices, it is a cumulative review of the delivery of hospitality. Albrecht and Zemke tell us that each guest has a "report card" in his or her head that is the basis of a grading system that leads the customer to decide whether to partake of the service again or to go elsewhere.

If a guest is to award an A+ to the hotel's hospitality report card, it is essential that all moments of truth be well managed. This challenge is not to be viewed as an impossible mission but rather as an organized and concerted effort by owners, management, and employees. Keep this customer report card concept in mind as you develop your ideas about service management.

Shortcomings in providing guest services at the front office in The Times Hotel have become critical in one particular aspect-knowledge of special events in the local area. Guests have complained that front desk clerks do not give clear directions, estimates of travel time, information on timing of events, cost of admission, or suggestions for public transportation. Guests approach desk clerks and receive only a brief response to their questions.

The front office manager has decided to use total quality management principles to resolve this situation. The hotel has stated a commitment to service and a financial commitment to this goal. If you were the front office manager, how would you proceed?

Employee Buy-in Concept

As Albrecht and Zemke note, "in any kind of retail or service business, the factor that has the biggest effect on sales is the 'last four feet.' It's up to the people in the store to take over at the last four feet." In other words, all the sophisticated marketing programs, well-orchestrated sales promotions, outstanding architectural designs, and degreed and certified management staff form only the backdrop for the delivery of hospitality. The frontline employee is the link in the service management program. He or she must deliver the service. It's a simple fact that still amazes many people. How can front office managers ensure that frontline employees deliver a consistently high level of service? Albrecht and Zemke offer the following suggestions:

To have a high standard of service, it is necessary to create and maintain a motivating environment in which service people can find personal reasons for committing their energies to the benefit of the customer. People commit their energies to the extent that what they do brings them what they want. What they want may be psychological-a feeling, a status, or an experience. Or it may be material-greenbacks are an excellent form of feedback. In any case the job of management is to engineer a motivating environment.

John W. Young echoes their ideas: "The challenge is to motivate your employees to deliver the required level of service to your customers, and do it consistently .... If we are to succeed in delivery of exceptional service, we have to convince every new employee of the benefit of 'buying in' to our philosophy and standards."

In short, a consistently high level of service is provided only by employees who are committed to the service management program. This commitment is fostered by management. It is such commitment that allows the front desk clerk to tell the newly registered guest about the special musical combo group playing in the lounge or to ask how the traffic coming in from the airport was or to suggest consulting the concierge in the lobby for directions to points of interest in the city.

Consider each employee in each hotel and determine how to stimulate his or her commitment to service. If money motivates them, financial incentive programs that reward positive expressions of hospitality are in order. Employee stock ownership programs also provide an incentive for employees to realize financially the importance of delivering a consistently high level of hospitality. Other reward systems may include preferential treatment in scheduling shifts, longer vacations, and extra holidays. Long-range rewards may include promotion opportunities.

Screening Employees Who Deliver Hospitality

Another factor to consider in developing a service management program is the employee character traits needed to provide hospitality. When candidates for frontline service positions are evaluated, interviews should be structured to screen out employees who are not able or willing to deal with the demands of guest service. Albrecht and Zemke offer these considerations for choosing frontline employees: "A service person needs to have at least an adequate level of maturity and self-esteem. He or she needs to be reasonably articulate, aware of the normal rules of social context, and be able to say and do what is necessary to establish rapport with a customer and maintain it. And third, he or she needs to have a fairly high level of tolerance for contact."18 And John W. Young notes:

The motivation process begins with the selection of employees, which is all important. The average person applying for a job is interviewed by at least four people. When Four Seasons opens a property every single employee hired is interviewed by the hotel general manager. First we look for people who are already motivated. Our compensation policies have been designed to support and reinforce our efforts in hiring, training, and development. We look on them not only as a motivator, but as a way of sending signals to our employees consistent with our philosophy and business strategy-almost as an employee communication program itself.

Group discussions among the managerial staff help highlight the attributes of a person able to deliver hospitality. These discussions should lead to a rather informal procedure for screening employees. Questions that determine whether candidates display maturity and self-esteem, are articulate, possess social graces, and have a high level of tolerance for continued guest contact can be discussed in group settings. Managers who are aware of what they are looking for in employees are better able to secure the right people for the right jobs!

Empowerment

Empowerment-management's act of delegating authority and responsibility to frontline employees, those people who deliver service to guests as front desk clerks, cashiers, switchboard operators, bellhops, concierge, and housekeeping employees-is the bedrock of service management programs. The process of empowering employees requires front office managers to analyze the flow of guest services and determine how the frontline staff interact with the guest. Are there any points of service at which the guest may request variations in the level of service provided? Might there be times when a guest questions standard operating procedures, such as billing, guest room access, or room accommodations? Do frontline employees constantly inform guests, "I don't have the authority to rectify this matter. You'll have to see the manager"? If the review of the guest cycle reveals opportunities for delegating responsibility and authority, then empowerment should be exercised.

The analysis of the guest flow (described earlier in this chapter) is the best way to start the empowerment process. However, this analysis must be performed by the front office manager in conjunction with frontline employees. If input from frontline employees is not included in the analysis, valuable data may be overlooked and an opportunity for employee ownership lost. The opportunity for employees to participate in the decision-making process ensures positive initiation of empowerment.

Empowerment tunities for a guest to question a billing amount, then the billing amount must be discussed. If the amount in question is less than $5, do cashiers have the authority to credit the guest account for that amount? Or the amount in question is less than $25; do cashiers have the authority to credit the guest account for that amount? Or the amount in question rises to more than $25; do cashiers have the authority to credit the guest account for that amount? Along with setting parameters for employee empowerment is a management feedback system that provides information on cashier financial activity and guest satisfaction. For example, a cumulative tally as well as individual tallies of a front desk clerk's authorization of refunding charges that have been disputed by guests should be reviewed by front office managers. Financial totals that exceed the parameters of employee empowerment should be questioned.

Training for Empowerment

Employees need training sessions to prepare for empowerment. Training sessions should cover the feeling that management has abandoned its responsibility by asking employees to resolve guest concerns. Employees may also experience anxiety in dealing with guests who are upset. Front office managers must develop flexible but relatively routine methods for employees to use to achieve a uniform delivery of service.

Training for empowerment begins by asking employees how they feel about providing guests with good service. Front office managers might ask employees how they think the hotel can make the guest feel most comfortable in this environment. Questions that pertain to employees' recent personal experiences at the time of check-in or checkout may yield some opportunities for discussion. Training continues with a list of empowerment policy standards, which describe the authority and responsibility included in their job description. Employee-manager dialog about these standards helps clarify employee understanding and concerns and identify manager communication issues. The manager should demonstrate and have employees go over the use of empowerment policy standards. Managers should also hold follow-up training sessions that include reviews of employee performance and opportunities for employee feedback.

Training for Hospitality Management

Part of a service management program involves employee training to deliver hospitality. Just as managers discuss what they want in an employee, they decide what must be done to convey hospitality to travelers who are away from home. Of course, this discussion is not performed in isolation and requires input from employees. Using the guest service cycle, the planning group determines what each frontline employee must do at each point to extend hospitality. The key to making training pay off is knowing what we want the trainees to be able to do when they have finished the program. An effective training process starts with a performance analysis. We must analyze the various jobs to be done in serving the customer well, and then spell out the knowledge, attitudes, and skills required of the person doing the job.

You cannot take it for granted that the desk clerk knows to maintain eye contact with the guest during the check-in procedure while using a computer, that the switchboard operator knows to alert a security supervisor when a guest mysteriously hangs up in the middle of a call for information, or that a bellhop knows to check the operating conditions of the heating, ventilating, and air-conditioning unit and television when he or she brings the guest's luggage to the room. The expressions of hospitality must be identified so that each employee can be trained to convey them.

Evaluating the Service Management Program

Any program requires methods for evaluating whether the program has successfully achieved its goals. This chapter opened by defining hospitality as the generous and cordial provision of service to a guest. How do the owners and managers of a hotel know that hospitality is being delivered?

Albrecht and Zemke base the development of a sound evaluation procedure on identifying the guest's moments of truth. This outline can serve as a guideline for what should be evaluated. The more work done to identifying the components of the guest service cycle for a specific hotel property, the more effective its managers and employees will be in evaluating service delivery. Specific desired behaviors can be identified and measured. For example, if part of the registration process depends on a prompt hotel shuttle van to pick up and deliver guests to the hotel, then complaints from guests about late or slow service tell the owners, managers, and employees that frontline employees are not delivering the necessary service correctly. Customer comment cards are one way hotel management and staff can receive feedback. However, not all satisfied or dissatisfied guests complete these cards. Owners, managers, and employees who are committed to a service management program must develop additional methods for determining guest satisfaction.

Another method that can be used to obtain useful feedback is to have frontline staff, such as a desk clerk, inquire about the guest's visit during checkout. Simply asking "Was everything all right?" is not sufficient. If the guest folio indicates the guest charged meals, beverages, room service, long-distance calls, or valet services, the front desk clerk should inquire about the delivery of service for each: "Was your food delivered hot, on time, removed from the hallway promptly?" or "How did you enjoy the live entertainment in the lounge?" A method of communicating guest responses to the appropriate departments, which can rectify the errors or reward the frontline employee, completes the process of evaluating the success of a service management program. For example, a quick call to the manager on duty that relates the information received from the guest can assist in remedying a potential guest service problem.

An inquiry from the desk clerk at checkout provides feedback about service quality after the fact. Supervisors of the dining room, lounge, bell staff, housekeeping department, maintenance crew, and the like must develop communication procedures with their employees to monitor the guest's experience as it occurs. The host or hostess must develop a sensitivity to a guest's reaction to menu items and prices; the bellhop must constantly be aware of the guest's needs for information, directions, or assistance with luggage; the housekeeping employee must be aware of the guest's needs for additional amenities, linens, or cleanliness of the public areas. All feedback must be communicated to the frontline employee for continuous improvement of service.

Follow-Through

Vital to every service management program is the continued management of the program over time. In the hospitality industry, continued management can be difficult. A hotel operates every hour of every day, and innumerable jobs are involved in keeping it running smoothly and profitably. Managers can begin a service management program with the best of intentions, but too often it is dropped or neglected in the day-to-day flurry of operations. Albrecht and Zemke remind us that "isolated change and improvement programs tend to run their course and then to run downhill toward the performance levels that existed before the program. The difference between a program and continuous commitment is management." Management is the key to implementing an effective guest service program. The commitment to hospitality is not a casual one; it requires constant attention, research, training, and evaluation. Only with this commitment can a hotel ensure hospitality every day for every guest.

Interfacing with Other Departments in Delivering Hospitality

One of the many benefits of employing total quality management is the participant's ability to understand fellow team members' job responsibilities. Teams composed of various departments in the hotel provide opportunities for insights into other employee's jobs. Sometimes the process of TQM can seem like a maze of charts, processes, interactions, and the like, which tend to confuse the uncommitted. But from that process rises a thorough understanding of how the guest moves through the hospitality system and the jobs of the providers of these services.

Participants in TQM come to realize that the delivery of hospitality is not the responsibility of any one person. This may come as a startling revelation to employees who feel alone in bearing the responsibility for guest satisfaction. TQM allows all participants the opportunity to see how employees from other departments share in the hospitality activity.

The "that's not my job" attitude is easy to adopt in a management system in which TQM is not used. Employees who feel they have distinct job duties within and between departments and are not paid to venture beyond them may contribute to the delivery of unacceptable service. Department managers who use TQM have the opportunity to prioritize service concepts and methods to deliver service with employees. This interaction gives managers and employees the occasion to air concerns about how restrictions resulting from narrowly written job descriptions affect their ability to provide service to the guest. A typical TQM team assigns representatives from various departments in a hotel to work on improving a particular guest service. For example, guests may complain that there are not enough towels in a guest room. This complaint, especially after housekeeping has closed down for the evening, causes a reduction in guest satisfaction and additional work for the lone front desk clerk on duty.

At the outset, the answer may be to "just put a few more towels in each guest room." The controller of the hotel may see this as additional costs of inventory purchase and laundry. Housekeepers realize that excess supplies in guest rooms have a tendency to vaporize and result in an increase in costs. However, a team approach to this seemingly simple problem uncovers a list of possible solutions that an individual employee might overlook. A team of desk clerks, housekeepers, bellhops, servers, cooks, switchboard operators, cashiers, and supervisors reviews this particular service and how it is delivered. Objective analysis of the components of the service gives employees insight into how departments interact to accomplish their tasks. Brainstorming sessions identify possible improvements that can be debated by team members. Additional meetings find team members crystallizing concepts and gaining insights and respect for jobs performed by team members.

The team may decide to have front desk clerks alert the housekeeping staff when more than two people check into a guest room. The housekeeping staff can then routinely bring additional towels. This decision not only solves the problem of guest dissatisfaction caused by too few towels but provides an opportunity for frontline employees to develop and deliver a guest service. It is no longer a front desk problem or a housekeeping problem but a team effort to produce a satisfied guest.

An example of a service management program is Hilton's "Hilton Pride Program," which recognizes exceptional hotel performance and customer satisfaction. "The Pride Program reinforces our pledge to maintain exceptional levels of customer satisfaction while building pride in the workplace. This sense of pride enables us to create a level of service that brings our customers back," says Dieter H. Huckestein, executive vice president, Hilton Hotels Corporation, and president of the company's owned and managed hotel operations.

The performance criteria include the following items:

- Customer satisfaction tracking studies
- Guest comment card responses
- Mystery shopper evaluations
- Team member surveys
- EBITDA (earnings before interest, taxes, depreciation, and amortization)
- Room RevPAR
- RevPAR index
- Brand management and product standard"

Delta Hotels received the Canada Awards for Excellence Trophy 2000 from the National Quality Institute (NQI). John Johnston, president, Delta Hotels, remarked, "Not only does this award recognize our ongoing commitment to excellence, but more importantly our commitment to our guests." The selection process included "[NQI] assessors [who] visited six Delta hotels and the Corporate office to review examples of quality in action. Delta Hotels met the rigorous criteria in the Excellence Framework by demonstrating outstanding continuous achievement in Leadership, Planning, Customer Focus, People Focus, Supplier Focus, and

Performance." Prior to this award, Delta Hotels established an internal quality control program called Quality Business Assessment. "With this process, Delta Hotels trains internal assessors to conduct individual hotel assessments and develop a quality improvement plan. Every two years, a hotel will undergo an initial three-day assessment and a subsequent five-day assessment to ensure that ongoing quality measures are incorporated into Delta's culture and all aspects of [its] operations. External assessors are also invited to conduct assessments, ensuring that assessments meet the professional standards of NQI." William Pallett, senior vice president, people and quality, says, "Our goal is to ensure a seamless approach to quality, so that it is part of our culture. Problem Solving Teams regularly monitor process for improvement opportunities." Tangible results of Delta's program include a one-minute check-in guarantee for guests and a guarantee for employees "to receive their review within 30 days of their anniversary date or receive one week's vacation with pay."

Customer Relationship Management

Customer relationship management (CRM) is a system that allows hotel managers to integrate technology to support customer service techniques that lead to top-notch customer service. The technology that is so apparent in CRM has to play a secondary role because one-on-one interaction with the guest continues to support reasons for return visits. Neil Holm, president of hypen, describes CRM as follows.

Often referred to as a type of technology, CRM is first and foremost a business philosophy-a way to consistently treat your guests right. Technology is the enabler that helps get useful information into the hands of your management and staff so that they can more powerfully foster guest satisfaction and loyalty.

Haley and Watson list (1) guest recognition, (2) data capture and maintenance, (3) channel integration and consistency, (4) ranking and discrimination, and (5) two-way personalized dialogs as the five elements of CRM. Guest recognition on a routine basis is easy, but when the guest customer base is sporadic or international, then we need assistance with data on relevant information. This is where the computerized information of the guest's coffee or golf time preferences is important. Data capture and maintenance is essential to keeping this system working properly. Every time a guest indicates that something has changed, it should be reflected in the system. Channel integration and consistency means that we have to provide guest recognition depending upon the various channels guests choose to use-the property level or Internet. Guests want that same type of recognition. Ranking and discrimination is a business decision; some guests will bring more profit into your organization, and you must decide how you are going to use your financial resources to attract them. (Author's note: In the business world you should treat all customers equally; you never know who your kindness has affected.) Finally, two-way personalized dialogs allow for a communication process between the customer and the hotel. Yes, the customer is asked to take action to the specialized sales offers produced by the hotel. Many computer programs interface with a hotel's PMS, and a student of hospitality management can easily locate them on the Internet.

Solution to Opening Dilemma

An immediate response to correct this guest service situation is to have the desk clerk register the guest at $95 per night, discuss the situation with the supervisor after the guest leaves the front desk, and then have the front desk clerk call the guest to confirm the room rate. However, a more effective way to handle future situations is to work with the general manager and owner to develop a service strategy statement and obtain financial resources to support a service management program. Exploration and application of employee motivation and empowerment are necessary to make a service management program work. Total quality management teams will help employees determine tasks required to deliver service. New front office managers should not take the delivery of good service for granted. Quality service is planned, not happenstance.

10

Training for Hospitality

Enrique Garcia, a hotel general manager, has heard the last complaint about his staff! He is tired of writing letters of apology and comping guest stays because of poor delivery of service. Recently, a guest complained that after he left the front desk area in his wheelchair, a desk clerk was overheard making an unkind remark. Two days before that, another hotel employee took 45 minutes to respond to a guest's request for assistance in moving a heavy box from his room to the lobby area, and that same person said it took 10 minutes to go through the check-in process. Mr. Garcia wants to contact an advertising agency that will assist him in cleaning up the hotel's image.

Determining Employee Hospitality Qualities

Assessing personnel needs requires identifying the skills and character traits required to do a particular job. Frequently, the front office manager can recite a list of problems with front desk personnel but cannot identify their strengths. The ability to recognize positive traits-skills of present employees as well as skills a potential employee should have- helps not only in choosing the right candidate for a particular position but also in assigning tasks to employees that match their abilities. If you do not know the skills of your current staff and the skills future staff will need, you cannot assemble a staff that will meet your needs or make effective use of their skills.

Job Analysis and Job Descriptions

A front office manager should begin by preparing job analysis and descriptions of each position in a department. Identify the responsibilities and objectives of each and then consider the personal qualities, skills, and experience needed to perform those duties. For example, a front office manager may want front desk clerks to sell the more expensive suites or rooms and other services of the hotel. To accomplish this objective, an individual must have an outgoing personality or be willing to accept new responsibilities as a challenge or an opportunity to grow. The front office manager may wish the front desk clerks to be more efficient in handling clerical duties neatly and accurately. These qualities may be found in a person with prior experience in other clerical or sales positions. Previous experience outside the labor force-for example, as an officer in a service club or a community group-may indicate the person's leadership skills and ability to organize projects. These and other traits should be viewed as a whole. The motivational concepts discussed later in the chapter will help a front office manager identify and develop an employee's positive attributes.

Positive Hospitality Character Traits

A front office manager must think about the character traits necessary to deliver hospitality on a daily basis. These traits include maturity, an outgoing personality, and patience as well as a willingness to accept constructive criticism. The employee should also feel comfortable selling, as he or she must promote the hotel's services.

Outgoing employees are able to seek out other individuals and make the initial effort to set a relationship in motion. Employees who are extroverts enjoy meeting guests and making them feel welcome. This is the type of employee who, in many cases, can turn a difficult situation into a challenge. For example, if a guest says there is no way he or she will be walked to another hotel-"After all, a reservation is a commitment"-an outgoing person may be better at persuading the guest that the alternative hotel will surely "meet your highest standards" than saying nothing at all.

Mature employees are able to assess the big picture and quickly analyze a situation before acting. Instead of reacting to a situation, this type of employee allows a guest to vent his or her concerns before offering a response. Mature employees also possess and exhibit patience in situations that require guests be allowed time to think or carry out a request. Guests may be confused about geographic directions in an unfamiliar surrounding; a mature employee gladly repeats and offers written directions or sketches to allow the guest time to absorb the information.

Practicing Promotional Skills

Employees who possess a positive attitude toward constructive criticism prosper and progress in a hotel career. All employees occasionally make errors in judgment and fail to meet standards. Employees who want to continue to learn seek a supervisor's insights into why a particular situation resulted from their actions.

Front desk clerks who are comfortable with practicing promotional skills are a great asset to a front office manager. This type of person accepts the challenge to sell products and services throughout the hotel and seek ways to meet or exceed sales quotas. This quality allows a front desk clerk to understand the total effort necessary to produce a profit for a hotel.

Screening for Hospitality Qualities

Composing questions prior to interviewing to determine if an applicant has the personal qualities needed to fulfill a job's requirements is usually effective. The interview should have some structure but be flexible enough for both the interviewer and the applicant to freely express their concerns.

The front office manager begins to develop a list of questions based on the job description to guide the interview. He or she wants to determine if the candidate has an outgoing personality, patience, the ability to accept constructive criticism, and the ability to sell. These are only a few of the qualities for which a front office manager wants to screen in an interview.

An Outgoing Personality

The first question attempts to determine if the applicant is outgoing. Although observing the person during the interview gives some indication of how he or she deals with others, you could get more insight with this question: "Tell me about the last time you went out to dinner. What did you like about the host or hostess?" A response that indicates appreciation for a friendly welcome shows the candidate is aware of the concept of hospitality.

Patience

To learn about the level of patience a job candidate possesses, ask a question such as "Tell me about your recent participation in an event (sporting, social, work) at which you received less than what you had expected." A response that indicates that small details were overlooked but overall the experience was rewarding may indicate the person is willing to be a team player.

Ability to Accept Constructive Criticism

To assess a candidate's ability to accept constructive criticism, a question such as "At your previous job, how did your manager handle a situation in which you did not meet stated goals?" may be used. A candidate's response to this reflects the degree of understanding the interviewee had about why he or she was reprimanded, and how the situation was corrected may indicate how the person accepts constructive criticism.

Interest in Selling

A question that allows a candidate to express his or her openness to soliciting donations for a charity assists an interviewer in understanding the applicant's desire to sell products and services for the hotel.

These questions do not guarantee that the front office manager will choose wisely, but the effort will produce a more effective track record of screening for hospitality.

Developing an Orientation Program

The person who is hired to work in the front office is in a unique position. In no other department of the hotel is each employee expected to know the operations, personnel, and layout of the facilities of every other department. The front office employee is constantly bombarded with questions from guests and other employees concerning when a certain banquet or reception is being held, where key supervisors are, or how to find the lounge or pool area. The orientation process introduces new hires to the organization and work environment and is vital in providing employees with background information about the property. This program helps new hires become aware of the activities, procedures, people, and layout of the hotel. It is a critical first step in training new employees.

Of the utmost importance is ensuring that orientation is thorough and well designed. An employee who is given a brief introduction to the people who work the same shift, a quick tour of the location of the guest rooms, and information concerning the time clock can hardly be expected to be competent. By the time orientation is complete, new employees should be able to answer guests' questions easily. If they don't have answers at their fingertips, they should know how to find them quickly. For example, if someone asks for the general manager by name and the new front desk clerk responds, "Who is that?" an inefficient and unprofessional image of the organization is conveyed. The new employee should know who that person is and how to reach him or her. Moreover, orientation should prepare all new hires to provide correct and complete information to guests, the general public, or other employees.

Orientation programs for front office employees differ from one establishment to another. However, the following outline can be used to develop a program for any establishment. This outline incorporates factors common to all properties, such as economic position of the establishment in the community, overview of the hotel, the employee handbook, the policy and procedure manual, and an introduction to the front office environment.

Economic Position of the Property in the Community

A new employee benefits from knowing how a hotel fits into the economic scheme of the community and the region. He or she may be impressed to learn, for example, that a particular hotel is responsible for 10 percent of the employment in the area. Information concerning the value of the tax dollars generated by employees, significance of the tourism market, number of conventions and subsequent guests who rely on the services of the operation, significant growth accomplishments, and other economic contributions not only reassure new employees that they have chosen the right employer but also instill a sense of pride in the organization. These and other economic indicators help the new hire think of the employer as a well-respected member of the business community. Larger organizations can prepare a slide or multimedia presentation to demonstrate their commitment to the business area.

Overview of the Lodging Establishment

An overview of the lodging establishment includes the number of rooms (accompanied by a detailed printed handout concerning layout), a list of services offered in the establishment, an organization chart of the staff in the various departments, and, of course, a tour of the property.

Guest Rooms The guest rooms are an important part of the day-to-day activity of the front office staff. The sooner the employee is aware of the location and contents of the rooms, the quicker he or she feels comfortable with the job. Floor plans for each floor and a printed summary of the typical contents of the rooms are handy references that the new person can review at a later time. For instance, if the odd-numbered floors have three suites and the even-numbered floors have study areas for businesspersons, including this information in the printed material assists in the training process.

Service Areas

The services offered by the hotel (restaurants, banquet facilities, room services, lounges,pool, athletics room, and gift shops) should be identified during the orientation program so the new employee can assist and direct guests. Listing the hours of operation for each department helps the new employee learn about the systematic operation of the hotel.

The people listed on the organization chart should be pointed out to the new hires. These people and their responsibilities should be explained. This background information assists in decision making and communication of information to department heads. It also gives the new hire a sense of belonging to the group.

Tour of the Property

The overview of the lodging establishment is not complete

without a tour of the property. This tour should include the guest rooms and guest room areas, major departments, and service areas such as restaurants, banquet rooms, gift shops, and recreational facilities. The tour can be informal yet specific in content. It allows the new employee to see the establishment as a place of work and a place of recreation for the guest. These tours also help the employee understand the front office's relationship to the entire establishment.

Employee Handbook

The employee handbook provides general guidelines concerning employee conduct and is a valuable resource for new hires. In this publication, hotel managers describe many topics related to personnel issues, including:

- Pay categories
- Evaluation procedures
- Vacation time
- Sick leave
- Holidays
- Paydays
- Use of controlled substances
- Social interaction with guests
- Resolving disputes with guests and other employees
- Insurance benefits
- Uniform requirements

Sometimes people being interviewed for positions at an establishment or new hires do not ask questions about these policies because they feel the employer may think them greedy, lazy, or overconcerned with a certain issue. On the contrary, these questions form the basis for a good employment contract. Employers should make the effort to discuss and explain their personnel policies.

Policy and Procedure Manual

The policy and procedure manual outlines how the specific duties of each job are to be performed (this is also known as standard operating procedures [SOPs]). This is another specific set of guidelines that is valuable for employee training. The policy and procedure manual addresses such concepts as the following:

- Operation of the PMS and other equipment in the front office
  - Reservations
  - Registrations
  - Posting
  - Written and oral communications with guests and other employees of the hotel
  - Checkouts
- Preparation of the night audit
- Safety and security measures

The front office manager who takes the time to develop these guidelines will have prepared a useful supervisory tool. Providing materials in writing to supplement the spoken training session allows new employees to review the skills they must master and to retain more of what they are taught.

Introduction to the Front Office Staff

The final segment of the orientation process is an introduction to the front office itself. This introduction prepares new hires for the training program that will follow. It familiarizes them with coworkers, equipment they will be using, personnel procedures, and interdepartmental relations.

New employees should be introduced to the current staff of front desk clerks, bellhops, telephone operators, reservation clerks, night auditors, supervisors, and others. A little planning on the front office manager's part is required to ensure that the new employee meets the entire staff in the first few days.

Saying a few words about the role of each employee during the introductions not only makes new hires feel more comfortable with their coworkers but also makes each current staff member feel like a special part of the team. Current staff members also appreciate meeting the new addition. This procedure is often overlooked, and new employees feel awkward for days or weeks.

Equipment Overview

The equipment in the front office should be described and shown to the new employee. Brief remarks about each piece serve as a reference point when needed skills are explained in detail during the training program. This part of the orientation program can be slowed somewhat to allow the new hire to become familiar with the equipment. The operator of the call-accounting system may have the new person pull up a chair to watch how calls are handled. The new employee may be encouraged to observe how a fellow desk clerk processes registrations and checkouts. The front office manager should assure the new employee that specific training will follow. This is a time for familiarization only.

The new employee should be shown how to check in for a shift on the PMS or the time clock. The location and timing of the posted schedule of shift coverage should also be indicated. The importance of reporting for duty on time and its effect on fellow employees should be explained at this time.

Interdepartmental Cooperation

Interdepartmental cooperation must be stressed during the introduction to the front office. This is an ideal time to establish the importance of harmony among the housekeeping, maintenance, marketing and sales, food and beverage, and front office departments. The front office must take the lead in establishing good communications among departments. Because the front office is the initial contact for the guest, obtaining status reports, maintaining communications, and knowing the functions being hosted each day are the responsibilities of the front office staff. Overlooking trivial misunderstandings with other departments sometimes takes colossal effort, but the front office must keep the communication lines open. Guests benefit from and appreciate the work of a well-informed front office.

Administering the Orientation Program

Administering the orientation program requires planning by the front office manager. The front office is a hectic place, and there is much for the new employee to learn. Concern for the guests and the services and information they require must be a priority. The checklist ensures that the new employee is properly introduced to the front office. It should be initialed by both the new employee and the orientation supervisor after the program is complete to verify that all policies were covered. Thus, no one can claim to be ignorant because there is written evidence that the material was covered in the orientation program.

Selection of Orientation Leader

The orientation program should be delivered by a member of the supervisory staff or a trained senior staff member in the front office. This person must have the ability to convey the attitude of the organization as well as the tasks of the employees. Whoever handles the orientation should not be on duty at the same time; it is impossible to explain so much about the property to a new employee while performing other tasks as well.

The orientation program helps the employer-employee relationship begin on the right foot. It introduces the workplace, guidelines and procedures, coworkers, and management staff to the new hire. The orientation program also introduces new employees to their work environment and encourages them to be a part of it.

Developing a Training Program

Training is an important management function and is required to develop and ensure high-quality performance.1 In the hospitality industry, some hotel organizations take training seriously; others talk about it extensively but have no real program in place. Those that have developed, instituted, and continued to update their training programs consider them great assets in human resources management. They allow the management team to develop qualified employees who can perform jobs according to predetermined standards. A good training program ensures that errors are reduced because all procedures are explained and demonstrated.Planning and developing a training program for front office employees includes identifying the tasks performed by the front office staff, preparing step-by-step procedures for each task, determining who will train employees, administering the training program, and reviewing the steps in the training process.

Identification of Tasks and Job Management Skills

The tasks performed by each employee are usually identified through the job description. The job description is based on the job analysis (discussed in chapter 2), which lists, in chronological order, the daily tasks performed by the employee. For example, the front desk clerk performs the following tasks on the day shift:

6:00 A.M. Enters start time with PMS.

6:05 Talks with night auditor about activities on the 11:00 P.M. to 7:00 A.M. shift; checks the front desk message book for current operational notes.

6:10 Obtains cash bank, a specific amount of paper money and coins issued to a cashier to be used for making change, from controller; counts and verifies contents.

6:30 Reviews daily report concerning occupancy rate and daily room rate.

6:35 Obtains function sheet (list of activities and special events, receptions, and the like) for the day.

6:37 Obtains housekeeper's report for the previous day.

6:40 Calls housekeeping and maintenance departments to determine the communications list (a log of unusual occurrences or special messages that the front office personnel should know about) from the previous shift(s).

6:45 Calls restaurant to learn specials for lunch and dinner.

6:50 Reviews expected checkouts and reservations for the day.

6:55 Checks out guests until 9:30 A.M.

All of the tasks identified in the job analysis must then be broken down further into specific skills to build a sound training program. This may seem like a laborious procedure. It is! But the first step is always the most cumbersome. Using the job analysis for each of the jobs in the front office ensures that all tasks required to deliver hospitality to the guest are included in the training program.

Preparing Step-by-Step Procedures

Step-by-step procedures for each task help the trainee understand how to perform tasks correctly. This approach also helps the trainer prepare and deliver training sessions more efficiently.

If a hotel front office has a PMS, the operator of the computer terminal must learn to enter data or commands sequentially. Documentation, written instructions on how to operate computer software, accompanies all property management systems. Documentation can be used as a basis for developing the step-by-step training procedure for using the PMS, and it can serve as a model for preparing step-by-step procedures for other tasks.

A step-by-step procedure to complete a guest checkout on the PMS might include the following:

1. Inquire about the guest's accommodations.
2. Enter the guest's room number.
3. Inquire about late charges.
4. Confirm method of payment.
5. Print a hard copy of the folio.
6. Allow the guest to review the folio.
7. Accept cash or credit card or bill-to-account.
8. Enter amount of payment.
9. Enter method of payment.
10. Enter department code.
11. Check for zero balance.
12. Give the guest a copy of the folio.
13. Inquire if additional reservations are needed.
14. Make farewell comments.

Each of these procedures can be subdivided as necessary. For example, as part of step 6, the new desk clerk could be trained to point out major sections of the folio and charges incurred by the guest so the guest is aware of all the charges that make up the total. The guest can then ask questions about any of the charges at this time, rather than after the bill is produced, thus eliminating extra work for the controller's department.

Management Concepts

In addition to task performance, other, less tangible skills must be addressed in a training program for front office employees.

Stress management, time management, and organizational skills are some of the areas that should be discussed. Although these skills are often covered in seminar formats, they cannot be considered in isolation. These skills are better understood when integrated into the training program as a whole, so they can be applied to task performance. For example, the employee being trained to check out a guest should be made aware that this process may occur under stressful conditions; he or she could face long lines, many guests questioning charges, and pressure from other guests to keep the line moving. Learning to remaining calm under these circumstances does come with experience, but the tenets of stress management will help even the new employee handle difficult situations. Self-control and concern for the guest's welfare are paramount.

Mastering time management is another important skill that enables employees to perform particular tasks at required times. For example, various departments depend on front office employees on a regular basis to relay messages to guests and other departments; if the front office does not come through, a great deal of confusion results for all concerned. Organizational skills help employees deal with their workload systematically rather than jumping from one task to another without completing any of them. Completing paperwork on a regular basis, rather than allowing it to mount into an intimidating pile, is one example of an organizational skill that can improve performance.

Presenting a skill requires the trainer to demonstrate the step-by-step procedure with the needs of the trainee in mind. This is not the time to show off how quickly the trainer can check in a guest. The trainer must be patient and consider the task from a beginner's point of view. First, the trainer must explain what the trainee is expected to learn. Next, he or she must repeat key instructions, particularly when demonstrating complicated equipment. The trainee must also be informed about where he or she can find assistance if help is needed (in printed instructions, with the user-friendly Help program on the terminal, or from another employee). Trainers should always explain slowly and check that the trainee understands all explanations as he or she goes along.

The trainer should also keep in mind what is best presented to trainees in various areas of the front office or hotel and at specific times of the day. Will the area be free of distractions and available for training? Is the time to present this skill better scheduled for the midmorning, early afternoon, or late evening? Training a new employee to use the PMS at the height of the morning rush almost guarantees failure. Of course, new employees must work under distracting and disorderly conditions, but during training they require a distraction-free, orderly area so they can concentrate on mastering skills.

The trainer should also be sure the materials needed to deliver the session are in order. Have DVDs, CDs, and videotapes been ordered and received? Have they been previewed? Does the VCR work? Has the room been scheduled for the satellite or PictureTel reception, the use of telephone lines to send and receive video and audio impressions? Have telephone initiation and reception agreements, contracts between senders and receivers of PictureTel concerning specifications of the telephone call and who pays for the call, been set? Have the coordinates been set for the satellite dish reception? Has the printed material required for training and follow-up been duplicated? Are enough copies available? These preparations are essential to a professional presentation. They allow in-depth training to take place without interruption and provide the trainee with a means for review after the session is over.

Training Is a Communication Process: You have to help them think through it.

Explaining how the skill being presented relates to other parts of the employee's job improves learning, enabling the trainee to understand how a particular task fits into the job as a whole. Trainees remember more when they understand why a task is important. Such explanations also teach new employees the importance of performing individual tasks correctly; this, in turn, forms the basis for a series of jobs.

When demonstrating skills, the trainer must consider the presentation from the trainee's point of view. For example, present the skill with the trainee to your right or left so the trainee can observe as it is presented. The trainee who cannot see the skill being presented has a much harder time understanding and retaining the skill. If the trainee is left-handed, special presentation planning is required. Perhaps standing in front of the left-handed person for the presentation will allow him or her to reverse some of the items mentally. If the trainer is aware that the trainee is left-handed (in a right-handed operation), training time and employee errors decrease.

The trainer must speak clearly and distinctly. Mumbling or talking too quickly only confuses the trainee. The trainer must consider not only what he or she says but also how it is stated. If the trainer's tone of voice implies that the trainee is incompetent, he or she alienates the trainee. Instead, the trainer should encourage the trainee's efforts, offer praise when a skill is mastered, and always be patient.

Every industry has its own jargon. Trainees should learn hotel jargon during training. For example, house count, no-show, sleeper, full house, and late arrival are all terms used in the industry. Even if the trainee has previous experience at another lodging property, it is still necessary to review these terms to be sure he or she understands each term as it is used at the current establishment. For example, at a former job, the term late arrivals may have referred to guests who arrive after 9:00 P.M.; at the current establishment, however, late arrival may refer to anyone arriving after 4:00 P.M.

The presentation should be broken into logical, sequential steps. The step-by-step procedure that was previously prepared allows the front office manager to present the material in an orderly fashion. Trainees understand such straightforward instructions as "Press this key on the keyboard to activate the registration menu" more easily than they understand "Here is the registration menu. . . . Oh, wait a minute. Let's go back to the reservation menu for a minute ..." Printed material that outlines the procedure helps the trainee learn the skill with practice.

After training is complete, the front office manager should watch how the employee performs on the job. Skills performed correctly are a good indication that the training was successful. Conversely, if the employee is confused or makes mistakes, it is possible that a trainer wasn't stopping to make sure the trainee was following along. As is true of all skills, being a good trainer comes with experience.

Planned training sessions must be incorporated into on-the-job training if this approach is to be successful. This method trains the new employee to perform tasks on an as-needed basis; the employee learns a skill only when he or she has to use it on the job. With this method, however, the demands of the business come first, and training takes a back seat. A consequence of failing to follow through is that the employee is never taught the correct procedures for performing a task. When this occurs, it means that the ground on which a good training program is founded-planning, development, organization, delivery, and follow-up procedures-is undermined. The consequence is an employee who does not have all the skills necessary to do the most efficient job.

Role-Playing

Role-playing gives the trainee an opportunity to practice a customer service situation by acting out the role before actually being required to do the job. The front office staff must often act as a sounding board for complaints and as a problem solver, even when the problem has nothing to do with the front office. Experience teaches that, sooner or later, every front desk clerk will have a customer with a guaranteed reservation when there are no vacancies, a customer who was given a key to a room that was not cleaned, or a customer who must wait a long time to gain admittance to a guest room. The options available for handling such situations are often not communicated to new employees. Only by trial and error do they learn to find accommodations at another hotel when the hotel is overbooked, to offer a sincere apology and provide another room to the guest who was sent to a dirty room, or to suggest a snack in the dining room or provide directions to the patio lounge to the guest who must wait an hour to get into a room. Role-playing allows the new employee to confront these situations before they actually occur. The goal is that when such situations really do crop up, the employee is able to act professionally and offer service with a smile.

If the hotel has the equipment to videotape employees, trainees can be taped during role-playing sessions. The tape can then be reviewed with the employee to provide feedback on his or her performance. The trainer can analyze the employee's eye contact, clarity of diction, talking speed, poise, manner of dress, and posture. This method is valuable in preparing new employees to handle the stress of a busy front desk or an irate telephone caller.

Trial and Error: Let Me Do It

At this stage of the training process, the new employee demonstrates the skill to the trainer, who observes the attempt and offers constructive criticism. Here, the behavioral objective is useful, as the trainer can use it to determine whether or not the employee is performing the skill according to desired standards.

The trainee should be encouraged to perform the procedure as often as necessary to master it and meet the objective. The trainer may note how much practice other employees needed to learn this particular skill; for example, saying "Many employees must practice this five or six times before they catch on and come up to speed" lets the trainee know that instant mastery of the skill is not expected. The trainer should specify how long the trial-and-error period will last. Additional training may be required. The step-by-step training procedure is helpful to the trainee in learning to perform the skill. The parts of the skill demonstration that were confusing or fuzzy are clarified through individual effort.

Follow-up: Check My Progress

The trainer must follow up with trainees after the program is completed. This is a necessary final element in a sound training program. The trainer may develop a training tickler file, a database that keeps track of training sessions and alerts trainers to important upcoming dates for each new employee, listing the name of the training session, date of the session, comments, and date for follow-up. This type of information can be processed in a separate database program on the PMS or maintained in an index card file.

The follow-up completes the training session because it provides the feedback the trainee needs to meet the behavioral objective. It also assures management that the skills necessary to deliver hospitality have been planned, demonstrated, practiced, and mastered.

Administering a Training Program

Planning the training program includes making provisions for administering it. Many details must be coordinated. Accurate but flexible schedules for training sessions must be set and maintained. Progress charts on employee training should be produced and displayed. Content preparation and duplication of training materials must be completed in a timely fashion.

The responsibility for administering the training program rests with the front office manager. If this responsibility is delegated to an assistant in the front office or human resources department, details of administration must be discussed with that person.

Even the most basic training programs must make provisions for developing employee skills that are useful to the organization. The unpredictable nature of business volume and employee availability in the hotel industry calls for a versatile staff. Cross-training, which means training employees for performing multiple tasks and jobs, is key. A front office staff member who is able to perform multiple jobs has rescued many a front office manager during a crisis. The front office manager who discovers that one front desk clerk and one telephone operator are unexpectedly absent on the same day can attest to the value of cross-training. If a bellhop knows how to operate the PMS and the reservationist is trained to use the switchboard, the day can be saved. However, cross-training will get a front office manager out of a tight situation only if he or she has planned for it. If cross-training is to be provided, it should be built into a job description and pay rate. Note, however, before planning for cross-training, that some labor unions prohibit the practice of assigning noncontractual duties; in this case, cross-training is not viable.

Developing a Trainer

Careful consideration should be given to selecting the individual who trains new employees. This person should have a professional attitude and provide trainees with a positive attitude and enthusiasm for their positions. The selected person should be in management or be a senior staff employee. The trainer must also be well versed in all procedures pertaining to the employee's job and familiar with training methods.

Job Knowledge

Knowledge of performing tasks comes with practice after formal training. There is no substitute for experience. The trainee inevitably has specific questions about particular tasks, and the trainer must be able to answer them accurately and completely. Such answers are not always found in policy manuals and training handbooks; they are often learned only through hands-on experience.

The trainer should be familiar with all front office equipment and know how to prepare printed instructions and how to operate audiovisual equipment. He or she should be familiar with the basic steps of the training process (discussed earlier in this chapter). Finally, trainers should try to empathize with the new employee, perhaps by recalling how inadequate they felt when they were new on the job. Patience is important, as is careful explanation. Trainers who give hurried explanations discourage questions and, as a result, end up with trainees who feel unprepared to do their jobs.

A professional attitude is evident in the way an employee handles his or her job responsibilities: explaining a foul-up in a room reservation, helping a guest locate another department in the hotel, participating in programs to increase room rates, and controlling operating expenses. The desk clerk whose responses to these duties are "This company always overbooks at this time of the year," "Follow the signs on the wall to find the restaurant," "I wouldn't help this place get higher room rates," and "Take an extra 15 minutes on your break-this place can afford it" does not exhibit a professional attitude.

Experienced managers are well aware of the skilled senior employee who has mastered the skills involved in a job but holds a negative attitude toward the company or the management that represents the company. It is best not to enlist the assistance of such employees in training new hires. Managers are responsible for molding attitudes, teaching skills, and passing knowledge on to their employees. Exposing new employees to an unprofessional, negative attitude during training undermines the purpose of the training sessions. The trainer should represent the company and demonstrate good employer-employee relations.

Training for Empowerment

Empowerment, which was discussed in chapter 11, must be applied to training employees. The act of delegating authority and responsibility concerning specific tasks to frontline employees, empowerment is an essential element in operating an efficient front office. As part of the training program, a front office manager must specify the dollar amount within which an employee can credit a guest's folio without the intervention of the front office manager. The trainer must discuss this empowerment concept so the employee knows when the dollar amount and the guest's satisfaction are in harmony. Yes, there are times when the front desk clerk may have to stretch the dollar amount because of extenuating circumstances. However, a daily review of credits that allows an opportunity for employee explanation makes empowerment work for the guest, the employee, and the front office. According to Lawrence E. Sternberg, "Contemporary management thinking is that the greatest gains in efficiency, productivity, and guest satisfaction are generated by making improvements in the system. Those improvements are most likely to occur when employees are empowered to recommend and implement changes on their own."

11

Promoting In-House Sales

The food and beverage manager has spent several thousand dollars on a marketing study to determine the dining needs of in-house guests. The chef has rewritten each menu to reflect those needs. However, the bell staff and front desk clerks continue to recommend the MidTown Deli around the corner as "a nice place to get something good to eat anytime of the day."

As the hospitality industry grows more sophisticated, with greater concern for delivering high-quality services, maximizing sales in all profit centers of the hotel is important. Additional sales to current guests-in the form of future reservations, in-house dining, room service, lounge and entertainment patronage, gift shop purchases, and the like-assists in producing a favorable profit-and-loss statement. The front office plays a key role in promoting these sales, and the front office manager must develop and implement a plan to optimize the sales opportunities available to the front office staff. This plan includes focusing on areas for promotion; developing objectives and procedures, incentive programs, training programs for personnel, budgets, and tracking systems for employee feedback; and profitability.

The Role of the Front Office in Marketing and Sales

The front office is often seen as an information source and a request center for guests and hotel employees. Front office staff may need to field questions such as "Has the front office manager produced the room sales forecast yet?" "Is a block of rooms available for June 3 to 7?" "To which rooms is this seminar group assigned?" "Is someone on duty who can greet and provide information for the tourist group arriving this afternoon?" "Has the daily event board been set up in the lobby?" and "Has the daily message been set on the great sign?" These are typical questions asked of the front office by other departments in the hotel. Answering them is a necessary part of any hotel's operations. Today, more than ever, hotel management demands a great deal of the front office. In an article published in Canadian Hotel and Restaurant, Avinash Narula reports:

As market conditions have changed, the nature and importance of the functions performed by the front office have also changed from being an order-taking department to an order-generating or sales department. If one looks at the balance sheet of any hotel, it will become obvious that the major portion of the profits, on average 60 percent, come from room sales.

This change in the nature of the front office's role, from a passive order taker to an active order generator, challenges the front office manager to review the front office staff's established routine. The front office manager must figure out the best way to direct the energies of the staff to support the efforts of the marketing and sales department.

The front office manager must first consider the attitude of the front office staff. These employees have been trained and rewarded for accurate performance of clerical tasks, playing a passive role in the sales of services. How easy will it be to transform them into active salespeople, persuading guests to purchase additional reservations, services in the dining room and lounge, or products in the gift shop? At the outset, most front office managers would say this is a tall order. Established, routine habits are comfortable and unstressful. However, the front office manager is a member of the management team and must interact with members of the team as well as the employees as a plan is developed.

Planning a Point-of-Sale Front Office

To be a point-of-sale front office, a front office staff must promote profit centers of the hotel. Planning includes setting objectives, brainstorming areas for promotion, evaluating alternatives, drawing up budgets, and developing an evaluation tool for feedback. Without a plan, a point-of-sale front office has little chance of success. The plan should be developed in consultation with hotel management, department managers, and frontlineemployees from various departments. Team members are selected to assist in ensuring that a workable, profitable plan is developed.

Some of the goals Narula provides for the front office as it adopts a sales department attitude include the following:

- Sell rooms to guests who have not made prior reservations.
- Upsell (encourage a customer to consider buying a higher-priced product or service than originally anticipated) to guests with prior reservations.
- Maintain the inventory of the product-that is, the rooms.
- Convey information to guests about other products available for sale at the property-for example, food and beverages. The objective of the front office is to sell all available facilities at the hotel to the guests. Front office staff are probably the most important means of letting the guest know what services are available.
- Ensure that maximum revenue is generated from the sale of rooms by striking a balance between overbooking and a full house.
- Obtain guest feedback.

If we take these goals as well as Narula's other goal of increasing communication between the front office and marketing and sales, then the planning can begin. Valuable information about the guest, essential for formulating an effective marketing strategy, can be conveyed by the front office staff. Changing market conditions require that such information be used by the marketing and sales division. Based on this suggestion, we can infer that the marketing and sales department needs the vital feedback regarding customer satisfaction with the availability of hotel products and services.

Set Objectives

The ultimate goal of a sales-oriented front office is an increase in revenue from room sales, food and beverage sales, and sales in other hotel departments. A front office manager who wants to develop a plan for a point-of-sale front office must set realistic objectives. What is it that he or she wants to accomplish? Should restaurant sales be increased by 10 percent, lounge sales by 15 percent, gift shop sales by 20 percent, or business center sales by 25 percent?

Developing these objectives is carried out in consultation with the general manager and other department managers. The result of these consultations may be one realistic objective that states: "Increase profit center sales by 15 percent." This may be the objective for the next several months. A new objective is then planned for future months.

Brainstorm Areas for Promotion

When developing a program to increase front office sales activity, the front office manager, in conjunction with other department directors and employees, should identify as specifically as possible the hotel products and services to be promoted. A typical outline of promotional areas follows:

I. Front office
- A. Reservations
  1. Upselling when reservation is placed
  2. Additional reservations during registration and checkout
- B. Rooms
  1. Upgrading reservation during registration
  2. Promotional packages
  3. Office rentals
  4. Movie library rental
  5. Computer games for children
- C. Office services
  1. Photocopies
  2. Dictation
  3. Typing
  4. Fax transmission
  5. Laptop computer rental
  6. In-room videocassette recorder rental

- D. Personal services
    1. Babysitting
    2. Shopping
    3. Bell staff assistance with luggage and equipment
    4. Concierge
        - a. Theater/music/art tickets
        - b. General tourist information
        - c. Tours of the area
        - d. Airline reservations
        - e. Emergency services
        - f. Information on local transportation

II. Food and beverage department

- A. Restaurants
    1. Special menu items of the day
    2. Signature menu items
    3. Special pricing combinations for diners
    4. Reservations
    5. Gift certificates
- B. Room service
    1. Meals
    2. Early-bird breakfast service
    3. Party service
    4. Snacks
    5. Beverages/alcohol
- C. Banquet service
- D. Lounge
    1. Specials of the day
    2. Special theme of the day
    3. Featured entertainer
    4. Promotional package

III. Gift shop

- A. Emergency items
    1. Clothing

2. Toiletries

B. Souvenirs

C. Promotional sales in progress

IV. Health facilities

A. Swimming pool

1. Availability to guests
2. Memberships/gift certificates

B. Jogging paths and times of organized daily group runs

C. Health club

1. Availability to guests
2. Memberships/gift certificates

Evaluate Alternatives

Planning teams must determine which concepts produced in a brainstorming session warrant further consideration. This task is not always easy, but if the team refers to stated goals and objectives, then the job is much simpler. In this case, the overall purpose of the program is to maximize sales by the front office staff of front office, food and beverage department, gift shop, and health facilities products and services. The team must decide which area or areas will be most profitable to the hotel and to the employees.

Devise Incentive Programs

During the brainstorming part of planning for a point-of-sale front office, the team should consider supporting incentives as an important part in the success of a sales program. The point-of-sale plan should include an incentive program, which entails understanding employees' motivational concerns and developing opportunities for employees to achieve their goals. This encourages cooperation among the frontline employees who must implement the point-of-sale plan.

The front office manager is responsible for determining how each employee is motivated. Many motivational strategies require a financial commitment by management. These costs must be included as a budget line item. When the owner can see additional sales being created as a result of these programs, the idea of sharing some of the profit is more acceptable.

Motivation, or understanding employee needs and desires and developing a framework for meeting them, is an essential part of developing a point-of-sale front office. The question becomes, How does a front office manager discover what employees want? A number of theorists have explored this area; the theories of Douglas McGregor, Abraham Maslow, Elton Mayo, and Frederick Herzberg provide insight into what motivates employees to behave in desired ways. Once a front office manager knows what employees want, he or she must develop a means of meeting these needs in return for the desired behavior. The front office manager must work with the general manager and human resources department to develop effective programs that meet the employees' needs. In this process, effective programs are defined by the employee.

The objective of the sales incentive program for front office employees is to encourage the front office to promote products and services in various areas of the hotel, including the front office, the food and beverage department, the gift shop, and the health facilities. Each promotional area may be considered, or the front office manager might choose only a few areas, perhaps those that generate the most profit, as incentive targets. A few examples follow:

1. *Upgrading a reservation during registration*: If a desk clerk can sell a room package costing $95 to a guest who has a reservation for a $75 room, a percentage of that $20 increase in sales is awarded to the desk clerk.
2. *Selling a meal in the hotel's restaurant*: If a desk clerk successfully encourages a guest to patronize the hotel's restaurant, a percentage of the guest's check is rebated to the desk clerk. At the restaurant, when the guest presents the VIP Guest Card signed by the desk clerk to the waiter or waitress and receives VIP service, the desk clerk receives the rebate.
3. *Selling room service*: If a desk clerk succeeds in convincing a guest to use room service, a percentage of the guest check is rebated to the clerk. The guest presents a VIP Guest Card

signed by the desk clerk to the room service person, which proves the sale was the result of that clerk's efforts.

Theories of Motivation

Douglas McGregor

Douglas McGregor theorized that management views employees in one of two ways. These theories are referred to as Theory X and Theory Y. Theory X states that the average human being has an inherent dislike of work and will avoid it if he or she can.4 Theory Y states that the expenditure of physical and mental effort in work is as natural as play or rest.

These two views of how human beings approach their jobs are vastly different. Theory X states that the supervisor must constantly expend direct effort to force the employee to do the job. Theory Y states that the employee brings to the job innate skills and talents that the supervisor can develop through an effective administrative and communication network.

Supervisors who give serious thought to these two views discover that sometimes they feel that one employee works best under Theory X, another employee works best under Theory Y, and yet another requires a combination of Theory X and Theory Y. This is exactly the intent of McGregor's efforts. He wants the supervisor to look at each employee as an individual who responds to a particular type of supervision.

Abraham Maslow

Abraham Maslow theorized that an individual's needs can be categorized by levels of importance, with the most basic need being the most important. The hierarchy of needs he identified was:

Fifth level: self-actualization, self-realization, and self-accomplishment

Fourth level: self-esteem and the esteem of others

Third level: love, affection, and belonging

Second level: safety (security and freedom from fear, anxiety, and chaos)

First level: physiological (food, clothing, and shelter)

Maslow further theorized that individuals strive to meet the first level of needs before even considering the second, and so on up the ladder. The physiological needs of food, clothing, and shelter must be provided for (by the paycheck) before the employee can be concerned with safety, stability, and security. The need for love cannot be a concern until the individual has satisfied his or her physiological and safety needs.

The front office manager can use Maslow's theory to identify the needs of individual employees and design programs that are appropriate. If an employee's wages do not cover his rent, he will want this physiological need for shelter met and will find a tuition-assistance program meaningless.

Through formal and informal communications, the employer should learn which needs are of utmost importance to each employee. Every employee has reached a different level in the hierarchy of needs, and it is important that supervisors recognize this. The front office manager should consider what levels of need each employee has met before attempting to provide for the next level of needs.

Elton Mayo

Experiments conducted at the Hawthorne plant of the Western Electric Company in Chicago, Illinois, from 1927 to 1932 led Elton Mayo to conclude that supervisors who recognize each employee as being special will achieve greater results than supervisors who treat employees as a group.7 The employee who is recognized for special talents and skills will find this recognition an incentive to continue to do a good job. The front desk clerk who is recognized for being able to sell additional services in the hotel may find this rewarding; it may fit into his or her career progression plan. This recognition may motivate the employee to duplicate the task in other areas and at other times.

Frederick Herzberg

Frederick Herzberg contends that factors such as "supervision, interpersonal relations, physical working conditions, salary, company policies and administrative practices, benefits, and job security are actually dissatisfiers or hygiene factors. When these factors deteriorate to a level below that which the employee considers acceptable, then job dissatisfaction ensues. The factors that lead to positive job attitudes do so because they satisfy the individual's need for self-actualization in his work."

According to Herzberg, minimum hygiene factors must be set to prevent a nonproductive environment. He believes organizations that provide less than these create an atmosphere for dissatisfied employees. However, a truly productive organization requires improvement in the motivation factors: achievement, recognition for achievement, responsibility, interesting work, personal growth, and advancement. Herzberg questions whether, if a hotel provides five vacation days a year, that will be a motivational factor for a front desk clerk if all other hotels in the area also offer five vacation days to their front desk clerks.

Applying Motivation Theories

Applying these motivation theories is a managerial challenge for the front office manager. It offers the opportunity to review the needs of the employees to establish a framework for day-to-day contact and incentive programs.

Maslow

The front office manager who reviews these motivational principles learns that each member of his or her staff requires a different style of motivation. For example, Maslow's hierarchy of needs provides a way to determine motivational techniques based on level of need. The employee who works to be with people, the employee who is moonlighting to earn additional income for a family, and the employee who is working toward becoming a supervisor of the department each require different motivational strategies. Someone who works to maintain social relationships is not concerned with an additional 50 cents per hour; this person might be more motivated by knowing that he or she can work the holiday shift. The person who is moonlighting is not motivated by health insurance benefits if his or her primary job provides that benefit. An additional 50 cents per hour will motivate this person, as will the assurance of a specified number of scheduled work hours. The person working toward a supervisory position is not motivated by a better work schedule, but rather the chance to be trained in all the various jobs in the front office or the opportunity to sit in on a general staff meeting.

Mayo

Mayo's work in recognizing the efforts of the individual gives the front office manager the opportunity to explore the connections among communication, satisfaction, and cost savings. A few words of encouragement about continuing to do a good job, an expression of personal concern about the employee's family or close friends, or recognition of an outstanding performance makes the employee feel special, even in a large hotel.

Heizberg

Herzberg offers the supervisor a different approach to motivation. He claims that the chance for self-actualization-personal growth and fulfillment-improves performance. While the employee needs an adequate salary, job security, benefits, and the like, these are expected to be present in the job. Anything less than what is expected causes dissatisfaction.

Applying this theory requires the supervisor to analyze both the hygiene factors of a job and the opportunities for self-actualization. What is the hotel providing that should be appreciated but is not? Why doesn't the company picnic or holiday party get the group together? The answers to these questions are at the crux of employee motivation.

Training Programs for a Point-of-Sale Front Office

Another supportive concept to consider during the brainstorming part of planning is the training required to allow the successful delivery of sales techniques.

Train in Salesperson Skills

It is not safe to assume that all front office personnel are born salespeople; indeed, it is probably safer to assume that no one is a born salesperson. The fear of rejection or of intruding on others when pitching a sale is far too real for many people. The front office manager must reduce this negative perception of sales by training and encouraging the staff; otherwise, the program is doomed to failure. The objective of training is to develop and teach employees methods to use to promote various profit centers of the hotel.

Develop an Attitude of Presenting Opportunities

The job of selling is more attractive if employees believe they are presenting opportunities to the guest. Front desk personnel who believe their suggestions are intended primarily to improve the guest's visit feel more comfortable with the idea of selling. Confidence in selling develops if the point-of-sale program is introduced gradually, promotion by promotion, giving employees a chance to try out various techniques. Incentive programs strengthen employees' commitment.

Let Employees Experience Hotel Services

An often overlooked but effective practice is to allow front office employees to experience the services and products they sell. Familiarity with and appreciation for the chef's specials, the luxury of an upgraded room, the equipment in the health club, the new merchandise in the gift shop, and the personal assistance provided by the concierge enable the employee to promote these areas knowledgeably and enthusiastically.

Training concepts for each of the areas listed in the promotion target outline must be detailed. It is not sufficient simply to tell a front desk clerk to sell a higher-priced room to a guest with a reservation during registration. Employees should receive suggestions on what to say and when to say it; timing is an important part of the sales opportunity.

Use Role-Playing to Create Your Own Training Video

Using the video techniques discussed in chapter 12, such as videotaping role-playing episodes of the desk clerks promoting hotel products and services within the hotel to the guest, is an extremely effective training procedure. These episodes do not have to be elaborate. They only need to highlight simple approaches to presenting opportunities that enhance the guest experience.

The front office manager who wants to use video as a training option must do a little homework first. Preparation for video training requires some thought as to just which skills and behaviors call for teaching or reinforcement. Discussions with the directors of other hotel departments (marketing and sales, food and beverage) provide a basis for promotional concepts. The front office manager should take an objective look at the salesmanship skills of the front office staff. How outgoing are they? How adept are they at recognizing the needs and wants of the guests?

The front office manager must then decide which specific promotional areas to highlight in the video. At the outset, the front office manager may want to choose only one or two areas. With these promotional areas in mind, the front office manager should write a script for the role-playing episode. It should include the specific behaviors or skills the employee is expected to master.

Producing the video involves scheduling a time that is conducive to shooting. Employee work shifts must be adjusted accordingly. Time for rehearsal must also be planned. The planning should take into consideration budgetary issues regarding the rental or purchase of a video camera and related equipment.

Budgeting for a Point-of-Sale Front Office

The front office manager incurs costs in operating a point-of-sale front office, including expenses involved in implementing incentive programs, producing training materials, and spending time to plan. These costs, while not overwhelming, should be anticipated. If all appropriate steps are taken, the income from increased sales should far outweigh the additional costs. The projection of sales and related expenses is useful when deciding which marketing ideas to explore.

Feedback

Feedback on the evaluation of the success of the front office staff in promoting other areas of the hotel is an important consideration in preparing a point-of-sale front office program. How can the front office manager know if the staff is using the sales techniques in which they were trained? How does the front office manager determine how the staff feels about this program after the novelty wears off? How does the guest feel about being presented with all these alternatives? How financially successful is the program? Front office managers cannot tell exactly how effective this promotional strategy is, but they must make an effort to obtain as much feedback as possible from staff and guests. This information is valuable in planning future promotional ideas, incentive programs, and training programs. The objective for this part of the plan could be stated thus: "To develop feedback systems concerning employee performance, employee attitude, guest perception, and profitability."

Guest Test

The standard guest test is one in which an outside person (known as the plant) is hired by the hotel to experience hotel services and report the findings to management. This test enables the front office manager to evaluate the sales performance of the front desk clerk. If an unknown plant presents herself with a reservation and is greeted with "Yes, we have a reservation; please sign in," the front office manager knows the front desk clerk is disregarding the sales procedure. The front office manager should discuss with the employee why the procedure was not followed. Perhaps the goals of the employee have shifted from a larger paycheck to a more reasonable work schedule. Or maybe he or she forgot there was a choice of incentives for the job. Perhaps too many guests were responding negatively to the promotion, and the clerk gave up trying. This information may indicate that unwanted goods or services are being targeted for promotion.

When the management of the hotel prepares the written information on the guest comment cards, questions concerning alternative promotion targets should be listed. Choices offered by hotel staff, such as upgrading reservations or information received about restaurants, gift shops, additional reservations, or other areas of the hotel may be included. This yields feedback as to whether the suggestions were made and how they were received. There is always the chance that guests may perceive an offer as pushy.

Financial Results

Another method for evaluating the program is reckoning the actual financial results. Were the anticipated profits outlined in the budget achieved? Use of a VIP Guest Card indicates to the restaurant manager that the guest was referred by the front desk clerk. Similar types of controls enable management to pinpoint the origins of room reservations, gift shop purchases, and other sales. A recordkeeping system must be established to reflect the amount of money awarded to front office employees as incentives to increase sales in targeted areas. The details of this recordkeeping system must be worked out with the department directors and the controller.

Planning a Point-of-Sale Front Office-An Example

A typical session for preparing a point-of-sale plan might be as follows: The front office manager has scheduled an informal meeting with the director of marketing and sales, the director of food and beverage, and a few frontline employees from each of the respective areas. Prior to the meeting, she has asked each of these members of the planning team to think of a few promotions they would like to stress in the next quarter. The food and beverage director begins the discussion by mentioning the following promotions that will run in the dining room:

1. Eat Wisely in January: Choice of entrée from the Eat Wisely lunch or dinner menu includes a free pass to the hotel health club.
2. Valentine Special in February: Dinner for two with choice of appetizer, dessert, or house wine at no charge.
3. Luncheon Special in March: Soup and salad bar free with entrée.

The director of marketing and sales wants to increase room sales during this quarter and suggests the following:

1. Increase convention bookings with I've Been There referrals.
2. Develop Weekend in the City packages.

After discussing these promotions, all team members agree that the Eat Wisely menu and the I've Been There promotions should be the targets of front desk sales efforts.

Incentives such as cash awards to front office employees for participation in Eat Wisely and I've Been There will be used. The team agrees that an in-house video should be developed to assist in training employees. The front office manager has scheduled a time to shoot the training video, selected and scheduled a few senior employees to be the actors, arranged for rental of a video camera and related equipment, and received approval for the projected costs. After several days of writing and editing, the following script is ready:

- Desk clerk: Good morning! Welcome to The Times Hotel. Did you have a pleasant trip to our city?
- Guest: The airport was pretty busy, and getting a cab was unreal. Is it always this busy out here?
- Desk clerk: At this time of year, there are usually several conventions in town. The city schedules extra public transportation, but sometimes delegates who arrive early get caught in the crunch. Do you have a reservation?
- Guest: Yes, I'm Thomas Renton, with the Investment Group Conference. My reservation is for a room to be shared with Michael Dodson.
- Desk clerk: Yes, Mr. Renton, I have a reservation for you, with departure scheduled for Friday, January 28. Mr. Dodson will be joining you tomorrow. All charges will be billed to Lawson Brothers Investment Firm. I have your room ready for you. Please sign the registration card.
- Guest: Thank you. That certainly didn't take long. After that wait for a cab at the airport, I do appreciate this service.
- Desk clerk: We appreciate your deciding to stay at The Times Hotel. Sir, I see from your reservation that you are on the board of directors of the Investment Group Conference. Our marketing and sales department is pleased to provide you with this special weekend pass, good for room and meals on another weekend. Perhaps you will be able to return to see how our new convention hall is progressing. It's scheduled to open this summer. The general manager told us that it will hold up to 10,000 delegates.
- Guest: That sounds great. I'll have some free time later this month to use that weekend pass.

A budget for this plan includes the following revenue and expense categories. When the hard facts of projected revenues and related expenses are visualized, the plan becomes more concrete and realistic. Projected budgets that show how a small cash outlay can produce significant revenue are effective in convincing owners and senior management that a point-of-sale front office program is a realistic and potentially profitable concept.

The data the team gathered in deciding to use the two promotional concepts are also useful in deciding whether or not these ideas will produce a profit for the efforts involved. The incentives, training, and budgets developed support the operational efforts of the plan. Feedback mechanisms include the standard guest test, comment cards, and monitoring of the source of sales for both promotions.

Solution to Opening Dilemma

Recommending outside restaurants is common in many hotels. The reason is that front office employees have not bought in to the hotel's profitability goal. It is management's responsibility to include frontline employees in developing a point-of-sale front office. In this situation, promoting the hotel's restaurant facility becomes the focus of the point-of-sale. Frontline employees also should have the opportunity to decide which promotional programs will be most beneficial to the hotel and to each employee.

12

Security

The act of delivering hospitality is thought to occur naturally. However, throughout this text, delivering hospitality is discussed as a planned concept, complete with research on guests' needs, policy and program development, establishment and delivery of training programs, and follow-up information systems. Hospitality also includes providing a safe environment for guests, which requires a well-organized department to oversee and implement safety programs. The security department of a hotel is vital to delivering hospitality to guests. This department is responsible for establishing the details of the following systems:

Importance of a security department to effective front office management

- Organization of a security department
- In-house security department versus contracted security services
- Hotel law
- Room key security system
- Fire safety
- Emergency communication procedures
- Employee safety programs
- Guest and employee safety
- Room key security
- Fire safety systems
- Bomb threat action
- Emergency evacuation plans

- Employee safety training plans
- Emergency communication plans

These operational procedures are never really appreciated until a crime occurs or a disaster strikes a hotel. They are assumed to be in place but somehow take second place to accommodating guests' more immediate needs and meeting the financial objectives of the organization. The terrorist attacks of September 11, 2001, in New York City and Washington, D.C., have affected security concerns like no other situation. Rebecca Oliva reports the following.

[A] recent survey of hoteliers found that one in three hoteliers fear for the safety of their properties. Even more shocking was the fact that nearly 50% of respondents admitted they had not increased investments in security-more than a year after 9/11. The security survey was conducted by Hotel Asia Pacific magazine and Pertlink, hospitality technology consultants.

Even so, many hotels are working to make their properties more secure in other ways-installing state-of-the-art camera surveillance systems in public spaces and conducting more staff security briefings. Properties have hired extra security guards, created security desks and are asking guests for identification cards. Results of these processes are twofold: they create an awareness of security issues among staff; and they tell guests that the hotel is concerned about their safety and security.

National, state, and local safety codes and ordinances require the hotelier to provide a safe environment for guests. This chapter discusses safety awareness as it relates to the front office manager's job and how the front office helps provide this essential service to guests.

Importance of a Security Department

The front office is a hotel's communication center; it is the vital link between the hotel management and the guest. When a guest calls for assistance because of fire, illness, theft, or any other emergency, it is usually the front office that must respond. The staff on duty at the front office cannot leave and resolve the emergency because they must continue to provide communication services and process financial transactions. The security department staff must react with speed and efficiency to serve the guest.

The security department is often regarded as a passive department, acting only when called on. In reality, it is an active department, setting policies, organizing programs, and delivering training programs to promote guest and employee safety. The director of security is a trained professional who must ensure that a busy hotel filled with guests, employees, and equipment stays safe. One of the department's goals is to prevent emergencies through planning. Another goal, however, is to train all hotel employees to respond to emergencies.

The importance of security to a hotel is emphasized in the following Hotel Security Report article by Patrick M. Murphy, CPP, director of loss prevention services at Marriott International, Inc., Washington, D.C., who reports on Marriott International's adoption of Crime Prevention Through Environmental Design (CPTED) in its chain of 1,900 owned and managed properties worldwide:

CPTED is part of a total security package. It can include anything and everything from the presence of security or loss prevention officers at a property to plans for protecting the interior, lobby, and guestrooms; exterior and parking area; and the surrounding neighborhood. Its goal is to keep the criminals from breaking into any area of the property; it accomplishes this by subtly making the environment uncomfortable for them.

The hotel priority areas in CPTED include the following.

- Building entrances-When reviewing a property we look to see that all entrances are inviting, brightly lit with no obstructing shrubbery. At night, side entrances should be restricted by use of card readers so that non-registered guests must pass through the lobby and past the main check-in desk.
- Hotel lobbies-They should be designed to be visually open, with minimal blind spots for front desk employees. Lobbies also should be designed so that persons walking through the front door must pass the front desk to reach the guestroom corridors or elevators.

- Guestrooms-These [electronic locking systems] create an environment where keys are automatically changed when a new guest checks in; locks also can be interrogated to determine the last person to enter the room.
- Guest amenities-Marriott designs its new properties with glass doors and walls to allow for maximum witness potential when providing swimming pools, exercise rooms, vending areas, and laundry facilities. Adding house phones in these areas makes it possible for guests to call for help if they feel uncomfortable or threatened by anyone.
- Exterior of the property-CPTED principles call for bright lighting at walkways and entrances. Traffic should be directed to the front of the hotel property to make would-be criminals as visible as possible. Entrances to the hotel grounds should be limited. Landscaping, such as hedges and shrubbery, can also create aesthetically pleasing barriers to promote the desired traffic and pedestrian flow.
- Parking-The preferred lighting is metal halide. High-pressure sodium should be avoided because it casts a harsh yellow light. The optimal parking lot or garage has one entrance and exit with well-marked routes of travel for both cars and pedes-trians. Garages need to be as open as possible, encouraging clear lines of sight. Elevators and stairwells that lead from the garage into the hotel should terminate at the lobby level, where a transfer of elevators or a different set of stairs should be required to reach guestroom floors. Other CPTED features in the garage should include CCTV (closed-circuit television) cameras, installation of emergency call boxes, and painting the walls white to increase the luminosity of light fixtures while creating an atmosphere that is appealing to the eye.2

In today's litigious society, an environment in which consumers sue providers of products and services for not delivering those products and services according to expected operating standards, it is important to maintain a well-organized security department. The cost of a human life lost because of negligence or the financial loss due to a fire far outweighs the expense incurred in operating a security department.

The following case illustrates the expense that can result from security breaches:

Perhaps the most significant [of high-visibility hotel crimes] was the 1974 rape of singer/actress Connie Francis in a Westbury, N.Y., hotel, which resulted in a much-publicized trial culminating in a multimillion-dollar verdict against the hotel. The case is still considered the industry's "wake-up call" in terms of legal liability.

Organization of a Security Department

The security department of a hotel is organized like any other department. At the head of the department is the director of security, who is responsible for maintaining a safe environment for guests and employees. The security director needs personnel, technology, and a budget to operate a 24-hour control system for the hotel. Depending on the size of the hotel, there may be an assistant director of security who acts in the absence of the director and assists in the administrative and supervisory functions of the department.

The director of security reports to and works with the general manager and interacts with each department director. Each of the shifts (7 A.M. to 3 P.M., 3 P.M. to 11 P.M., and 11 P.M. to 7 A.M.) is staffed with shift supervisors and security guards who are responsible for patrolling the grounds to watch the activities of the guests and employees and check on safety and security equipment. The number of people required to staff this department depends on the size of the hotel.

Job Analysis of the Director of Security

The job analysis of a director of security outlines the administrative and supervisory tasks of this member of the management team. Active planning to ensure quick and effective reactions to problems and emergencies is the basis for successful job performance. A typical job analysis is as follows:

8:00 A.M. Reports to the hotel.

8:05 Discusses the activities of the previous night with the parking garage attendant.

8:15 Discusses the activities of the previous night with the security shift supervisor or security guard on duty.

8:30 Obtains notes concerning the activities of the previous night from the night auditor. Obtains the daily function sheet, which lists the events of the day.

8:40 Checks the audit report of fire and safety equipment located at the front desk.

8:45 Discusses the status of heating, ventilating, and air-conditioning equipment with the director of maintenance.

9:00 Meets with the security shift supervisor or security guards for the first shift to communicate activities and duties of the day.

9:30 Meets with the executive chef to be updated on special functions of the day and incidental activities in that department.

10:00 Meets with the housekeeper to discuss incidental activities in that department.

10:30 Returns to the office to review the daily security shift reports.

10:45 Updates the general manager on the status of security within the hotel and incidental departmental activities of importance.

11:00 Discusses the activities of the day with the restaurant manager.

11:30 Returns to the office to prepare the weekly schedule.

11:45 Responds to a call from the front office that a guest is stranded in the elevator. Assists maintenance in keeping order. 12:45 P.M. Meets with the director of marketing and sales to determine the security needs for an upcoming high school prom and an insurance executives convention.

1:00 Returns to the office to work on the budget for the next fiscal year.

1:30 Lunches with the city fire marshal to discuss plans for renovating the sprinkler system in the new wing.

2:15 Meets with the front office manager to discuss the fire emergency and bomb threat action plan for front office personnel.

2:45 Meets with the security shift supervisors for the first and second shifts to discuss operational procedures.

3:15 Conducts a fire emergency training program for fourth- and fifth-floor housekeeping personnel.

4:15 Returns to the office to revise the fire emergency and bomb threat action plan for front office personnel.

5:00 Meets with the general manager to discuss the status of fire safety training in all departments.

5:30 Responds to a call from the front office that a guest has fallen on hotel property. Assists the guest with first aid and arranges for transportation to a medical facility. Completes an accident report. Assists the family of the guest in making arrangements for an extended stay.

6:00 Confers with maintenance personnel on the operational status of fire safety equipment.

6:15 Prepares a to-do list for the next day.

6:30 Checks with the banquet captain on the status of guests at scheduled banquets.

6:45 Checks with the lounge manager on the status of guests.

6:55 Checks with the front office manager on the status of guest check-in.

7:00 Checks with the garage attendant for an update on activities.

7:05 Checks with the shift security supervisor for an update on patrol activities.

7:10 Departs for the day.

This job analysis shows the security director to be involved with managing details concerning the whereabouts of people and showing a proactive concern for their safety. The job calls for constant interaction with department directors, employees, government officials, guests, and operational equipment. All of these tasks add up to a highly responsible position in the hotel. The following comment on hotel guest safety outlines the objective of a hotel's obligations to guests: The hotel is not the insurer of guest safety but it must exercise the care of a reasonable and prudent operator in protecting the guest. This duty extends to an innkeeper's obligation to protect guests from:

- negligent or deliberate acts of hotel employees
- acts of other guests
- acts by nonguests committed on the premises

Failure to conform to the reasonableness standard in these three areas provides a liability risk for the hotel.

The responsibilities outlined in the job description for the director of security may be assigned to other workers in some hotels due to budgetary reasons. The general manager in a limited-service property, for example, may assign the crisis management role of maintaining control of an emergency situation to the manager on duty. The administrative role may be shared with the assistant manager, reservations manager, or housekeeper.

In-House Security Departments versus Contracted Security

The events of September 11, 2001, urged hotel operators to take the responsibility of guest security very seriously. However, general managers of hotels must determine how to make operating an in-house security department cost-effective. Operating a well-organized security department must be the primary concern when considering hiring an outside security firm. As the job analysis for the director of security indicates, there is more to the position than patrolling the halls and grounds of the hotel. Foot patrol- walking the halls, corridors, and outside property of a hotel to detect breaches of guest and employee safety-is an important feature of security, but it is a preventive measure, not an active means of organizing security. However, in some situations, a general manager is forced, for economic reasons, to consider the purchase of an outside service. Administrative and planning procedures for operating a security department are delegated to other department heads. The cost consideration must be weighed against planning and coordinating a safe environment for the guest and employee.

The hourly rate charged by the security service for security escort service, or having a uniformed security guard escort a hotel employee to a financial institution to make bank deposits; for performing regular hall patrol; and for maintaining surveillance of the parking garage may seem attractive compared to the annual salaries and administrative overhead associated with operating an in-house security department 24 hours a day. But more than cost must be considered. Who will work with the other department directors to establish fire safety and security procedures? Who will plan and deliver fire safety and security training sessions? Who will monitor fire safety devices? Who will work with city officials in interpreting fire and safety codes? Who will update management on the latest technology to ensure a safe environment? These and other questions must be answered if owners and management are committed to security.

If an outside security service is hired, the role of maintaining security is parceled out to the department directors. The director of maintenance operates the fire safety and security equipment, maintains operating records of fire safety equipment and elevators, and reacts to hazardous situations. The general manager, if time permits, establishes a safety committee that responds to government guidelines and potential hazards. Each department director, if time permits, establishes security guidelines based on personal experience. Under these circumstances, safety and security become low priorities. The lack of coordination almost guarantees disaster when an emergency strikes.

The following excerpt discussing a bombing in a hotel in Jakarta, Indonesia, emphasizes the wisdom of adopting a proactive operational position on guest security.

As terrorism continues to pose a threat to soft targets such as hotels, as evidenced by the recent bombing outside the JW Marriott in Jakarta, security has never been more important. With this reality, global hotel companies are no doubt concerned with how to strike that delicate balance between security and guest convenience. Although this is an issue that hoteliers grapple with daily, many hotel companies continue to shy away from talking about their security procedures. Understandably, part of the issue is that hotels do not want to compromise their security by disclosing what measures they are taking. However, another issue is that hoteliers must learn to think of security as a positive rather than as a necessary evil.

"Our challenges far exceed appearing to be negative or painting dooms-day scenarios," says Jimmy Chin, director of risk management, The Peninsula New York. "We need to hammer away at the message that something else can happen, and we need to address it and examine what steps we can take to either protect or respond to it. It should be positive because guests see us as a deterrent against possible crime and terrorism. Guests today expect to be protected. The hotel industry should be discussing security measures openly, sharing best practices instead of worrying about how it looks."

Meeting the challenges of providing security for guests and employees requires a full-time approach. Part-time efforts to control crises in a hotel may be shortsighted. The following story shows the consequences of not providing adequate security.

The security department in a hotel works closely with the front office manager. Photo courtesy of Pinkerton Security and Investigation Services.

The verdict against Hilton Hotels Corp. in the Tailhook case could have far-reaching implications for hotel liabilities in providing security for guests, according to hospitality legal experts. In this case, former Navy Lt. Paula Coughlin sued Hilton for failing to provide adequate security during the Tailhook Association convention at the Las Vegas Hilton in 1991. Jurors awarded Coughlin $1.7 million in compensatory damages and $5 million in punitive damages. Hilton claimed that three security guards were adequate for the 5,000 people at the event.

Room Key Security

One of the responsibilities of the director of security is to establish and maintain a room key control system, an administrative procedure that authorizes certain personnel and registered guests to have access to keys. One court found that "as a general proposition, a guest has an expectation of privacy in his or her room and a hotel has an affirmative duty not to allow unregistered guests, unauthorized employees, and third parties to gain access to a guest's room."

Although issuing and filing keys are duties of front office employees, there is more to room key control than these two tasks.

According to Rizwan Saferali, owner of Super 8 Motel Kissimmee in the Orlando, Florida, area, who recently installed eSecure and Gibraltar locks from SAFLOK, "Having electronic locks has improved all aspects of the property, from guest services to employee satisfaction. We are proud to have been able to guide the property through its electronic access management experience."

eSecure [is] a user-friendly, Windows-based front desk system [that] requires no capital investment-properties just pay a monthly usage fee and receive the system software and electronic locks. The system works in conjunction with the Gibraltar170 lock by SAFLOK, an extremely durable lock that provides unparalleled electronic security. SAFLOK will install the system and locks and provide technical support and service for the entire system throughout the life of the program contract.

A significant benefit of eSecure is the fact that the monthly usage fees are based strictly on occupancy; therefore, properties pay only when they are receiving revenue from bookings. This structure is even more beneficial for properties operating on only a partial year business cycle.

To make keys or perform other transactions on eSecure, a user simply logs into SAFLOK's remote server via dial-up or other Internet connection and follows the point-and-click prompts. The request to encode a new keycard is completed within seconds.

With eSecure, SAFLOK can offer the opportunity to upgrade guest security to properties who may otherwise lack the immediate capital to do so. The combination of an advanced front desk system, top-of-the-line locks and affordable monthly pricing truly demonstrates that SAFLOK delivers access management solutions based on customer needs.

Usually one of two lock systems is used-the hard-key system or the electronic key system. Hard-key systems consist of the traditional large key that fits into a keyhole in a lock; preset tumblers inside the lock are turned by the designated key. The electronic key system is composed of:

battery-powered or, less frequently, hardwired locks, a host computer and terminals, keypuncher, and special entry cards which are used as keys. The host computer generates the combinations for the locks, cancels the old ones and keeps track of master keying systems. The front desk staff uses at least one computer terminal to register the guest and an accompanying keypuncher to produce the card. An electronic locking system allows the hotel to issue a "fresh" key to each guest. When the guest inserts his or her key into the door, the lock's intelligent microchip scans the combination punched on the key and accepts it as the new, valid combination for the door, registering all previous combinations unacceptable.

Smart Card

Another version of the electronic key is the smart card, an electronic device with a computer chip that allows a hotel guest or an employee access to a designated area, tracking, and debit card capabilities for the guest. Bruce Adams reports the following on smart cards:

Keeping track of room access by hotel management has never been easier. Employees have smartcards that grant them access to different levels of security. The cards track what level of key was used, who was there, and creates an audit trail that is easy to manage.

Beyond state-of-the-art locking and tracking capability, the smartcards serve as guest identification cards, which include the guest's name and dates of stay at Portofino Bay Hotel at Universal Studios theme park. "Their card functions as an ID card, which gives them special privileges at the theme park," [said Michael] Sansbury [regional vice president for Loews Hotels]. "Some of those benefits include front-of-line privileges at rides and events, early admission to the park and priority seating in restaurants. The smart cards also serve as charge cards at the hotel and park." "The smartcard is linked to the guest account in the hotel," Sansbury said. "The credit limit in the hotel is transmitted to the smartcard. Merchants at any shop or restaurant at Universal Studios can swipe the smartcard the same way they swipe a credit card. It works the same way as a credit card," [reports Sansbury]. "If they lose their smart-card, it is very easy to invalidate," Sansbury said.

Terence Ronson reports on an additional security measure-biometrics-that hotels are considering and some are using to control access to.

Biometrics is a term used to describe a measurement of uniqueness of a human being such as voice, hand print or facial characteristics. Some of you may have seen mock-examples of such devices in James Bond movies, Mission Impossible and Star Trek. Card-based access systems have been around for a long while and control access using authorized pieces of plastic, but not who is in actual possession of that card. Systems using PINs (personal identification numbers) such as ATM's only require that an individual knows a specific number to gain entry. Who actually enters that code cannot be determined. Biometrics devices, on the other hand (no pun intended), verify who a person is by what they are, whether it's their hand, eye, fingerprint or voice. I expect Hotels would be more inclined to be interested in fingerprint or hand-recognition access control systems-probably because of the cost and relative simplicity in which they can be implement[ed] into an existing operation.

For example, when captured, a fingerprint image is converted into a digital form by extracting a set of unique characteristics. The abstract data taken from the recording is then encrypted and stored in the database as a template, to be later used as a reference for comparison purposes.

Users are authenticated by extracting and comparing information derived from unique arches, loops, markings, and ridges of a fingerprint. This set of information, called minutia, is a mathematical representation captured as a series of numbers and relationships of the whorls and ridges of the fingerprint. No actual image of the fingerprint is stored, ensuring privacy and security, the prime concern of users.

Hard-Key System

The hard-key system is less expensive at the time of initial purchase. However, the costs of purchasing additional keys and rekeying locks must be considered over the long run. Also, reissuing the same key to guest after guest presents a security problem. Often, the guest fails to return the key at the time of checkout. If a careless guest discards a room key or a criminal steals a key, guest safety is jeopardized. If regular maintenance and rekeying lock tumblers are not part of the preventive maintenance plan (and budget), guest security is compromised.

The electronic key system, smart card, and biometrics can be used for guest rooms as well as other areas of the hotel; they are an investment in guest security and safety. As each new guest registers, a fresh plastic key or minutia is produced. The new combination for the guest room lock or public/storage area responds only to the new guest room key or pass key. This procedure almost guarantees guest and employee safety. The initial investment in these types of systems must be evaluated against overall maintenance and replacement costs of a hard-key system and increased guest and employee security.

Electronic key access is one of many alternatives from which facility managers can choose. The system includes an electronically coded key and door controllers that can be easily programmed to recognize one or more codes. Since the electronic keys are assigned codes from one of several billion possible combinations, they are virtually impossible to duplicate.

High-end electronic access control systems can be equipped with numerous . . . features . . . [such as] recording who entered an area and at what time . . . [and can] link this information with a central computer, allowing facility managers to provide reports on the activities of thousands of users through thousands of doors. These reports are extremely helpful during the investigation phase of a crime incident. Access control systems also can be equipped with a panic alert that allows the individual to send a distress signal in the event they are being coerced to open the door.

While the hard-key system is the traditional method that hotels have been using for many years, its cumbersome and costly maintenance indicates that it should be replaced with advanced technology. This may be a slow process, but it will greatly improve guest, employee, and inventory safety. The economies of scale make the electronic key system an affordable necessity.

Fire Safety

Hearing someone shout "Fire!" panics anyone who is unprepared to deal with this dangerous situation. Well-orchestrated safety procedures that are well managed at the onset of a fire can save the lives of guests and employees. The front office manager and the director of security must develop effective fire safety and evacuation plans as well as training programs for employees to ensure their effectiveness.

Fire Code General Requirements

Fire safety plans begin with the fire safety codes of the municipality where the hotel is located. These codes stipulate construction materials, interior design fabrics, entrance and exit requirements, space limitations, smoke alarm installation and maintenance, sprinkler system installation and maintenance, fire drill testing, fire alarm operation and maintenance, and the like. These extensive codes were developed to ensure guest safety. They may require extra financial investment, but they are intended to protect the guest and the occupants of the building.

Guest Expectations

Hotel guests expect, either consciously or unconsciously, to find a safe environment during their visit. Some guests may ask for a room on a lower level or inquire if the rooms have smoke alarms. However, most guests are concerned about other matters and do not ask about fire safety procedures. When the guest settles into a guest room, he or she may give a passing glance at the fire evacuation procedure posted behind the door. Some guests may even count the number of doors to the nearest exit. Is this enough? Will human lives be in jeopardy because guests' pressing concerns have caused them to place their safety in the hands of the management and employees of the hotel?

Fire Safety Plan

The front office manager who wants to take active measures to ensure guest safety must develop a simple fire safety plan, communicate it to employees and guests, and train employees and guests to handle a stressful situation. This includes the following com-monsense elements:

1. Equip all guest rooms and public areas with smoke detectors that are tied to a central communications area.
2. Regularly test and maintain smoke detectors; keep up-to-date records of the tests.
3. Install, maintain, and test fire alarms as required by local fire code regulations; again, keep up-to-date records of the tests. Constantly monitor smoke detectors and fire alarm systems, preferably at the front desk.

5. Prepare and post floor plans showing fire exit locations by area-public areas, work areas, and guest room areas.
6. Tell employees and guests where the nearest fire extinguishers and fire alarms are located and how to evacuate the building. Instruct them in fire safety guidelines.
7. Develop a fire action communication procedure for front office personnel.

Employee Training in F :e Safety

Providing training programs for employees on the locations of the fire exits, fire extinguishers, and fire alarms and on methods of building evacuation greatly increases the chances that all occupants will escape the building safely when necessary. After new and current employees are taught the locations of fire exits, extinguishers, and alarms throughout the building, supervisors can spot-check the effectiveness of the training with random questions such as: "Where is the nearest fire exit when you are cleaning room 707? Where is the nearest fire extinguisher when you are in the bakery? Where is the nearest fire alarm when you are in the laundry?" These simple questions, repeated often enough, impress employees with the importance of fire safety.

Local fire departments or the director of security can train employees to use fire extinguishers. These informal training sessions should include operational procedures and information on applying the appropriate type of fire extinguisher. The time to start reading directions is not during the fire. These training sessions give employees confidence in their ability to handle an emergency.

Guest Instruction in Fire Safety

Often, instructing guests on fire safety is overlooked. They are at the hotel for a relaxing, enjoyable visit. But fire can strike at any time, even during relaxing, enjoyable visits. Inform each guest that all rooms are equipped with smoke detectors, that the nearest fire exit from any room is, at the most, four doors to the right of the room, that a fire extinguisher is located next to the elevator on each floor, and that a fire can be reported by dialing 0 for the hotel operator. Guests appreciate that the hotel cares about their well-being and that it has taken every precaution to ensure equipment is available and in working order. Management may want to encourage guests to read the fire evacuation guidelines posted on the door of the guest room by offering enticing promotions. For example, on registering, the guest is informed of a special coupon attached to the fire evacuation plan located on the door. This coupon may be redeemed for a two-for-one breakfast special, a free cover charge in the lounge, a free morning newspaper, a discount in the gift shop, or some other incentive. Hotel fire safety procedures should be displayed in guest rooms.

1. When you check into any hotel or motel, ask for a copy of the fire procedures plan. If they do not have one, ask why.
2. Check to see if there is a smoke detector in your room. If there isn't any, ask for a room that has one.
3. Familiarize yourself with the locations of the fire exits and count the number of doors from your room to the nearest fire exit. (If the corridor is smoky, you may not be able to see the exit, but you can feel your way along the floor.)
4. Get into the habit of keeping your key in the same place every time you stay at a motel or hotel so that you'll always know exactly where it is. Then, if you have to leave your room, be sure to take your key with you. (If you cannot reach the exit, you may have to return to your room because of fire or smoke in the hallway.)
5. If you wake up and find your room is beginning to fill with smoke, grab your key, roll off the bed, and head for the door on your hands and knees. You'll want to save your eyes and lungs as long as possible, and the air five or six feet up may be filled with odorless carbon monoxide.
6. Before leaving your room, feel the door with the palm of your hand. If it is hot, or even warm, do not open it! If it is not warm, slowly open it a crack, with the palm of your hand still on the door (in case you have to slam it shut), and peek into the hallway to see what's happening.
7. If the coast is clear, crawl into the hallway, feeling your way along the exit side of the wall. It's easy to get lost or disoriented in smoke. Count the doors as you go.

8. Do not use an elevator as a fire exit. Smoke, heat, and fire may put it out of operation.
9. When you reach the exit, walk down the stairs to the first floor. (Exit doors are locked on the stairwell side, so you cannot enter any other floor.)
10. If you encounter smoke in the stairwell on the way down, the smoke may be "stacking" on the floors under it, and the stairwell would be impassable. Do not try to run through it. Turn around and go up to the roof.
11. When you reach the roof, open the door and leave it open so the stairwell can vent itself. find the windward side of the building so you won't be caught up in the smoke. Then, have a seat and wait for the firefighters to find you.
12. If you cannot get out of your room safely, fill the bathtub or sink with water. Soak towels and stuff them under the door and between the cracks to keep the smoke out. With your ice bucket, bail water onto the door to keep it cool. If the walls are hot, bail water on them, too. Wet your mattress and put it up against the door. Keep everything wet.
13. If smoke does begin to seep into your room, open the window. (Keep the window closed if there is no smoke. There may be smoke outside.) If you see the fire through the window, pull the drapes down so that they will not catch fire. Also, wet a handkerchief or washcloth and breathe through it.
14. DO NOT JUMP unless you are certain of injury if you stay in your room one minute longer. Most people hurt themselves jumping, even from the second floor; from the third floor, quite severely. If you're higher than the third floor, chances are you will not survive the fall. You would be better off fighting the fire in your room.

Accommodations for guests who are physically challenged should also be a concern for hotel managers. Visual alarm systems, flashing lights that indicate a fire or other emergency in a hotel room, should be installed to alert hearing-impaired guests. A report of the locations of physically challenged guests should be easy to retrieve from the PMS registration module in case of an emergency.

Fire Action Communication Procedure

The front office employees must take the lead in controlling the panic that may arise when a fire strikes. The fire communications training program developed by the front office manager must be taught to all front office personnel. If fire strikes during the middle of the day, more than one person will probably be available to assist in maintaining control of the situation. But if the disaster occurs at 10:30 P.M., there may be only one person on duty to orchestrate communications.

The communications procedure begins when a guest or an employee calls the switchboard to report a fire. Unfortunately, in many cases, some time has already been wasted in attempts to extinguish the fire. Seconds are important in reporting the fire to the local fire company. At some properties, the fire company is immediately notified via the interface of the hotel's fire alarm with the municipal or private monitoring station. But front office personnel should never assume that the fire company has been notified and should immediately call the fire station to report the fire. The call may duplicate an earlier report, but it is better to have two notifications than none.

After the fire is reported, security and management should be alerted. Guest and employee evacuation procedures must be initiated and organized. Established procedures stipulating who should be informed and in what manner, as well as who is to assist the guests and employees in evacuating, result in an efficient evacuation. The front desk clerk must produce a list of occupied guest rooms immediately. The rooms located on the floor where the fire is reported and the rooms located on the floors immediately above and below the fire room are of vital importance to firefighters and volunteers who assist in the evacuation.

On arrival, firefighters immediately report to the front desk. They need to know where the fire is located and what guest rooms are occupied. Copies of the list of occupied rooms and special notes on whether the occupants are children or physically challenged aid in the rescue effort.

Front office personnel must remain calm throughout the ordeal. The switchboard will be active, with calls from inside and outside the hotel. Requests for information from the fire emergency crew and first-aid and rescue squad will be mixed with phone calls from the media and persons related to hotel guests. Switchboard operators should keep phone calls brief so the phone lines are open.

Security should not be forgotten during crises. Some people take advantage of such confusion to loot and pilfer. Cash drawers and other documents should be secured.

Each hotel must develop its own communications procedure for a fire. Each plan will vary based on the strengths of the employees in the front office. Training the staff with fire drills aids all employees in handling the emergency; everyone must be part of the drill, no matter how calmly they react to ordinary crises. Holding fire drills on each shift gives employees practice and is worth the effort.

The following stories highlight the importance of being prepared to react in an emergency situation:

[James T. Davidson, executive director, Training Services, Educational Institute] was working as a front desk clerk in Bermuda during the arson riots in 1976. Rioters set fire to the top floor of the hotel. [The hotel's] communications tower was on the roof and [it] lost communications within moments, even though [the hotel's management] thought [that it] had a fool-proof system. Several people were killed, including some guests who tried to use the elevator-it took them straight to the blaze. There was an emergency plan for evacuating guests, but no real plan for getting them a safe distance away from the burning building.

Years later, [he] was general manager of a property on the Seychelles Islands during two attempted coups d'etat. A total curfew was imposed during both coup attempts, but the second was worse because it happened during the middle of the night when [the] staff was limited. For six days, [the hotel] made do with a staff of 13 for 300 guests and lived off the food that was at the hotel. The 13 staff members worked in just about every department at one time or another. [They] enlisted guests to help keep the hotel running, and most were glad to pitch in.

Each incident taught [him] the importance of planning and communications, and how essential it is to have regular emergency procedure drills.

Even though these stories are pre-September 11, 2001, planning for a general disaster and communications within that disaster were and are still very important.

Emergency Communication

There are times when guests and employees must evacuate a building in a nonemergency situation. Although it is imperative that the building be emptied, evacuation is not as urgent as it is during a fire. Examples of such situations include a bomb threat, a fire in an adjacent building, a gas leak, or an electrical power outage. When these situations occur, an emergency communication system must be in place to ensure an efficient evacuation.

The director of security, in conjunction with the front office manager and civil authorities, should develop a plan for all departments. The role of the front office is essential in directing communications with guests and employees. The front office staff is responsible for alerting employees and guests that an emergency situation exists. The emergency communication plan should establish a communications hierarchy, which is a listing of the order in which management personnel may be called on to take charge; emphasize cooperation between the hotel and civil authorities; and provide training.

The 1993 bombing of the World Trade Center provides a cautionary lesson in preparedness:

When disaster strikes, inadequate or incomplete preparation becomes painfully evident-and costly. These hard lessons became clear in the immediate aftermath of the February 26, 1993, bombing of New York's World Trade Center, when the staff of the adjacent Vista Hotel reacted heroically to a very daunting situation. Loss of the facility's main telephone switch made it impossible to communicate with management and arrange emergency recovery services. Cellular phones could have fetched thousands of dollars apiece that day. Drawings illustrating how the hotel was built were not easily accessible, creating confusion among the rescue teams.

Here is another incident of a more urgent nature:

A natural gas explosion tore through the [Embassy Suites Outdoor World at Dallas/Ft. Worth International Airport] swimming pool maintenance room at 6:25 P.M., August 6, 2000, just four days after the hotel's opening, forcing guests to flee the property. Rapid response by the hotel's staff, led by GM Bill Bretches, as well as police, firefighters and paramedics, helped clear the property swiftly and minimize injuries. Two hundred fifteen of the hotel's 329 guest suites were occupied at the time of the explosion, with many of the guests in the property's atrium for the evening reception.

Guests were brought to the hotel's parking lot, where they were given water and clothing provided by Bass Pro Shops Outdoor World, a part of the hotel complex. Staff accounted for guests by matching names with the registration list. All guests, accompanied by Embassy Suites staff, were relocated within 90 minutes to nearby hotels.

The following discussion of planning for effective emergency communication outlines the most important features of such a plan.

Developing the Emergency Communication Plan

The emergency communication plan is developed in cooperation with the director of security, the front office manager, and local civil authorities. These individuals are responsible for developing a plan to be used in the event of an impending life-threatening emergency that includes training staff and employees.

Emergency Communications Manager on Duty

The job description of each management position includes a task entitled "emergency communications manager on duty." This duty requires the person to act as the liaison between the hotel and the civil authorities. Each member of the management staff receives adequate training in the responsibilities of the job. The role of emergency communications manager on duty is assumed in the following order:

- General manager
- Assistant general manager

- Director of security
- Director of maintenance
- Food and beverage manager
- Banquet manager
- Restaurant manager
- Director of marketing and sales
- Controller
- Housekeeper
- Front office manager
- Front desk clerk on duty
- Night auditor
- Responsibilities of the Front Office

On receipt of a call informing the hotel that the guests and employees are in danger, these procedures are to be followed:

1. Remain calm. Write down the name, phone number, affiliation, and location of the person making the call.
2. Immediately alert the emergency communications manager on duty to the impending danger. If main telephone service to the hotel is inactivated, use a cellular phone.
3. Inform the front desk clerk of the impending danger. Produce a room list of all registered guests in the hotel. Produce a list of all social functions in progress.
4. Alert the emergency communications leaders on duty in each hotel department. These people report to the front office immediately. Hold an emergency action meeting with the emergency communications manager on duty. The lists of registered guests and social functions in progress will assist in the evacuation.
5. The emergency communications manager on duty will advise you which authorities should be alerted.
6. Respond to phone inquiries as directed by the emergency communications manager on duty.
7. Remain at the front office to manage emergency communications until directed to evacuate by the emergency communications manager on duty.

Responsibilities of Other Hotel Departments

Training

Delegating the task of emergency communications leader on duty to other responsible members of a department requires the following considerations:

- Each department director develops a hierarchy of positions to assume the responsibility of emergency communications leader.
- Each emergency communications leader on duty receives adequate training in the responsibilities of this job duty.
- Upon receiving information indicating that the hotel guests and employees are in immediate danger, immediately relay the information to the front office-dial 0.
- All emergency communications leaders on duty report to the front office for an emergency communications meeting. Directions are given for assisting guests and employees to evacuate.
- Employees on duty take direction from the emergency communications leaders on duty on assisting guests and employees in evacuating the hotel.

The emergency communications managers on duty should receive ten or more hours of training in leading a crisis situation. This training must be documented, with two hours of refresher training every year.

Current employees receive two hours of training in emergency evacuation procedures. New employees receive training in emergency evacuation at the time of orientation. Refresher training, two hours every year, is required of all employees.

Employee Safety Programs

The hospitality industry is rife with opportunities for employee accidents. Behind the scenes are many people crowded into small work areas, busy preparing food and beverages and performing other services for the guests. The employees who are most in danger include those whose equipment is in need of repair, who work in areas that are too small, or who depend on other employees who are not attentive to the job at hand. The front of the house also provides opportunities for accidents. Employees and guests must use public areas that may be overcrowded or worn from continual use. The following information on hotel law provides insight into an innkeeper's responsibility:

The innkeeper must periodically inspect the facility to discover hidden or latent defects and then to remove or repair those defects. During the time prior to repair the innkeeper has a duty to warn the guests about the existence and location of the dangers.

How does hotel management begin to develop guidelines for employee safety?

Employee Safety Committee

The best way to begin is to establish a safety committee, a group of frontline employees and supervisors who discuss safety issues concerning guests and employees. Frontline employees know the details of day-to-day hazards. They deal with the faulty equipment, traverse the crowded banquet rooms, work next to one another in a poorly laid-out kitchen, process soiled laundry, push carts through busy public corridors, and hear guest complaints during checkout. Moreover, these people make up part of the group that employee safety procedures are supposed to protect. Why not give them an opportunity to make their environment better? Although some employees do not want this responsibility, other employees will welcome the opportunity. With positive results, there may be a few more volunteers the next time. Management is a necessary part of the committee, not only because it is used to carrying out long-range plans but because it supplies the clout and support needed to implement the procedures.

Composition and Activities of the Safety Committee

The safety committee should include representatives from all departments in the hotel. If this is not possible, then co-committees for each shift might be an option. Management should convey the importance of the safety committee. Every comment received from the members is worthwhile and should be noted in the minutes of the meeting (Figure 14-7). Checklists with assignments for fact-finding tours, to be reported on at the next meeting, should be distributed to begin the process. The meetings should not be mere formalities, quickly conducted with little thought about their content. At each meeting, the minutes of the previous meeting should be read, and progress made in accomplishing goals should be reported. Members should see that the tiles in the laundry room, the leak in the stack steamer, and the worn rug in the lobby have been repaired or replaced as suggested.

Department Supervisors' Responsibility

Each department director must encourage a safety-conscious attitude. Management members can set an example by following safety procedures themselves when operating equipment and by scheduling adequate staff during busy time periods and following up on requests for repairs. If employees know that you place safety first, they will also adopt that attitude.

Safety Training Programs

Specific safety training programs should be developed by each department director. The directors review their departments to determine where safety training is needed. Security, equipment operation, sanitation, chemical use, transport of materials, and movement of equipment are areas to examine in compiling a program. The orientation program is the best opportunity for providing employees with safety training. Films, handouts, and booklets produced specifically to teach the safe way to perform a task reinforce on-the-job training and practice.

Regularly scheduled training sessions with notations of progress for use in the annual employee review are a necessity; otherwise, the employee gets the impression that management is showing that same old film again just to meet the insurance company's requirements. Safety training sessions should be scheduled when the employee is able to concentrate on the session and is not distracted by other duties. This may mean that sessions must be scheduled before or after a shift, with additional pay. If management wants to enhance safety with training programs, then this must be a budget item. Planning for safety takes time and financial investment.

13

Executive Housekeeping

Guests return to a hotel, in part, because of its cleanliness-not the initial advertising efforts of the hotel marketing department to attract guests with price, product, and service features. This basic operating concept therefore requires a special consideration of how housekeeping fits into the marketing effort. The focus of this chapter is the executive housekeeper's management of the people, processes, communications, and interactions that affect the guests' stay. These operational procedures have an enormous impact on the financial position of the hotel. Guests who have a negative first experience-a messy lobby, a dismal-looking bathroom, or worn bedding-will not be impressed; the possibility of a return visit are minimal. Also, negative word-of-mouth advertising will become another problem to manage.

John Hendrie reports that the major hotel chains are now using housekeeping concepts in their marketing campaigns to attract customers:

In print and television, the consumer is no longer battered by the flash, pizzaz and glitter for their travel dollars. Rather, we are now shown the "glamour" and receptivity of a wonderful, welcoming, warm bed, home-like furnishings and restful color schemes. Quite a turnaround in marketing strategy, but, after all, at the end of the day, we travelers do spend significant time in our guest room, and it should be comfortable, tasteful, clean and safe-a return to hospitality basics.

All Hospitality operators need to pay attention to what leading hotel companies, such as Westin, Radisson, Sheraton and Hilton, are doing and demonstrating in the marketplace. They have the marketing clout to research, in-depth, Guest Satisfaction and expectation, gather reliable data, and present to the public what their research has uncovered. For this round, the results show that the consumer wants a Quality Experience in their room. And, you know what, they are right! One large hotel concern, Westin, even has beds and appropriate linens for sale on their Website, and these products have become a new cottage industry for them. Talk about Branding!

Barbara Worcester writes about the importance of housekeeping to the guest:

Sheets, blankets, pillows, towels and shower curtains aren't just soft goods ... If sheets are soiled, blankets are rough and scratchy, pillows thin and nonsupportive and shower curtains are moldy and stained, the entire image of the hotel is tarnished, and the guest most likely will not return.

All of this advertising effort encourages a profitable financial bottom line for the hotel. Now let's review the organization of the housekeeping department.

Overview of a Housekeeping Department

The housekeeping department is usually organized with an executive housekeeper as its leader. This person's job, even in limited-service properties, is usually rather standard. In full-service hotels, an assistant executive housekeeper with floor supervisors manages the duties of the room attendants (housekeepers or housemen). Also, in limited service as well as full-service hotels, additional housekeepers are assigned to clean and maintain public areas. The responsibility for operating the in-house laundry also falls to the housekeeping department. The staffing of this housekeeping subdepartment includes a supervisor, shift supervisors, and attendants.

Shifts vary from hotel to hotel because of guest checkout times. Some executive housekeepers schedule a few room attendants from 7 A.M. to 3 P.M. and stagger the starting time of other room attendants depending on the size or nature of the group in the hotel. Laundry attendants may start earlier in the day depending on banquet and restaurant linens that must be laundered or laundry that was held from a previous day.

Relationship of the Executive Housekeeper to the General Manager

The executive housekeeper facilitates the work of the general manager by coordinating operational efforts that affect the customer satisfaction level-which, in turn, has an enormous impact on the financial position of the hotel. For example, when a group of businesspersons that represents $100,000 in gross sales to the hotel is pleased because the executive housekeeper's staff was able to provide quick turnaround service on room entry the day they arrived, keep the hallways free of room service trays, respond rapidly to requests for extra towels and toiletries, and maintain exceptionally clean bathrooms, then the executive housekeeper's staff can appreciate how important their role is in producing a profit for the hotel.

Some of the part-time jobs she held while she was in college included front desk at the former Sands Hotel, inventory control, mystery shopper, and catering attendant in various hotels in Las Vegas hotels.

Her lodging career began with Marriott as the front desk manager at the 1000 room Los Angles Marriott. She then traveled to New York and was promoted to the front office manager position at the 1800 room Marriott Marquis. She traveled back to the west coast and went to work for the San Antonio Marriott as the front office manager. As Marriott began to expand their brand, Ms. Cannon expanded her career and used her background to become the training manager for Courtyard by Marriott in Dallas, TX. Not wanting to reject a challenge, she went into another segment of the hospitality business and operated her own private business for 10 years-Cannons' Pub, which was an Irish pub in New York City. Her next move was back to the hotel business, but this time into the role of executive housekeeper at the 250 room Hotel Hershey in Hershey, PA. She continued building her career as executive housekeeper at the 750 room Hyatt Regency in San Francisco, CA and the 250 room Inn At Reading, located in Reading, PA.

Ms. Cannon describes her role as executive housekeeper in relation to the general manager as one that allows him to concentrate on issues of operating the hotel. He knows that rooms will be clean and guests will be satisfied with their rooms. If her department was not run efficiently, then it would take away time that the general manager would have to use on other projects such as marketing the hotel.

She belongs to the International Executive Housekeepers Association (I.E.H.A.) and feels that this organization provides useful information for her through their monthly trade journa- Executive Housekeeping Today. She also remains current by reading Hotel &C Motel Management Magazine, Laundry Today, and she logs on to the web site www.hotel-online.com each day.

Some of the "big issues" she would like to pass along to students who should consider the role of an executive housekeeper on their way to the role of a general manager include knowing how to prepare budgets, costing payroll, and managing employees. She elaborated on managing employees to include motivating employees, working with them sometimes on the job, and developing loyalty with them on a one on one basis.

This job analysis indicates that the job of an executive housekeeper is focused on the small details of running a department, yet at the same time is concerned with the department's interaction with others, such as the front office and security. The executive housekeeper realizes that his or her department provides a service to the guest, and this service relies on good communication efforts with staff and departmental managers.

MANAGEMENT OF A HOUSEKEEPING DEPARTMENT

The executive housekeeper is a manager first and foremost. This department, like any other in the hotel, requires the ability to plan, organize, control, direct, and communicate with people. There are many systems to develop, details to oversee, and people to supervise to ensure a well-run department. The job analysis indicates a diverse array of staffpersons, department heads, and hotel procedures that make up a typical day in the life of an executive housekeeper. In this section, we review topics that support management practices for executive housekeeping, including:

- Room assignment/workload
- Training
- Room inspection

- Housekeepers report
- Communication-English as a second language
- Inventory control-linens, guest supplies, cleaning supplies, furniture
- Cleaning control
- In-house laundry versus outsource laundry
- Occupational Safety and Health Administration
- Material Safety Data Sheets
- Going green
- Professional associations

Room Assignment/Workload

The number of rooms assigned to a room attendant has particular significance to the hotelier and general manager, the executive housekeeper, and the room attendant. The hotelier and general manager look at this number as a measure of effective use of human resources, daily income, and guest hospitality. The executive housekeeper views the number as an indicator of how efficient his or her staff are in meeting daily goals and providing guest hospitality. The room attendant views the number of rooms assigned to him or her as "the work of the day"-something that provides an opportunity for fulfillment of his or her biological, safety, and social needs as well as an expression of hospitality to the guest.

Determining the number of rooms a room attendant can clean during a day takes into consideration the design of the room, room furnishings, fabrics, number of people occupying the room, nature of the guests in the room, training provided for employees, and incentives. The usual number is between 15 and 20, depending on the hotel and its policies.

The method of assigning room attendants starts with the executive housekeeper or the assistant to the executive housekeeper retrieving the number of rooms occupied the previous night (let's say 180 rooms) from the PMS housekeeping module. This number is divided by the number of rooms assigned to each room attendant (let's say 18). This quotient equals 10; therefore, the schedule for the day is adjusted to reflect the need for 10 room attendants.

However, room characteristics like those previously mentioned usually detract from the chart's usefulness.

Training:Training is an essential supervisory practice of the executive housekeeper. Each moment and movement of the staff is under the watchful eye of the guest for the production of hospitality and the hotel owner for efficiency and safety. Robert J. Martin, in his text Professional Management of Housekeeping Operations, lists the following areas for skill training: bed making, vacuuming, dusting, window and mirror cleaning, setup awareness of the room, bathroom cleaning, daily routine of the worker, caring for and using equipment, and industrial safety. These major areas provide focus points where time, labor, safety, and cost savings can be evaluated. Training should be viewed as an objective of a goal for delivering hospitality; a plan must be developed to carry out that objective.

How can the executive housekeeper most effectively train his or her staff? The answer reflects such factors as time available, skilled people in the department to train, resources for purchasing VCR or DVD equipment and materials, room available in which to hold training sessions, etc. However, the underlying question is whether or not the hotel owner or general manager believes training will improve hospitality. If so, then the small financial investment in training will pay large rewards.

It is important to provide training to both new and experienced employees. Training gives new employees the opportunity to strengthen skills brought with them, and it helps them adapt to their new environment. Training helps employees of all levels of experience take on new responsibilities with confidence, helping them to be more productive.

Inspection: inspection, a final review of the room to assure that all housekeeping tasks are completed and room furnishings are in order, can be approached with a positive management strategy. In some hotels, one person is appointed to inspect rooms in each area prior to releasing them to the front desk for occupancy. This person, usually a supervisor, goes around to the rooms and inspects their cleanliness, orderliness, and operational details. Although this system may work well in some hotels, executive housekeepers should consider having room attendants inspect their own work. This saves time and builds employee confidence. If a motivational system is built into this option, then it will probably work. As for any good plan, an evaluation mechanism must be in place; examples include guest comment cards and a front desk staff who asks random guests at checkout for feedback on cleanliness of bathroom, bedding, proper working order of electronics, etc.

Another department that works closely with housekeeping in producing hospitality is maintenance. The following article describes how one hotel chain combines the talents of the employees of both these departments to self-inspect guest rooms. An incentive program is built in.

At PMHS hotels, managers empower their housekeepers. In addition to cleaning supplies and fresh linen, housekeepers also carry a small yellow "Zero Defects" kit containing fresh light bulbs and batteries for remote controls, and a small screwdriver to fix a loose toilet seat. Although housekeepers never do major repair work, all are equipped with the necessary training that allows them to discern what repairs they are able to do, and what repairs need a work order.

Jim Lowe, Director of Facilities for PMHS, explains the logic behind Zero Defects. "During the half-hour that a housekeeper spends cleaning a room, he or she uses all of the appliances, remote control, air conditioner or heater, and the faucet. Housekeepers are in a better position than anyone to evaluate whether or not a room is functional. And if there are any small repairs that need to be made, such as a new battery in a remote or a new filter for an air conditioner, the housekeeper is in the prime position to make them."

If there are any problems the housekeeper is not able to fix, he or she fills out a three-part International Work Order. A maintenance technician takes it from there, treating the work order as if it were a guest complaint. The Zero Defects program, [PMHS chief operating officer Greg] Miller explains, anticipates and eliminates guest complaints.

To reward their housekeepers for taking a proactive stance, PMHS offers a bonus for every room that is inspected and found to have zero defects. The housekeeping department also receives a team bonus for every problem-free room. For every work order completed in a timely manner, maintenance technicians receive the same bonus.

One result of the Zero Defects program has been greater unity between the housekeeping and maintenance departments. "Instead of only communicating with each other by paperwork, our employees are free to consult one another and work together to make their jobs easier," explains Miller. "These departments are indeed the 'Heart of the House,' and the Zero Defects program really makes that clear."

In addition to bonuses and other incentives, the Zero Defects program includes a yearly event, the Heart of the House Olympics, in which staff from every hotel, as well as the corporate office, gets together for games, prizes, food, and fun. These programs make sure that keeping properties free of defects is profitable for both employees and employers.

Housekeeper's Report

This report verifies the number of rooms sold on a particular night as well as rooms vacant and rooms out of order. This is an essential communication tool for the night auditor as he or she compiles the financial data for the current day's activities.

This report is compiled from the housekeeping status transmissions that are relayed to the front office throughout the day via the PMS or telephone calls, voice messages, text messaging, emails, electronic data submission, or, in some hotels, a visit to the front desk to transfer the current housekeeping status. The executive housekeeper or his or her representative assembles data like that displayed in Figure 10-6. This function, provided by the executive housekeeper, is a safeguard in the accounting process.

Communication

English as a The hospitality industry has always provided individuals with an initial access to their Second careers. Working as a bellperson, front desk clerk, receptionist, or in the food service Language (ESL) areas of the hospitality industry allows people to earn funds for furthering their academic career or supporting a growing family. The hospitality industry also continues to attract many people for whom English is a second language. Executive housekeepers are challenged to manage employees with limited English communication skills in areas such as issuing daily duties, training, and communication. How can these communication bridges be crossed with ease?

Some of the strategies that an executive housekeeper may develop would be to initially locate an English-speaking group leader with whom the minority feels comfortable and communicate with that person to get your strategy developed with others in the minority-speaking group. Try to develop a rapport and a trust level that communication is important for delivery of hospitality to the guest, performing their job, and their safety. Next there are several English as second language resources on the market that could serve as a reference for the minority-speaking employees.

Communication between the front office and the housekeeping department is most important in the delivery of hospitality to the guest. After room attendants complete their tasks, they must relay this information to the PMS. If their work is delayed-and, hence, the transfer of the information-then so is the delivery of hospitality. Review the following scenario to see how a small gesture to fulfill a need for a group of guests caused great turmoil.

Situation 1: Why Can't Room Attendants in Housekeeping Get Those Rooms Cleaned More Quickly, or, If That Guest Asks One More Time ...

It is a busy Tuesday morning at the front desk. The Rosebud Flower Association (350 guests) is checking out of the hotel. The Franklin Actuary Society (250 guests) is beginning to arrive for registration. Yesterday, the president of Rosebud, Jose Rodriguez, requested a late checkout for all his members because they had to vote on an important legislative issue. The president asked a desk clerk, Samantha (a new member of the front office staff), to approve the late checkout. Samantha, unaware of any reason not to grant this request, OK'd a 2:30 P.M. checkout time.

It is 11:15 A.M., and the front office manager is on the phone with the housekeeper asking why some of the rooms have not been released. The housekeeper assures the front office manager that he will investigate the situation immediately and goes to the first, second, and third floors of the hotel to speak with the floor supervisors. They tell him that there are DO NOT DISTURB signs on the doors of the majority of the rooms. One of the guests told the supervisor on the second floor that he had permission to stay in his room until 2:30 P.M. When the housekeeper relays this information to the front office manager, a nasty exchange takes place concerning the delivery of professional hospitality.

It is now 3:15 P.M., and the hotel lobby is jammed with people checking out and checking in. Only about 20 percent of the rooms needed have been released by housekeeping. The food and beverage manager arrives and suggests to the front office manager that he announce the availability of the hotel coffee shop and lounge to the waiting guests. The front office manager feels this is a good idea but that, with such chaos, no one would hear the announcement. Therefore, he does not make the announcement.

At 7:20 P.M., the last guest is checked in. The front office manager breathes a sigh of relief and happens to notice a gift box addressed to Samantha, who opens it and reads the card out loud: "Extra thanks to you for your kind consideration." The front office manager reminds Samantha that gifts from registered guests are not encouraged. Samantha replies that this is from a former guest- "You know, that nice Mr. Rodriguez from the flower association. All he asked for was a late checkout time for his group."

Analysis: The miscommunication in this case was the fault of the front office manager. At some time during the orientation and training of new employees, the front office manager must communicate the policies, procedures, and limits of authority. Well-developed operational policies and procedures and documented training enable communications to flourish.

For example, new employee orientation should include a discussion on the policy for communicating requests for late checkout to the supervisor on duty. An in-depth review of the clearance procedure that the supervisor on duty must follow would further help the new employee understand that the front office does not act alone. A decision made by one employee affects the work of many people. A typical review of procedures could include the following:

1. Consult with the reservations manager to determine the expected time of departure for the guests or groups of

guests currently in the hotel and expected times of arrival of those who will be registering the next day.

2. Consult with the director of marketing and sales to determine if any special group requests concerning checkout departure on arrival times have been granted.
3. Consult with the housekeeper to determine the effect of a delayed checkout time on daily operations of the housekeeping department.
4. If the request for a delayed checkout time will conflict with another group's check-in time but the situation warrants approval of the request, ask the food and beverage manager to set up a special snack table in the lobby for guests unable to check into their rooms.

When the front office manager takes the time to explain the policies and procedures of the department, the new employee can think through situations rather than responding with a knee-jerk reaction. The delivery of service in a hotel requires the employee to be able to meet the needs of the guests by exercising his or her authority and taking responsibility for conveying an atmosphere of hospitality.

Inventory Control

Inventory control is a major responsibility of the executive housekeeper. Linens, guest supplies, cleaning supplies, fixtures, and furniture all require attentive review for timely replenishment and replacement.

Linen Control Linen control is based on a par system-an established level of inventory that provides adequately for service. The par system is established by the hotel general manager because linens are a major expense for the hotel. For example, if the hotel decided to have a par of four (one set of sheets in the wash, one set of sheets on the bed, and two sets of sheets on the shelf ready for use) rather than a par of three (one set of sheets in the wash, one set of sheets on the bed, and one set of sheet on the shelf ready for use), the additional set of sheets could tie up several thousands of dollars each year in inventory. The same reasoning is applied to bath towels, bath mats, hand towels, face cloths, pillowcases, blankets, bedspreads, and so on.

Guest Supplies Guest supplies, more commonly referred to as guest amenities-personal toiletries or care items-are another cost to the hotel that requires close attention because they support guest hospitality but are open to theft. Guests enjoy and appreciate the small bottles of shampoo, hair conditioner, lotion, soap, mouthwash, shoeshine cloth, mending kit, and other amenities. However, supplying these goods costs the hotel at least $1.50 per guest room per room-night. If this figure is extended for a hotel with 250 rooms and an annual 65 percent occupancy, the expense rises to $88,968.75.

(250 x 0.65 x 365 = 59,312 rooms x $1.50 = $88,968.75)

Keep in mind that this is a minimum, and some hotels spend more. Not only is the hotel spending that amount of money on a guest service, these types of products are easily removed from the premises by guests and employees from storage rooms and house-keeper's carts parked in hallways during cleaning time. For these reasons, a workable inventory system must be initiated that ensures ease of use accountability.

Cleaning supplies

Cleaning supplies for guest rooms include cleaners, disinfectants, and polishers for windows, tile, bathroom fixtures, office furniture, kitchen equipment, living room furniture, and so on. These may be purchased in one-gallon to five-gallon or larger containers for economy, or in aerosol cans. The larger containers of the product are stored in the housekeeping department area, while the usable sizes for guest room cleaning are stored on the room attendant's cart. The product is dispensed into these smaller, more usable containers for the room attendants.

Bibliography

Auguste, E.: *Escoffier Cook Book: A Guide to the Fine Art Cookery*, New York, Crown, 1969.

Boissevain, J.: *Coping withTourists*, Oxford, Berghahn Books, 1996.

Clark, Mona: *Interpersonal Skills for Hospitality Managers*, London, Chapman Hill, 1995.

Donald E. : *Public Personnel Management: Contexts and Strategies, Upper Saddle River*, NJ: Prentice Hall, 1998.

Eberts, Marjorie: *Careers in Travel, Tourism, and Hospitality*, Lincolnwood, VGM Career Horizons, 1997.

Gisslen, Wayne: *Professional Cooking*, New York, Wiley, 1999.

Johnson, Hazel: *Financial Institutions and Markets: A Global Perspective*, NY, McGraw Hill, 1993.

Koontz, H.: *Management: A Global Perspective*, New York, McGraw Hill, 1993.

Lawrence, J.: *Principles of Managerial Finance*, MA: Addison Wesley Longman, 2000.

Michael, John: *Principles of Hospitality Law*, London, Cassell, 1999.

Nancy, N.: *Choosing a Career in Hotels, Motels, and Resorts*, New York, Rosen Pub. Group, 1997.

Peter, J.: *College & University Foodservice Management Standards*, Westport, AVI Pub. Company, 1985.

Rosemary, E.: *Managing Employee Relations in the Hotel and Catering Industry*, London, Cassell, 1995.

Thomas, F. : *Introduction to the Hospitality Industry*, New York, Wiley, 1995.

Walden, Richard: *Genetic Transformation in Plants*, England, Open University Press, 1988.

Index

□□□